P9-CFW-980

DATE DUE			
FEB 10			
FEB 24			
MAR 10			
MAR 24			
APR 15			
APR 29			
MAY 14			

74839
Lerche

St. Procopius College Library
Maple Ave. and College Road
Lisle, Illinois

Concepts

of International Politics

Charles O. Lerche, Jr. and Abdul A. Said

School of International Service
The American University

PRENTICE HALL
EMPLOYEE COPY
NOT FOR RESALE

Prentice-Hall, Inc.

Englewood Cliffs, N. J.

1963

JX
1308
·LL

To

Ernest S. Griffith

PRENTICE-HALL INTERNATIONAL, INC., *London*
PRENTICE-HALL OF AUSTRALIA, PTY., LTD., *Sydney*
PRENTICE-HALL FRANCE, S.A.R.L., *Paris*
PRENTICE-HALL OF JAPAN, INC., *Tokyo*
PRENTICE-HALL DE MEXICO, S.A., *Mexico City*
PRENTICE-HALL OF CANADA, *Toronto*

© 1963 by Prentice-Hall, Inc.
Englewood Cliffs, N. J.

*All rights reserved. No part of this book
may be reproduced in any form, by mimeo-
graph or any other means, without per-
mission in writing from the publishers.*

Library of Congress Catalog Card No.: 63–11099

Printed in the United States of America

C

74839

Preface

This book is an experiment. It is an attempt to present in a convenient and reasonably systematic form a conceptual framework for the study and the comprehension of international politics. This academic field, with no methodology uniquely its own and with no long history of illustrious scholarly pioneering, in recent years has exploded in a "conceptual revolution." An army of scholars using a broad variety of techniques of analysis and synthesis, has made a massive and many-sided effort to organize the familiar data of international affairs into an intellectually responsible discipline. It is out of this ferment that the present volume grows.

Contemporary students of international politics are often informally classified as "theorists" or "policy scientists," depending on whether their primary interests lie in the development of valid and broadly applicable generalizations or in the solution of particular problems of state relationships in the real world. This book leans to the first category in that its emphasis throughout is general and theoretical, with its goal one of contributing to a deeper understanding of the entire international political process on the part of its readers. The authors, however, must openly confess a bias: they feel that a sound theoretical grounding is as vital to the policy-oriented specialist as it is to the system-oriented generalist.

In this book, therefore, the authors attempt to develop a sufficiently useful—that is, teachable—view of the international political system and process to provide the student either with a base for more advanced theoretical studies or with the capacity to deal in a more sophisticated and competent manner with the data of ongoing international political relations. This is a formidable task, and the authors are as aware as their readers will be of the extent to which their aim was perhaps overambitious. The ideas and the organizational framework presented here, however, have been tested in classroom use for several years with considerable numbers of students. The results have been encouraging to an extent to justify the opinion that this approach may have general applicability.

The table of contents suggests the major divisions of the book. Part I focuses upon the individual state and is devoted generally to an elaboration of the broad idea of "foreign policy." Part II develops the notion of "politics" as the crucial form of interstate relationship. Part III includes a discussion of five critical areas of political action in the contemporary world that promise to retain their relevance into the future. Parts I and II together are intended to provide a theoretical base for the moderately more specific discussions in Part III. The short reading lists that follow each chapter emphasize works that are conveniently and inexpensively available in paperback format.

Acknowledgments

The familiar "debt of gratitude" that academic authors usually acknowledge to their students for "inspiring" or "provoking" a book in this case is to be taken literally; both the conceptual skeleton and the final shape of this book grew out of the day-by-day necessity both authors have experienced of confronting undergraduate students with basic yet meaningful materials in international politics.

Miss Thea Fund, Mr. Philip M. Burgess, and Mr. Bahram Farzanegan, while student assistants of the authors, gave of their time and enthusiasm to the preparation of this book far beyond the call of duty or the expectations of the authors.

Dr. Kenneth W. Thompson of the Rockefeller Foundation and Dr. William Olson of the Legislative Reference Service of the Library of Congress read the manuscript and contributed to the further education of the authors while sparing the readers many questionable generalizations and imprecisions of expression.

Mrs. Elizabeth Forrest, whose technical skill was matched by a fine editoral sense, prepared the final form of the manuscript with great speed, good humor, and finesse.

The authors, of course, recognize their ultimate responsibility for all errors of fact and inaccuracies of judgment, and express their hope that both categories of fault have been kept to a minimum.

C. O. L., JR.
A. A. S.

Washington, D.C.
January, 1963

Table of Contents

v

One

The Nature
of Foreign Policy

This book is a guide to the ideas that men use when they discuss, study, or practice international politics. Our subject matter is in the first place "international"; that is, it will deal almost entirely with the relationships that different national groups ("states") have with each other. It is also a "political" study: the kinds of relationships in which we are primarily interested are those that we shall define as political. There are many international relations other than political—economic, cultural, interpersonal, and so on—but we shall consider them less on their own merits than in terms of their impact on the political behavior of peoples, governments, and states.

Politics can usefully and instructively be analyzed from any of three points of view. We can, in the first place, inquire into the motivations and tactics of the individual political actor as he moves within the political system. Secondly, we can examine the political system itself—the social structure within which the political actor moves—in order to understand the processes of political action and the opportunities and limitations affecting its members. Lastly, we can focus on the substance of political action to discover what it is that the actors are concerned with and what the social consequences of their political maneuvering might be.

In this book we shall look serially at international politics from each of these points of view. Part I is a discussion of the individual political actor (the state) and its foreign policy. Part II centers on the international political system both in theory and in practice. Part III deals with the substance of international politics and is organized as a discussion of several major problems that grip the entire system and its members.

Politics: The Struggle to Maximize Values

"Politics" is a common word in the English language that refers to an equally familiar phenomenon. Everyone knows what he means by "politics," yet precise definition is usually rather difficult. Individuals have strong emotional responses to the concept; any definition cannot help but reflect the definer's biases. The words "politics" and "political" will appear repeatedly throughout this book. It is important at the outset that we make explicit what we mean. Our first undertaking, therefore, is a definition of politics and a demonstration of how political concepts find their eventual international expression in a state's foreign policy.

THE NATURE OF POLITICS

Politics consists of the organizational activity men engage in to maximize their deeply felt convictions about social values. By political action men attempt to realize their differing notions of the "public good." Thus politics is really a *process*—a means to a value-centered end—but the process is meaningless except in terms of the values that give rise to political action.

Such a definition of politics is broad in its applicability to the acts men perform in a political context; as indeed it must be, since political acts include virtually the entire spectrum of human activity. The definition is, however, quite explicit in emphasizing social values as the roots of politics. Since these shared ideas of "the good" are what make political action unique, almost any human action can, with an appropriate value motivation and organizational setting, be termed *political*. Without the value drive or the organizational nexus, the same action is in the strict sense *apolitical*.

Human beings do not, furthermore, agree on any single inclusive set of social values. Struggles reflecting differing value judgments are an integral part of the political process. Conflict and disagreement are the milieu of politics. When anyone achieves a political goal, it is normally at the expense of other political actors who have their own goals and aspirations. Thus the range of political action may extend from agreement and cooperation between political actors at one end through to the various twilight zones of partial agreement or total opposition and conflict at the other. The experienced political practitioner has at his command strategies and tactics to help him attain the highest feasible level of value satisfaction.

These two ingredients of politics—the value-rooted ends of action and the political climate of struggle and disagreement—are as clearly demonstrated in international politics as they are in the more familiar environment of electoral politics in a democracy. Foreign policy consists of a society's attempt to realize on the international plane certain notions of what it conceives as good. It is the value root of foreign policy that makes nationalism so intense today and that makes the resolution of conflict so difficult. That international politics takes place in a climate of disagreement and conflict would seem to require no demonstration. In its key aspects, then, international politics is the same sort of social process as politics at any level; with appropriate conceptual adjustments, insights derived from international politics are broadly applicable to internal political relations and *vice versa*.

One additional point should be made here. Within any political system, disagreement and conflict over value choices takes place within a larger value consensus that helps hold the system together. It is, indeed, such an agreement on fundamentals that gives rise to the system in the first place and makes political action possible. We shall see later that the international system incorporates such a consensus (although only imperfectly grasped by many states) and that political action on the international plane is feasible only in its terms.

SOCIAL VALUES AND FOREIGN POLICY

Each society, especially when it deems itself a "nation" and is organized into a state, has a social code that contributes to its peculiar identity. These value preferences activate and energize all political action. If the prevailing concepts of "good" and "evil" could be rationalized within the boundaries of the society itself, they would have little or nothing to do with international affairs. Ever since the Industrial Revolution and the dawn of modern nationalism, national value structures have impinged upon the world outside their borders. At this point, social values come to relate intimately with questions of foreign policy.

Certain aspirations, needs, and wants are widely shared in any society. Many of these require governmental action to attain even partial fulfillment, and men look to their political leaders to act on their behalf in attaining these goals. Obviously, one of these areas of value preference in which only public agencies can act effectively is that of international relations. Individuals or sub-groups of a society cannot adequately function in the interest of the entire group; only officials armed with the authority and the sanctions of the society at large can deal with extra-societal problems. Foreign policy, therefore, is the exclusive province of government because only government can act on behalf of all the people individually and of the society collectively.

The content of governmental action in the international arena is determined by the set of social values controlling the society at large. Before the birth of political consciousness in the states of Europe, international politics consisted only of the relations of kings; mass attitudes and preferences had no foreign-policy relevance. The rise of nationalism made foreign policy in one sense "democratic"; governments became obliged to structure their international efforts so as to reflect the mass value judgments of the people they represented. The analytical apparatus of statecraft is no more than a standardized technique for translating the value preferences of a society into a workable frame for governmental action.

THE VALUE CONTENT OF FOREIGN POLICY

From an analytical point of view, we must avoid becoming overly specific about the "social values" that underlie foreign policy. Values are seldom self-evident, and the particular concepts of good and evil that a government chooses to pursue always stem from a mixture of sources within the society. We can identify at least five differing versions of the "good" that are usually combined in a single foreign policy.

(1) The good of the individual citizen: primarily the wish to

be secure in his person, his beliefs, and his property as they become threatened by forces outside his society.

(2) The good of the society at large: collective values, normally including the preservation of the social system, the augmentation of its prestige, the protection of its ideology, and so on.

(3) The good of the state (the juristic personality) as such: the more common ingredients include self-preservation, security, well-being, and the "strength" of the political unit.

(4) The good of "special interest groups" in the state/society: these tend to be included to the maximum extent possible within the operative notion of the general interest and contribute largely to the shaping of public policy on specific issues.

(5) The good of the government itself and of its personnel: values peculiar to membership in a public community that inescapably find expression in the actualities of policy.

Thus the values the state maximizes in foreign policy are varied in their origin and their substance. It is the task of the officials charged with policy-making to shape this broad spectrum of needs and wants into some semblance of integrity and to apply the resulting value synthesis to the phenomena of international politics. The statesman may compromise among competing values, he may accept some at the cost of rejecting others, or he may find some other rationalizing device. He cannot, however, avoid the necessity of building his approach to world affairs on a foundation of value choices.

FOREIGN POLICY AND INTERNATIONAL POLITICS

The base of any foreign policy is a state's mission to maximize its value synthesis. Once it moves onto the international scene, however, it encounters other states, each seeking the accomplishment of its own value-derived goals. Thus international politics is at bottom an exercise in the prosecution of value differences and grows less from objective environmental conditions than it does from the judgments men make about those conditions.

In this respect, as mentioned previously, international politics is not dissimilar to domestic politics. There is, however, a significant difference between the two types of politics that makes the international variety peculiarly perplexing and fascinating to its students. Although domestic politics—at least in a stabilized society—goes on within a well-understood set of rules that cover the range of permissible action and are enforced by social and governmental mechanisms, no such structure inhibits the practice of international politics. States are free to pursue their value purposes as far as their wishes and their strength will permit; they are normally checked by the strength of other states and only occasionally by institutional mechanisms.

International politics, due to the highly internalized motivations of its practitioners and the lack of universally efficacious limitations on approved action, is ever on the verge of explosion. The values that go into foreign policy are deeply held and powerful; the restraints are relatively few and of imperfect effect. In many respects, therefore, international politics is a manifestation of the political process in its simplest form.

Interests, Goals, and Objectives

Our discussion up to this point has established that foreign policy is purposeful and that value judgments are the bases upon which a state proceeds in international politics. The state, however, must act in the real world; it cannot function effectively on behalf of values that remain abstract, absolute, and undefined. No foreign policy can really achieve "freedom," "power," "justice," "honor," or even "peace"—to cite a few of the more common values of foreign policy—except in concrete terms and in relation to specific situations. The statesman must, in a word, translate "values" into "objectives" before he can begin to act.

FROM "SOCIAL VALUES" TO "NATIONAL INTEREST"

The key concept a policy-maker uses in applying value judgments to the realities of political action is "national interest." Notoriously vague and difficult to define, the notion of national interest is nevertheless central to policy-making. It may be considered as the general, long-term, and continuing purpose which the state, the nation, and the government all see themselves as serving. It is rooted in the deepest soil of social consciousness and cultural identity of a people, and it includes all the disparate ideas of the good that we have earlier noted. In practice it is synthesized and given form by the official policy-makers themselves.

We cannot be more specific in defining the content of national interest, since both its value roots and the process of its synthesis are peculiar to a society, its history, and its institutional makeup. We can, however, be quite explicit about its function. As the overriding purpose governing the state's relations with the outside world, it serves two purposes: it gives policy a general orientation toward the external environment, and, more importantly, it serves as the controlling criterion of choice in immediate situations. The dominant view of national interest, in other words, dictates the nature of a state's long-term effort in foreign policy and governs what it does in a short-term context.

National interest thus flows from the application of a highly generalized value synthesis to the over-all situation in which a state is placed in world politics. It is thus, within the terms of its social origin, relatively slow to change, and change is "evolutionary rather than revolutionary." National interest provides the necessary measure of consistency to national policy; a state, consciously adhering to its national interest in a rapidly changing situation, is more likely to maintain its balance and continue to progress toward its goals than it would if it changed its interest in adapting to each new situation.

ENDS AND MEANS IN FOREIGN POLICY

The development of national interest (even if it is never verbalized) is the first step in formulating a foreign policy, even though it remains an abstract concept. Before the concept may actually serve as a guide to action, the statesman must grapple with a classic problem: the reconciliation of ends and means.

The ends of state action in international politics—the national interest and such national goals as may be derived from it—are postulated *a priori*. Before policy can be made, the statesman must somehow mesh the facts of his problem, including whatever means he has at his disposal, with the conceptual system formed by his set of ends. In specific policy situations, one of the most difficult problems policy-makers face is the determination of the most appropriate relationship between abstract ends and concrete means.

Ends, in theory, determine means; in a situation permitting several possible courses of action, that one should be chosen which most directly advances the national interest. In practice, however, there is always a real temptation to allow means to determine ends, to decide that that objective which is the most feasible to attain is actually the one that the state should seek. Intermediate ends—ends that, if achieved, are intended only to serve as means to still further ends—tend also to acquire an absolute relevance in themselves as ends.

Any confusion in the ends-means relationship, any loss of appreciation of the value roots of policy, or any reluctance to remain firmly committed to long-range concepts of interest, cannot help but deprive a foreign policy of vigor, effectiveness, and flexibility. Governments that succumb to these dangers quickly find themselves thrust on the strategic defensive and, to a major extent, placed at the mercy of others who know more precisely what it is they are trying to accomplish. There is no substitute for a clearly-rationalized and thoroughly understood purpose in foreign policy. This is especially true in the contemporary period, an era of great change in the international milieu.

THE NATURE OF AN OBJECTIVE

State action in foreign policy is always in pursuit of an "objective": that state-of-affairs that the state is seeking to bring about as being most in its national interest. An objective may call for some change in the existing situation or else for the protection and preservation of an existing set of relationships judged desirable. It is crucial, however, that an objective be formulated in concrete terms appropriate both to the conditions prevailing and to the effective range of action enjoyed by the state.

An objective flows from the application of national interest to the generalized situation in which the policy is being made. An intermediate value postulation antecedent to the choice of an objective is often made by the selection of a "goal," defined here as a quasi-Utopian formulation of what would be the most desirable state-of-affairs in the foreseeable future of a particular issue. The adoption of a goal, rooted as it is in the relatively fixed factors of the decisional milieu, assists materially in the evaluation of the dynamic forces that will shape the particular objective selected.

Thus within any single policy situation the relations of the national interest, the postulated goal, and the selected objective are largely functions of different time spans of analysis. National interest has at least an implication of perpetuity or ultimacy: its interest will presumably keep the state involved in the problem forever, or at least as long as the political system endures. A goal is set in terms of the maximum time span that can be anticipated analytically. As long as the general shape of the situation remains constant, the postulated goal will be controlling; any drastic change, however, would require the selection of a new goal more in harmony with the nature of the problem. An objective is immediate or short-range in its time component; the state-of-affairs that is the target of state action is attainable in terms of the forces operative at the moment of decision.

The ends-means relationship is central to the choice of an objective. The goal represents the best conceivable state-of-affairs, while the objective is actually the closest approximation to the goal that the decision-makers feel is feasible. The postulated end of state action in most situations does no more than point out the direction in which the state should move. How far it actually goes along this figurative "line of flight" depends on the means it has available for use in the situation.

It is essential that a policy-maker formulate his objective as precisely as possible, not alone because it gives him a means of concentrating his attention and his effort on issues that to him are crucial, but also because he can better appraise degrees of success or failure if he is quite clear about his aims. An objective stated in abstract and nebulous terms can never be "attained"; "peace," "prestige," and "power" alike are meaningless except with reference to a concrete context. Much state effort is wasted and many decisions rendered pointless because the objective is couched in fuzzy, abstract, and absolute terms.

THE COMMON OBJECTIVES OF STATES

After arguing as we have that each state's set of interests, goals, and policy objectives is unique to itself, it may seem somewhat contradictory to suggest that it is possible and useful to discuss "the common objectives of states." Although the uniqueness of state purpose is confined to matters of detail, the general problem of foreign policy presents itself to all states in the same fundamental terms. States are compelled by the logic of sovereignty and the inexorabilities of the political system in which they function to seek the same kinds of satisfaction. At least conceptually we may divide the objectives sought by any foreign policy into six categories, remembering of course that each state defines its purpose within each category in such specific language as suits its dominant interest.

1. Analytically, *self-preservation* must be considered an ubiquitous objective of state action. The "self," the preservation of which is deemed a supreme good, is the collective entity of the "state" and its human and territorial manifestations. A state's desire for existence, if it wishes to remain a state, is self-evident. States normally act so as to maximize their chances of survival in the world; for most this is simultaneously the highest and the most basic purpose of foreign policy.

2. Second in importance to self-preservation is the objective of *security*. The nature of the international political system is such that existence for any state is never certain. Each, therefore, is impelled to arrange its relations with the rest of the world so as to give itself the best possible opportunity for continued existence. This is usually called a "search for security," but real security is clearly unattainable under the conditions prevailing in the state system. What the security objectives of states amount to is no more than the reduction of all visible and conceivable threats to a practical minimum. A measure of insecurity is really an inescapable cost of doing business in the state system.

3. Third in the list of common objectives of states is what we call *well-being*. After the higher-priority objectives of self-preservation and security have been satisfied to the maximum permitted by the state's situation, the state then tries to improve the actual conditions of existence of its citizens. The well-being that is the object of state action is both conceptually and practically the welfare of the collectivity rather than that of individuals; the unit of calculation is "the economy" and the measures of prosperity tend today to be those familiar "macro-economic" concepts, "gross national product" and the "rate of economic growth." Of course there may be no real clash between collective well-being and the economic welfare of individuals, and even when such a conflict develops it is only seldom made explicit on any "guns or butter" basis. In cases of un-

avoidable divergence of interest, however, the normal pattern of political value choices dictates the intrinsic superiority of collective well-being over any individual or group interests.

4. Another common objective of state action is *prestige*. States normally act so as to appear impressive to others, and attempt to receive deference and status concessions from them. The achievement of a satisfactory prestige level is one of the more frustrating problems of foreign policy; how much prestige and status is enough in a given context? It is obvious that any politically self-conscious people has a strong urge to be well thought of by others and to wish concrete evidence of its prestige. One serious confusion that often complicates the search for prestige centers about the criteria of high status: a state may wish prestige in terms of certain aspects of its own ego-image, but may instead receive generous deference in other terms that do not meet its wants. A reputation for a high level of artistic achievement, for example, is of little significance to a state that wishes rank as a major military power. The difficulties implicit in any attempt to "win" prestige, however, have not served to deter states from the attempt.

5. Of somewhat less pervasiveness but of great importance to some states is the promotion and/or the protection of *ideology*. The present century is, far more than any since the sixteenth, an age of total belief systems, and a number of states, both large and small, have made both the protection and the promulgation of their ideologies a major element in foreign policy. Carrying within itself as it does implications of proselytization and messianism, ideology as a foreign-policy objective again raises questions of the explicitness and attainability of goals and of the criteria of success and failure in foreign policy. There is, furthermore, some contemporary evidence that even the more militant ideologically-oriented states have been having some second thoughts about the practicability of seeking ideological vindication by the processes of international politics.

6. Finally, we must take note of *power* as a common objective of states. As we shall be pointing out in a later chapter, power considerations belong more appropriately in a discussion of the means of foreign policy than in a catalogue of the ends of state action. Yet an indispensible preliminary step to the accomplishment of a goal may in fact be the accumulation of additional increments of power, and it is also true that for "reasons" of prestige or demands of se-

curity a state may overtly establish an increase in power as a major objective of policy. While it is a serious oversimplification to state flatly that all international politics is a struggle for power and that every state's primary motivation is the urge to augment its store, it is undeniable that for a broad variety of real or spurious reasons, many states do in fact legitimize power as an appropriate end of state action.

Policy and the Strategic Decision

The tension between ends and means is never more acute than when a state's policy-makers are approaching a decision whether or not to act and, if action is to be taken, what steps should be taken first. An objective must be selected and a course (or courses) of action launched. Officials must serve the interests and goals already formulated and yet must act in situations permitting only a limited range of means. The choices are often extremely difficult; policy decisions must be in the largest sense "strategic." Unable to accomplish everything they wish, states must weigh the competing claims on their resources and capabilities and decide not only what portion of their goals are susceptible of accomplishment at the moment but also the priority system that governs the relative emphasis given to different areas of action.

The Meaning of "Policy"

A "policy" is here understood to be a course of action designed to attain an objective. Although we shall defer the detailed analysis of policy-making until Chapter Two, certain larger aspects of the concept of policy are appropriately considered here.

We should first note a semantic difficulty. The "foreign policy" of a state refers usually to the general principles by which a state governs its reaction to the international environment; such catch-words as "isolationism," "balance of power," or "imperialism" are often, if somewhat inaccurately, used to characterize particular foreign policies. On the other hand, if a policy is, as we define it, a course of action oriented to a single objective, it follows that any state has many policies—as many as it has objectives. Thus "foreign policy" and "foreign policies" have completely different meanings. Probably the best way to avoid confusion is to keep in mind that foreign policy (singular) is usually phrased in terms of goals, whereas policies (plural) draw their relevance from objectives.

Second, a policy always involves both *decision* and *action*, with decision perhaps the more important ingredient. Action on behalf of an objective can result from policy only if the decision itself indicates clearly what the policy-maker had in mind both as to objective and as to procedure. As a result, the formalized decision (the "policy paper") normally includes at least three ingredients of clarification and guidance for the benefit of anyone who might be concerned with its implementation. These three elements of a decision are (1) the formulation of the objective in the most precise terms possible; (2) the nature of the action to be undertaken, stated with sufficient clarity to guide and direct the state's other officials; (3) the forms and perhaps the amounts of national power to be applied in the pursuit of the objective.

A third factor bearing on policy is reflected in the final point in this list. A policy decision normally calls for the commitment of resources, the assumption of a risk, or both. This is the "cost/risk" factor in policy-making which we shall examine later. Here we need only keep in mind that in foreign policy as in life, everything has its price. Often the most excruciating problem in policy determination is the decision about how much effort should be made in pursuit of an objective in view of competing claims of other goals and the limitations on the state's resources.

THE NEED FOR PRIORITIES

No state can accomplish everything it wishes in its foreign policy; almost by definition, a state's reach exceeds its grasp. Objectives and goals tend to formulation in absolute terms—a government speaks of "security," "peace," or "freedom," but never of "partial security," "relative peace," or "a measure of freedom" for itself. The ends of policy are thus unlimited, but the means are sharply limited both in logic and in fact. States, even large and "powerful" ones, have "champagne tastes and beer incomes," and must budget their effort as carefully as a housewife allocates her available funds.

Thus every state must have an operative system of priorities that governs its policy choices. Some questions are simply more important than others in terms of the social values on which the nation's approach is built. Some, indeed, are literally absolute, such as self-preservation; unless the state exists, any of its other purposes are really beside the point. Others, while clearly critical, must take second place to those of the highest priority. As the scale of priorities is elaborated, each intermediate objective takes its place in relation to all others, more important than some and yet inferior to others.

Priority ranking of interests, goals, and objectives is critical because it determines the relative claim that each has on the state's resources, energy, and "worry time." Such a set of criteria of intrinsic importance is a major determinant of policy. A state, for example, is always willing to suffer a setback with respect to a low-priority end in order to gain ground on a higher-priority goal. Over-all strategies are established on a priority basis; long-term commitments of power can only be made intelligently on the principle of "first things first."

A state that attempts to conduct its foreign policy without priorities, or with its priority system vague and imprecise, rapidly discovers that it has priorities imposed upon it by force of circumstance. With no real sense of the relative importance of the different problems it is called upon to deal with, all issues tend in practice to become equally significant; in many cases, each problem is dealt with as if it were of absolute priority. If all issues are of equal intrinsic importance, that one becomes operationally the most critical that is under consideration at the moment. Top priority thus tends to be assigned on the basis of recent occurrence rather than criticality.

The "importance" of issues is determined in every case by the internalized values of the state. No one outside a state can state unequivocally what ought to be the priorities of that state's policy; even self-preservation in fact has no more importance than a state chooses to give it, and cases can be found where states voluntarily chose to go out of existence in order better to achieve certain other values. The priorities that a state applies are its own, peculiar to its *Weltanschauung* and appropriate to no other society.

Thus far we have been using "importance" as if it were an

absolute, and as if priorities flow automatically from a single unified system of values. In practice, however, many kinds of concerns are important to a state, and the determination of the appropriate criterion of priority is frequently a serious problem in policy-making.

One of the more common conflicts that besets policy is between a functional or procedural priority on one hand and a substantive priority on the other. Priorities of means and priorities of ends, in other words, often apply in different ways and impose hard choices. A state, for example, may be vitally interested in the preservation of the principle and the practice of peaceful change in world affairs in general (a procedural priority) and yet may at the same time be under great pressure to use force to make an important gain in its level of security (a substantive priority). There is, unfortunately, no easy or simple answer to this dilemma; governments resolve it recurrently on an *ad hoc* basis.

In another dimension, priorities lend themselves to confusion: time. Every government often finds itself in a situation in which a particular move, if it is to be made at all, must be made immediately—even though the issue is intrinsically minor and the step will in some way be a blow to another enterprise of greater ultimate significance but of less immediate relevance. In most cases the officials concerned make every effort to avoid irreparable damage to their long-range and higher priority concerns while dealing with immediate issues; only by accident or by almost inexcusable carelessness will a government become so engrossed in its immediate problems as to permit more significant long-range issues to go by the board.

A final consequence of an unclear priority system should be noted. If a government faces a priority choice without being sure of its own criteria of importance, it may seek the easy way out by refusing to make any choice at all. Its policy effort will therefore be expended in an attempt to defer the necessity of decision, demonstrated most explicitly by maneuvering for the purchase of time. If the breathing space it wins is used to resolve its priority dilemma, it may deal effectively with the difficult choice when it arises again. If, however, the time bought is frittered away uselessly, the need for a decision might not only come again but the conditions of choice may be much less favorable.

THE CLASSIC COMPROMISE

The task of the statesman, as the cliché puts it, is to "reconcile the desirability of the possible with the possibility of the desirable." No other formulation of foreign policy has so aphoristically, yet inclusively, epitomized the operating mission of the responsible decision-maker.

Much of our preceding discussion has been leading up to this point. In any policy situation, the state has a range of ends, all of them desirable in terms of its interests, that can be arranged in order of preferability. Some of these are attainable with ease, some are attainable only by great effort, and others are beyond the range of attainability. On the other hand, the state also has a spectrum of action open to it. It has the capacity to produce a number of different outcomes. Some of these may be highly desirable, others neutral in desirability, and still others inherently undesirable. The two curves of desirability and possibility cross at the point of decision. The mission of the policy-maker is to ensure that the action takes place as far as possible along the curve of desirability.

Thus foreign policy normally consists of enterprises involving partial commitments of capability for the accomplishment of partial purposes. As a rule a state does not count on obtaining either all it wants or all it can get in any situation; rather it attempts *to get all it can of what it wants*. The policy decision is thus always a compromise.

INITIATIVES AND RESPONSES

The "strategic decision" is in all states marked by a relative emphasis on prudence and restraint. Strategy is a cautious enterprise; the consequences of failure in statecraft may be so destructive that rational statesmen refuse to give themselves the benefit of any analytical doubt in setting a course of action.

Thus it follows that for the vast majority of states, policy is more responsive than it is initiatory. In an environment so productive of dangers and threats, policy-makers attempt first to rationalize the conditions of existence within the system before they seek to bring about changes in the system in their own behalf. Only after a state has dealt adequately with stimuli arising from outside itself does it feel free to launch its own enterprises. Responses to challenges are a first charge on a state's resources. Initiatives are undertaken only with increments of capability thought surplus to its foreseeable needs.

Of course, the key notion in this relationship is—as it so often is in foreign policy—that of "adequacy." In one sense no state can respond completely to all the challenges produced by the external environment. Absolute security is, as we have noted, unattainable. But even within the limits imposed by the inevitable burden of risk a state carries, difficult decisions of adequacy and the allocation of resources and effort plague policy-making.

Some states, either because of especially fortunate situations or, more commonly, relatively optimistic interpretations of the nature and extent of the challenges they face and of the necessary responses, find themselves endowed with relatively extensive capability to undertake initiatives. In other words, states with greater prowess in scientific achievement, technological innovations, and military power, have greater freedom to assert themselves against lesser states. If powerful states have an interest in working environmental change, they are able to blend desirability and possibility at a comparatively high level. This is a common characteristic of the strategy adopted by Communist states. Others, however, interpret their requirements as demanding that a large proportion of their capability be committed to a range of responses with only a modest surplus left for the initiation of policies. Democratic states in the contemporary era are often accused of such caution in analysis that their policies are purely responsive. From such differences in the interpretation that each state makes of the effective environment and of its capacity for initiative, as well as from its internalized image of its world role, flow fundamental differences in policy. We shall examine these variations and their implications in the next section.

Types of Foreign Policies

Even after we admit that each state views its own international problem as unique and develops patterns of response and initiation that are peculiar to its situation, we can still conclude that it is possible and useful to classify the foreign policies of states. Our system of classification is not an elaborate one, since it includes only two categories. The conclusions that stem from them, however, are applicable in a significant way and cover a broad range of instances.

THE TWO CATEGORIES OF PURPOSE

Throughout this chapter we have stressed the basic role in foreign policy played by social values and the image of national and state purpose. We have identified foreign policy as the government's attempt to maximize those social values that require implementation on an international scale. We have identified "purpose" with the ends of policy and attempted to demonstrate the centrality of ideas of purpose to the totality of state effort in international politics. Now we examine the content of purpose so as to distinguish the different ways states structure their missions.

As a people, speaking through its leaders, applies its value structure to the generalized world environment, it cannot escape passing a fundamental judgment on the relationship between its society and all others. Such a verdict can be affirmative: the society may conclude that it is basically satisfied with its place in the world, and such readjustments as it wishes to make are minor and do not call for major change in the international structure. On the other hand, the conclusion may be negative: the society may decide that the place it is occupying in the world is unacceptable. Either decision determines all subsequent discussion of foreign policy.

If the society decides that it is willing to accept indefinitely the general shape of the world and its place in it, its over-all international purpose will become a conserving (not necessarily *conservative*) one. If, however, it rejects the role which it is playing at the moment, by that decision it may choose to bring about change in the international order in its own interest. Every state in the world, at some time or another and in many varying ways, has made such a choice and then based a foreign policy on it.

This selection of a generalized category of purpose is in the nature of a pure value judgment. There are no objective criteria by which an observer can anticipate what evaluation of the environment a people will make. The elements that produce the eventual conclusion are imbedded in the social dynamics of a people and assume unpredictable and often eccentric forms.

Some years ago, students felt that this duality of purpose could be meaningfully reflected by a classification of states into "have" and "have-not" categories. Unfortunately, this division was not sufficiently explicit about what it was that the "have" nations possessed that produced satisfaction or what it was that the "have-nots" lacked that made them dissatisfied. In some cases it was a level of material well-being that apparently served as the crucial criterion; in others, considerations of status and prestige; and in still others, obvious dissatisfaction with a historic role or a nostalgia for former eminence, and so on. The best we can say is that a nation is satisfied with its world role if its critical values are receiving adequate fulfillment. Dissatisfaction follows a conclusion that certain critical categories of value needs are not being met. Each state is the only final judge of what the determinants may be and how high a level of satisfaction is adequate.

It is from this idea of purpose that the controlling concept of national interest develops. The "general and continuing" end for which a state acts and sees itself as acting is derived from that state's interpretation of its role in the international order. It provides a large part of the filtering mechanism through which data from the external environment passes and in terms of which the information is given relevance and meaning. It is, finally, from the notion of purpose that the criteria of success and failure in foreign policy are derived.

THE POLICY OF THE STATUS QUO

From a concept of purpose that stresses satisfaction and conservation arises the policy orientation that we call "*status quo*." States that assume this international role develop policies that show a number of common distinguishing traits.

Before examining the content of a policy of the status quo, however, we must carefully define the sense in which we are using this very common but often misunderstood concept. The status quo a state seeks to preserve is its own status *vis-à-vis* the rest of the international system and its other members. The acceptance of a status quo posture does not necessarily imply an enthusiastic embracing of the details of the existing state of affairs, but rather only a judgment that the over-all pattern of value satisfaction the state is extracting from the international system is the most favorable it can hope for by any reasonable expenditure of effort. Thus a status quo policy by no means condemns the state to the inflexible defense of all the details of an established order; indeed, an enlightened status quo position—particularly when held by a major power—leaves ample room for extensive situational change and the exertion of initiatives by the state concerned. What is beyond major modification, however, is the state's own relation to the system as a whole.

Status quo policies, therefore, are defensive in strategic orientation, however much they may from time to time call for tactical offensives. Accordingly, the controlling notion of national interest is couched in terms of "defense," "preservation," and "neutralization" rather than those of "offense," "change," and "advantage." Status quo policies seek the stabilization of relationships rather than their modification. They normally press for the wide adoption of all manner of institutional and procedural restraints on the outer limits of state action.

A state following a status quo policy accepts conflict as a condition of existence, but only seldom initiates it. When caught in an overt struggle, it consciously attempts to avoid any escalation in the terms of conflict, works for a resolution of the dispute at as low a level of tension as possible, and is normally willing to accept an inconclusive outcome as being really a victory—since it is left in possession of whatever prizes it had at the beginning of the disagreement. It is axiomatic that status quo states never initiate major wars.

The policy of the status quo, whether followed by a large state or a small one, is directed toward the evolution of the international system into a stabilized and regularized set of relationships that incorporate the relatively advantageous situation the state enjoys at the moment. As a result, status quo policies tend to be marked by restraint in conception, caution in execution, and the acceptance of only a comparatively small burden of risk. Operationally, their strength lies in their capacity to anticipate situational change and to develop rapid and efficacious responses to it. When status quo policies are prevalent in the international system, the general atmosphere is one of relative quiet and relaxation; change is slow, evolutionary, and limited in extent.

THE POLICY OF REVISIONISM

The second type of foreign policy—that which flows from a rejection of the current status and role of the state—is known as "revisionism." It is in almost every conceptual aspect the antonym of the policy of the status quo.

Revisionism aims at the favorable modification of the state's over-all international position in the system. It does not necessarily demand the operating assumption that all international relationships are fluid and subject to change, but only those that it feels are crucial. As to those points which epitomize its dissatisfaction, however, it will accept no solution as final except one that gives it the measure of fulfillment it demands.

A policy of revisionism is strategically an offensive one. National interest demands major environmental change in the state's favor, and policy is directed toward the discovery or the creation of opportunities for effective action and their immediate and complete exploitation. Relationships are not amenable to stabilization until the state achieves what it seeks. Revisionist states, therefore, are normally cool to proposals for the organization of international politics in any way that might inhibit their carefully guarded freedom of action.

Revisionist states do more than accept conflict; they actively seek it as long as it offers a hope for the rational attainment of an objective. They will normally accept a higher level of tension in a dispute, are less averse to escalation (at least up to a point), and are much more resistant to accepting a stalemate or a draw than are status quo states. In a struggle between an exemplar of each type, it is normally the revisionist state that begins the conflict and sets its terms; in any such controversy that does not go to the limit of all-out war, furthermore, it is usually the revisionist state that also decides how long the dispute will continue. Major wars, therefore, have been usually begun by states that were revisionist in orientation, at least at the time the critical decision was made.

A revisionist policy is characterized by relative daring in con-

ception, an optimistic calculation of factors of cost, and a willingness to carry a relatively large burden of risk. Its operational advantage lies in its capacity to bring about situational change or
quickly to capitalize upon it. An historic period dominated by
revisionist policies, therefore, is marked by a high level of tension
in politics and a rate of change that is both rapid and extensive.

Bibliography

Beloff, Max, *Foreign Policy and the Democratic Process*. Baltimore:
    Johns Hopkins Press, 1955.

Buck, P. W. and Travis, M., Jr. (eds.), *Control of Foreign Relations
    in Modern Nations*. New York: Norton and Company, 1957.

* Coran, Melvin, *Soviet Foreign Policy Since the World War II*. New
    York: Frederick A. Praeger, 1963.

* Goldwin, Robert A., (ed.) *Readings in World Politics*. New York:
    Oxford University Press, 1959.

Gross, Feliks, *Foreign Policy Analysis*. New York: Philosophical Li-
    brary, 1954.

Hoffman, Stanley, *Contemporary Theories in International Relations*.
    Englewood Cliffs, New Jersey: Prentice-Hall, 1960.

* Kennan, George, *American Diplomacy 1900–1950*. Chicago: Chicago
    University Press, 1951.

* Lasswell, Harold D., *Politics, Who Gets What, When, How*. New
    York: The Meridian Books, 1961.

* Macridis, Roy C. (ed.), *Foreign Policy in World Politics* 2d ed.,
    Englewood Cliffs, New Jersey: Prentice-Hall, 1962.

Modelski, George A., *Theory of Foreign Policy*. New York: Frederick
    A. Praeger, 1962.

Morgenthau, Hans J., *In Defense of the National Interest: A Critical
    Examination of American Foreign Policy*. New York: Alfred A.
    Knopf, 1951.

————, and Kenneth W. Thompson, *Principles and Problems of Inter-
    national Politics*. New York: Alfred A. Knopf, 1950.

Osgood, Robert E., *Ideals and Self-Interest in America's Foreign Re-
    lations*. Chicago: Chicago University Press, 1953.

Rosenau, James N. (ed.), *International Politics and Foreign Policy*.
    New York: The Free Press of Glencoe, 1961.

* Young, Ronald (ed.), *Approaches to the Study of Politics*. Evanston,
    Illinois: Northwestern University Press, 1958.

—————
* Indicates paperback edition.

Two

Government
and Policy Making

W e have already established that states act purposefully in international politics and that an essential part of the process of foreign policy is making and implementing decisions. Our next inquiry, therefore, is into the ways states organize themselves for their international contacts and the considerations that influence their decisions.

State Organization for International Action

GOVERNMENT AND FOREIGN AFFAIRS

In the delicately balanced and perilous world of today, foreign affairs in some form is one of the principal concerns of all states. For a small state the problem may involve no more than the basic issue of survival; for larger ones, to the basic requirements of security are usually added a variety of positive objectives that each hopes to attain in its own behalf. Each state's task in the international arena is peculiar to itself, but for all states, foreign policy is a matter of high priority and major import.

As might be expected, therefore, all governments organize themselves for foreign affairs with considerable care and relative elaborateness. However inefficiently domestic policy may be framed and executed, and however casual may be internal political arrangements, no state or its government can afford to function internationally for very long except at its absolutely maximum level of effectiveness. Foreign policy establishments in any state reflect at any time the best of which the society is capable.

Organization for foreign policy is roughly identical in all governments. Atop the organizational pyramid stands the head of government, testifying by his active role to the basic significance of international affairs. He is directly assisted by whatever close advisory and administrative apparatus the government boasts, whether a "cabinet" of the British type, a "Presidium" as in the Soviet Union, or a less institutionalized Cabinet-Executive Office arrangement as is the case in the United States. The principal foreign-affairs specialist in the government is the foreign minister (in the United States, the Secretary of State), who heads the administrative department concerned with foreign policy and is the head of government's principal official adviser. In all states other departments participate directly in foreign-policy decision; financial and military experts almost always do, and economic ministers (on questions of trade or development) have become virtually as critical. Legislative bodies play roles dependent on their constitutional place, but by and large foreign policy is primarily an executive prerogative, only occasionally inhibited by legislative interference.

A real part in decision-making is played by the corps of representatives a nation maintains abroad. Diplomatic personnel are ubiquitous today, and economic, cultural, and military representatives are growing in number from every nation. The information they relay to their home governments obviously affects policy; in addition, they conduct many negotiations themselves.

THE HEAD OF GOVERNMENT

The head of government, be he President, Prime Minister, or Dictator, is the key figure in all foreign-policy decisions. By virtue of the special responsibility international practice confers upon him (only he may officially speak for the state in international relationships), and as a result of his internal status as political leader of his people, he merges in his person more of the nation's foreign policy authority than can be found anywhere else. No institutional arrangements can eliminate or blur his primary responsibility.

The head of government may of course structure his mission in any of a great variety of ways. He naturally seeks advice and information to guide his decisions, but he may either rely on the opinions of his subordinates or instead trust his own judgments and intuition. He may function entirely within the official apparatus; he may, on the other hand, rely more on informal and unofficial sources of recommendations—for example, the Communist Party in the USSR, the "kitchen cabinet" in the United States, or "the Establishment" in Great Britain. He may confine his personal attention only to issues of massive and general import and leave their detailed implementation to subordinates, or he may intervene into the decisional process in matters of great detail and short-run impact.

In general, we may pinpoint responsibility as the uniform foreign-policy function of heads of government. Each assumes a range of operational duties appropriate both to the internal and external political situation and to his own personality and interests. It is clear, however, that his place is indispensable; nothing can be done by a state in international relations except with his participation and his actual or tacit sanction.

The peculiar function of the head of government lies especially in the province of political leadership. Whatever the controlling internal dynamics may be, the head of government must somehow translate the prevailing value pattern and operative consensus of the mass public opinion into foreign-policy terms. Whether he be a dictator or a popularly-chosen leader, as the visible symbol of national unity it is his task to formulate national purposes and give them expression in the form of concrete objectives. Under modern conditions heads of government expend an ever-increasing proportion of their effort to maintain this nexus between an ever-changing international environment and the political community which they lead. Their policy decisions tend therefore to become increasingly general, symbolic, and direction-setting, and less concerned with immediate operational choices.

FOREIGN MINISTER AND FOREIGN OFFICE

Foreign ministers in most states have a peculiarly taxing role. On one hand, they must be specialists and technicians, concerned with the innumerable complexities of day-by-day decisions. They must also have an appreciation of the larger internal and external political problems with which their respective chiefs are faced. Simultaneously they must be administrators (as each is the head of the Foreign Office and foreign service of his state), policy-makers (insofar as they are permitted to be by their superiors), and advisers.

To this multiple responsibility has in many cases been added yet another task: that of high-level negotiation. New improvements in transportation and communication, and the need for quick decision have given the foreign ministers of all leading powers and of many smaller ones a roving commission to travel widely and to conduct all important negotiations among themselves, either bilaterally, before the United Nations, or in some form of "conference." Obviously, foreign ministers seized with complex and protracted discussions of a problem cannot always obtain workable solutions, and organizational strains and dilution of effort are predictable consequences of their profession. Whatever the disadvantages, however, foreign ministers' meetings (and their logical outgrowth, "summit" meetings among heads of government) have become a thoroughly normal feature of international political life.

The foreign office of each state constitutes the primary grouping of expertise on international matters to be found within the government. Generally speaking, its domestic personnel are relatively few in number, although—at least in free governments—some significant increase has taken place in recent years. It is normally organized for action into subsections that reflect the nature of its task. There is normally a breakdown by geographic areas corresponding to the nation's involvement in various parts of the world, and also what the U. S. Department of State terms "functional bureaus," each of which focuses on a special function in a global context.

There is thus a dual mission for a foreign office. It has an operational task to communicate with its own personnel abroad and with foreign diplomatic missions in its own country. In performing this dual role, foreign office personnel make a vast number of policy decisions at all but the highest level of importance. On the other hand, the foreign office acts as a source of policy recommendations that flow upward to the higher decisional levels: the foreign minister, the cabinet, the head of government and his staff. In this respect, foreign-policy bureaucrats often, by defining alternatives and selecting data, materially influence the ultimate decisions.

In most states, foreign-office personnel form a part of the inner bureaucratic elite within the government. The crucial as well as the esoteric nature of their responsibilities tend to confer an aura of preferment, and, in addition, create some residual envy and resentment in officials of other departments. As foreign policy responsibilities have become diffused throughout many executive agencies— as has been the case in most powerful states—intragovernmental rivalries have impeded the optimum mobilization of national effort. This has been particularly true in the United States.

THE DIPLOMATIC SERVICE

Every state maintains a network of diplomatic missions abroad; one in each state with which it conducts relations. It also acts as host for similar missions sent by other states. Thus communications flow in a dual channel: a message may go directly from the foreign ministry to the resident ambassador of a second state, or it may go to the nation's ambassador abroad for delivery to the other foreign minister.

Each mission abroad is led by a "chief of mission," usually titled "ambassador." His function is multiple: he represents his state before the host government; he acts as a channel of communication; he reports information to his own government; he performs a public relations task for his state before the people of his host country; he maintains contact with his own nationals who are subject to the jurisdiction of his host country; and he may from time to time conduct negotiations. The present century has seen a great magnification of the public-relations and representational roles of ambassadors, and a corresponding diminution of the function of negotiation. Though in some respects regrettable, the substantial elimination of the ambassador as an important decision-maker was inevitable as soon as instantaneous communication and rapid transportation made it possible for responsible officials to conduct negotiations themselves.

Embassies vary in size and structure according to the importance of the states to each other and the prestige figure each wishes to cut. Regardless of size or detailed organization, however, some degree of specialization of function among embassy personnel is the rule. For purposes of reporting and representation, different officers

concentrate on political, economic, cultural, labor, and other matters; specialized (non-foreign office) representatives for military,
scientific, commercial, agricultural, and various other kinds of
affairs are frequently found, at least in the embassies of larger and
more prosperous states.

Most governments rotate diplomatic personnel between assign-
ments abroad and tours of duty in the foreign office. There is much
to be gained by this practice. Policy-makers at home thus gain an
appreciation of the problems faced by diplomats abroad, while the
missions themselves gain insight into the larger dimensions of national policy and into the difficulties of decision-making which
confront their own governments.

Complicating the task of diplomats abroad in recent years has
been the proliferation of what the United States calls "operating
missions": task forces charged with executing within a country,
programs already negotiated diplomatically. The exact status of
the operating mission *vis-à-vis* the resident diplomatic staff, has
proved troublesome for American officials and has caused considerable tension. Other states that have adopted this device of implementing policy have encountered the same sort of problem. Since
the lines of control and authority of the operating mission and the
diplomatic mission do not coincide, the resolution of jurisdictional
conflicts often rotates upward to higher administrative personnel,
sometimes even onto the shoulders of the foreign minister or
similar head of government.

OTHER DEPARTMENTS

The centrality of foreign affairs to most governments is clearly
demonstrated by the wide involvement of other departments in
the matter. Every government brings a broad spectrum of insights
and capabilities into the process of making and executing foreign
policy.

Two departments are virtually universal in their participation:
the agency charged with raising and allocating public funds (the
Treasury Department in the United States, the Exchequer in Britain,
the Finance Ministry in many states) and the military establishment. Each brings its special orientation to matters of international
affairs.

Foreign policy for major states is very expensive. Questions of national survival, security, and interest are a top-priority charge on the state's resources. Thus any major foreign-policy decision (and most minor ones as well) involves some charge on public finance and requires the active or tacit approval of the appropriate department. Matters of taxation, furthermore, touch sensitive nerves in the body politic, and general political considerations cannot help but affect any decision to commit public funds to international purposes. In an era in which most governments are taxing their citizens to the practical maximum and any increase will touch off resistance, great caution is required before budgetary increases for foreign policy purposes can be undertaken.

By far the largest share of expenditure for foreign policy purposes—at least for the more important states—goes for the military establishment. Most governments today are deeply committed to the maintenance of as large a military force as is practicable. Motivations of security contribute to this urge in the majority of cases, but for others the dominant factor is clearly a search for prestige. We must also keep in mind that in many of the new and unstable states the military machine is an instrument of government and political leadership.

These various considerations all have the same effect: military leadership and the armed forces are actively involved in foreign-policy making in almost all states. They bring a special point of view—notably a distrust of "politics" as bargaining and a strong preference for direct methods—to all deliberations in which they take part. Usually they find themselves actually or potentially at odds with the foreign office.

Increasingly important in almost all states today is the economic ministry. For developed states its primary concern with foreign policy lies in the area of international trade; for underdeveloped ones, with the problems intrinsic to industrial development. From time to time its recommendations may be absolutely controlling. This is indeed the case with many young states in Asia and Africa today. Because the economic health of a nation has a direct effect on the amount of resources it may commit to international politics, no government can indefinitely ignore the economic consequences of its policy. This fact alone would make economic specialists important in foreign-policy making.

Other agencies usually play a role more periodic and irregular. Perhaps special mention should be made of whatever organization the government maintains for propaganda. Modern mass communications are a powerful tool of domestic leadership and an effective instrument of policy. Propaganda experts are thus of great relevance and often of critical importance. Other departments with foreign-policy responsibility tend to be called into the decisional process as their special orientation dictates and as the particular problem demands.

The Policy Process

The entire foreign-policy organization of a state exists for the purpose of making and executing decisions taken to advance its interests. Because the basic ingredients of the decision-making process are substantially identical in all states, we turn now to the policy process within any government.

THE PROCESS OF DECISION

Analytically we may conceive foreign-policy decisions as flowing from the appreciation of a fluid and only imperfectly perceived situation by the corps of official decision-makers. In this effort they use criteria of interest and purpose stemming from their social milieu and professional background, modified by their peculiar institutional setting. Although national interest as a concept has deep social roots, in any particular decisional situation its expression is undertaken by the responsible decision-makers.

Thus the steady input of information to the decisional hierarchy undergoes constant analysis and evaluation as the officials attempt to determine which of the various events so affects the nation as to require decision and possibly action. These stimuli come from the "external setting." For most states the majority of data are simply noted and disregarded as peripheral to the national interest; only a few major states have such widespread concerns as to make their involvement almost total. Only those matters that are judged to have policy relevance are actually put to analysis and enter the process of decision.

The bulk of state activity in international affairs, therefore, may be thought of as "reaction" or "interaction": responses to stimuli external to the state. A portion of any foreign policy consists of "action" in the pure sense: efforts undertaken in response to internal stimuli so as to modify the environment in a desired direction. The norms of strategic decision ordinarily make this a matter of lower priority than the crucial business of constant response and adaptation to external stimuli, many of which are actually or potentially inimical. A state's first responsibility is to ensure its continued existence and effective range of choice; only after it has done all it can to guarantee its sheer participation in the system can it safely attempt to bend events to its purpose.

If foreign policy thus consists of the application of a set of internalized criteria of judgment to a dynamic external situation, we may conceptualize the process as consisting of the following steps: (1) the establishment of the original criteria; (2) the determination of the relevant variables in the situation; (3) the measurement of the variables by the criteria; (4) the selection of an objective; (5) the elaboration of a strategy to reach the objective; (6) the decision to act; (7) the action itself; (8) the evaluation of the results of the action in terms of the original criteria.

We must keep in mind that this formulation is an abstraction applicable only to a single problem, and that in practice the procedure is never so clear-cut. States conduct many decisional operations simultaneously. Each analysis has its own peculiarities. Each affects all the others and is affected by them. Very few decisions go through to completion without being modified by changing circumstances and many enterprises are dropped without reaching fulfillment because time and new concerns have rendered them obsolete. In spite of these practical warnings, however, the schematic presentation above is valuable because it distinguishes the various intellectual operations involved in a foreign-policy decision.

THE ANALYSIS OF SITUATIONS

Having once decided that a situation merits decision, officials then undertake a situational analysis in some depth. Their purpose here is two-fold. They seek initially to discover the manner and the extent of their involvement in the situation under scrutiny in order to arrive at the most advantageous objective for their government to seek. (In Chapter One we noted that "objectives" derive from concrete situations in contrast to "goals" that are postulated *a priori*.) The second purpose of their analytical effort is to delimit the actional possibilities open, and to discover the different courses of action the situation makes possible, independently of their relative desirability.

Situational analysis ordinarily requires the consideration of three distinct sets of factors: (1) the general pattern of forces operative in the area of decision that lie beyond the control of any single state; (2) the particular policies being followed by other states—at least the important ones—in the given context; (3) one's own capabilities for action in the light of the first two factors. In theory, this analysis is as objective and cold-blooded as professional skill can make it. Only by the best possible comprehension and appreciation of the situation can successful policy choices be made. So many intangible factors must be weighed and evaluated that no government can be more than approximately accurate in this effort.

Only after situational analysis can an objective be selected. Only after the decision-makers understand what can be done can they decide what they will attempt to do. This point is of central importance in the decisional process. It is not until after the objective has been selected that the situation permits re-analysis with an eye to the selection of the optimum course of action designed to bring about the hoped-for-state-of-affairs.

It should be emphasized once more that the situational context of a decision is analyzed at least three times. The first stresses long-term factors so as to develop a working concept of interest. The second focuses on middle-range aspects in order to suggest an objective. The third concentrates on short-run and immediate variables; this emphasis is productive of alternative strategies and policy declarations in the narrow sense.

THE CHOICE AMONG ALTERNATIVES

The key concept in the analysis of policy is "choice": any decision-maker so conducts himself as to preserve at any stage in the process his maximum range of choice. In practice this results in formulating his opportunities (or his imperatives) as a set of alternatives of action.

Strategically the principle of alternatives is often formulated in negative terms: "Never put yourself in a situation in which you have only one possible course of action." As long as one state retains a choice of tactics, its opponent must go to the trouble of devising responses to each of the various lines it can follow, and thus dilute its effort. A lack of alternatives, however, condemns a state to a predictable response and to facing a predetermined counter-strategy. Formulating decisions as a choice among alternatives, in a word, is a way of examining all opportunities and of conserving whatever strategic advantages may flow from forcing uncertainty and risk on the decision-makers of other states.

Thus the approach to a decision is usually cast—with varying degrees of formalization depending on the elements of time and change in the situation—as a canvass of all the alternatives open to the state in the particular context, together with estimates of the probable outcome of each alternative. This spectrum of choice forms the ultimate agenda of the "decisional unit"—whether a single policy-maker or a group. From the open alternatives, that one is selected that promises the greatest gain or, as often happens, the least loss in terms of the criteria of choice that are controlling at the moment.

We must understand that the range of alternatives seldom includes many bad choices and only one "right" one. Most of the time, the real range of choice is fairly narrow and the policy and interest differentials among the various alternatives are relatively small. Selection of one is often difficult, especially when pressures of time or administrative necessity telescope the decisional process or eliminate certain steps altogether. No state can dispense entirely with alternatives, however obscure their differences may be in a particular situation. Policy cannot for long be made on an *ad hoc* basis, nor can any government cheerfully give up the flexibility the process contributes to decision-making.

Basing a decision on a choice among alternatives, especially if the several courses of action are not mutually exclusive, makes it much easier for a state to adapt itself to the consequences of an error or an unforeseen circumstance in its original decision. If the selected course of action fails to evoke the hoped-for response, an appreciation of the alternatives (and their consequences) originally canvassed will facilitate a shift to another line of policy. There will be no need to go through the entire process again. The decision-makers can better develop "fall-back positions" in advance of their being needed if the entire spectrum of choice is kept firmly in mind.

In rapidly-moving situations, it is not uncommon for a state to launch a course of action with no clear idea of its ultimate outcome. The general line of attack is itself the result of a choice among alternatives, and contains within itself further alternatives. One (perhaps several) of these will be adopted depending on the nature of the response to its initial initiative. Thus policy is kept abreast of situational change with—if implementation is forceful—a consequent gain in effectiveness. We must admit, however, that for most states such extreme flexibility is usually beyond their capability. Only relatively powerful states can afford to enter active maneuvering with several alternative approaches available, each equally within its competence to pursue.

The usual method of testing the validity of a choice is by taking its initial steps in a tentative fashion and leaving an escape route open for use if the judgment proves to have been faulty. In such a case, a state can hold its losses to a minimum while preserving freedom of action to strike off later on a different tack. Only after the correctness of its assumptions and the accuracy of its situational analysis have been reasonably confirmed does a state permit itself to become committed fully to its initial choice of action.

EVALUATING AND REVISING DECISIONS

Throughout this discussion of the policy process, it has been evident that state action is contingent for its effectiveness upon the extent to which it is responsive to the actual situation. Since decisions are always made upon incomplete and inaccurate information, it follows that prudence would demand a major effort at the constant evaluation of the results of decisions and immediate revision of policies that are not in fact producing the desired effect.

Here modern communications media are of great utility to the policy-makers. Where in an earlier age he would ordinarily be forced to wait weeks or months to learn the response to one of his moves, today he can get this information within a much shorter period—sometimes instantly. In this sense the process of evaluation and revision is much simpler.

But in another way, modern conditions complicate the task of making decisions. Events today move even more rapidly than decisions—which after all are made by human beings subject to fatigue and bad temper. Furthermore, the very complexity of foreign policy leads major states to implement their decisions by relatively fixed commitments and long-term "programs"—both extremely difficult to change even in circumstances of stress. A third factor vitiating evaluation is the sheer press of foreign policy business. When new problems, clamoring for decision, crowd in on the decision-maker, he is much more likely to deal with them than to turn to the tedious and often agonizing reappraisal of earlier decisions to see if they worked out as expected.

It is therefore not uncommon today for a particular policy to be utterly invalidated by an unexpected train of events that adequate evaluation and revision would have anticipated. Major powers with extensive and complicated networks of commitments are particularly prone to this danger. For them, constant evaluation is the most necessary, and yet for them it is usually the most difficult. Smaller states, with less margin for error, and with a narrower range of concerns as well, have proved much more adept at adjusting their policies to even modest situational evolution.

Factors Influencing Decisions

Foreign policy is not made by electronic computers. It is formulated by men who lack mathematical precision but who do possess judgment. We have seen that a policy decision incorporates a choice. What factors influence the selection of one course of action rather than another?

THE APPRECIATION OF THE PROBLEM

Decision-making must begin with an understanding of what the decision itself is about. No policy choice can be made without an appreciation of the problem the decision is to affect. This truism is often overlooked in much of the discussion of policy-making in the United States.

To begin with, it is probable that no two officials in any government see the same set of facts in identical "problem" terms. Each brings his own personality, professional and organizational bias, and intuitive skill to bear on his task, and each may have his own sources of information. It would be too much to expect all of them to identify the same variables as operative. A large part of the "Tower of Babel" effect in policy-making—especially in western democracies—flows from this variance in the over-all appreciation of the policy environment among those charged with responding to it. One significant task of leadership, whether political or professional, is to impose controlling criteria of problem identification upon all subordinate decision-makers.

Another confusion sometimes stems from the semantic trap laid by the word "problem." Strategy is a cautious business at best, and the natural tendency (at least in western languages) to conceptualize "problem" (as incorporating an obstacle to be overcome and pressures to be resisted) only reinforces this tendency. If "problem" is understood to be the factor in a situation that demands solution, and if it is borne firmly in mind that, in logic, a "problem" is as likely to constitute an opportunity as an obstacle, the possible deadening effect of the idea can be minimized. It is as problematic to determine ways of capitalizing on an unexpected advantage as it is to develop a strategy to lessen the effect of misfortune.

A crucial element in any problem analysis is the early selection of an objective to the attainment of which the nation's effort will be committed. This is the essence of "strategy," defined as a plan for the employment of resources for the attainment of a predetermined end. On the broadest foreign policy scale, such a plan may accurately be termed a "national strategy." Since all operational decisions are made in terms of postulated goals, the identification and evaluation of strategic objectives constitute a major step in the process of problem identification. This task, however, is more complex than it might seem at first sight.

Even if the decision-maker has a firm grasp on national goals and an adequate comprehension of the situation, he ordinarily encounters difficulty in formulating objectives. On one hand he is aware of ends derived from the *a priori* value postulates that underlie his nation's notion of interest. On the other, he sees other ends notable because their achievement seems feasible. One set of possible objectives, in a word, is attractive because of its intrinsic *desirability*, while the other group has *feasibility* in its favor. Only rarely will a single objective rank high on both scales. The task of the decision-maker thus beset by opposing constructions of the problem is to strike the best possible balance between the desirability and the feasibility of the various objectives he perceives and to act on the basis of this compromise.

THE COST/RISK CALCULATION

A second major factor that affects foreign-policy decision is the cost/risk calculation. No state can count on getting anything free in international politics. Any decision to take action will exact cost. Furthermore, even with the maximum intellectual and physical effort, any policy carries with it some risk of failure. The twin cautions of cost and risk tend sharply to delimit the real range of choice of the policy-maker.

In considering a possible line of action, the decision-maker dare not give himself the benefit of any doubt. In establishing a possible cost factor, he must assume the worst possible consequences of his move. He must, in other words, convince himself that the objective he is seeking is worth the highest price his nation might be called upon to pay for it. Only after he has made this decision is he free to take implementing action.

Of course, the "worst possible consequences" are actually those that are foreseeable in the light of the policy-maker's supply of information. Were "possible" to be taken literally, every decision would be a peace-or-war choice, for war is a *possibility* in any international confrontation. Cost factors are actually estimated in terms of the span of probabilities open at any time. A decision to act really means that the decision-maker feels that the objective sought is worth the highest price that anyone will actually charge him and his state.

Usually simultaneous with the calculation of cost, but analytically a second step in the analysis, is the determination of the risk involved in the projected course of action. "Risk" here refers to the relative odds in favor of success, and is necessary in decision-making simply because of unforeseen contingencies that perpetually endanger the peaceful interaction of states. The evaluation of risk is a recognition of the generous element of guesswork in all foreign policy.

For each alternative that demands a decision, the state establishes an "acceptable burden" of risk: the amount of failure that its policy will tolerate. Obviously, how acceptable such a "calculated" risk will be is determined by two sets of interlocking factors: how important is the objective being sought (a value judgment), and how serious will be the consequences of failure (an analytical conclusion). For important objectives, a state will bear great risk of failure. Lesser objectives are sought after with a corresponding decrease in the burden of risk.

The factors of cost and risk as determined by the decision-makers establish parameters within which decisions must fall. No rational policy choice would dictate action in behalf of an objective that might cost too much if the risk of having to pay that price is beyond the level of acceptance. Thus policy-makers find themselves hemmed in by analytical inhibitions and practical counsels of prudence.

THE DOMESTIC ASPECT: CONSENSUS

Another parameter within which the decision-maker must operate is internal (domestic) in its effect. Regardless of form of government or political philosophy, any foreign-policy apparatus is bound by popular consensus and limited to whatever area of permissibility mass attitudes may allow. This is not to encourage the unsophisticated view that "all foreign policies are democratically inspired." The consensus that restricts decision-makers may be entirely synthetic and the result of a planned campaign of deceptive mass propaganda. But regardless of its origin or its degree of sophistication, consensus plays a key role in staking off the area of free decision the policy-maker enjoys at any given time.

As long as war remains the ultimate sanction of state policy and as long as wars are fought by entire populations, consensus will govern decision-making. No government will risk popular repudiation of a decision to go to war. No government can safely be divorced from the active support of its populace. Mass identification with foreign-policy issues, although an enormous source of strength to all governments, is also in this sense a debilitating factor that often deprives officials of the capacity to follow their best professional judgment.

Again, we must note that in practice, consensus operates with varying degrees of constraint. With a wide area of permissibility and on matters of lesser import, decision-makers may and often do operate without specific reference to mass reaction. The more narrowly and the more specifically consensus focuses, however, the more officials feel its impact.

There is an interesting relationship between the dimensions of breadth and intensity of consensus. A broad grant of discretion to government ordinarily also implies a relatively low level of mass identification. When a government increases the intensity of its popular support on a particular issue, it pays a price by the narrowing of its permissible alternatives, at least as interpreted by the consensus. Thus the paradox: the closer to war a situation drifts, the more public attitudes become inflamed, and the less control over events statesmen exercise. In gaining popular support against the worst, governments often sacrifice their ability to capitalize affirmatively upon more favorable circumstances.

Consensus is most obvious when it is most specific. Periodically—especially in moments of crisis—mass attitudes will seize upon a particular issue or problem of policy and insist on a (usually oversimplified) position. Granted that only rarely does mass response to problems take into account either enough relevant data or practical range of choice, almost always such manifestations are bugaboos to decision-makers. Policy personnel in democratic and dictatorial states alike dread such developments and make considerable effort to keep popular attitudes adequately excited but safely below the boiling point. When consensus does break out of control, policy-makers may ignore and defy popular demands only at their own great risk, and even then for a brief time span.

THE INCOMPLETENESS OF INFORMATION

We owe to the mathematical *theory of games* the insight that decisions can be made under any of three sets of conditions: conditions of certainty, conditions of uncertainty, and conditions of

risk. In conditions of certainty each action has one predictable outcome. In conditions of uncertainty each action may have more
than one outcome but their relative probabilities are unknown. In
conditions of risk each action may have more than one outcome
but their relative probabilities are known. Decisions made under
conditions of certainty are so rare in foreign policy as to be analytically insignificant. Decisions made under known conditions of
uncertainty do not occur in a government of rational men. Almost
all foreign-policy decisions taken by states, therefore, are made
under conditions of risk.

"Risk" in this sense has almost the same meaning as in the cost/risk
calculation, and for the same reason: any foreign-policy decision
is made in a context of incomplete information. This is by the
nature of the case; the built-in time lag between event and decision
makes it futile for any policy-maker to wait until he has the complete facts. He must act on the information available to him and
arrange his decisions so as to reduce the risk to a practical minimum.

The inadequacy of information available to the policy-maker
manifests itself in either of two ways: he may not have enough data,
or he may indeed have too much. In the first instance he lacks the
one or the several crucial informational inputs that will enable him
to construct a meaningful and valid decision. If data are unavailable
or if he cannot wait for more complete information, he fills the
gaps with estimates, extrapolations, or assumptions and goes ahead
anyway. In the second situation, he has the information he needs,
but it lies buried under mountains of extraneous and only mildly
relevant data. Again, either because of time pressures or because he
lacks immediately applicable criteria of relevance, the decision-
maker often finds himself little better off than he would have been
without the elaborate accumulation of unsifted information.

Under the heading "intelligence," governments today constantly
exert themselves to improve both the quantity and the usefulness
of the information upon which they must base their decisions. As
more and more areas of human life and action have become relevant
to foreign policy, more and more kinds of information are gathered
up and funneled into the decision-making apparatus of each government. Once swept into the analytical net, the information is di-
gested, evaluated, correlated, and distributed to all decision-makers
whose responsibilities make these data useful and necessary to them.

Those officials who consume the end-product of this information gathering and disseminating network are known in the United States as the "intelligence community."

The purpose of this greater emphasis on information is of course to reduce the risk factor in decisions; that is, to minimize as much as possible the extent to which the outcomes of any action are unknown and to amplify what is known of the relative probability of their occurrence. This may be classified conceptually as a "search for certainty" in policy-making, but of course the realistic goal is much more modest. Any effective substitution of knowledge or informed insight for pure guesswork in foreign-policy decisions is a net gain, and every state is convinced that enough improvement is possible to justify a major effort.

THE PRESSURE OF TIME

Still another factor that materially affects foreign-policy decisions is the simple phenomenon of time. Modern technology has speeded up the pace of international politics. With improvements in transportation and communication, events occur more rapidly than in past eras, and their outcomes reach the decision-maker in a much shorter time. This combination of forces cruelly burdens the policy-makers' task.

In the first place, responsible officials lack the time needed to analyze situations, compare alternatives, and consummate choices. They operate under the lash of an unceasing whip of events, and can avoid being flogged to death only by dealing with most issues in a summary (therefore usually routine and unimaginative) fashion. The best they can ordinarily do is conserve their analytical skills for the really important questions. Even in this modest and creditable effort they face difficulties. So pressed for time are they that often a crucial issue—if in any way difficult to identify—slips by as "just another problem."

In an attempt to cope with a larger and more rapidly moving flow of business, many governments have expanded their policy-making organizations. This has proved to be a self-defeating expedient: the turgidity of bureaucracy has more than offset the gain in manpower commitment. Lateral communication within the bureaucratic structure and the need for "clearances and concurrences" often slows down decision-making unbearably and normally deprives it of focus and force.

An unfortunate consequence of the pace at which most foreign-policy decision-makers drive themselves (or are driven) is the disappearance of reflective thought in a climate of tension. With no time to "waste in just thinking," officials lose a quality of perceptiveness and flexibility ordinarily considered an advantage in a policy-maker. Men under pressure tend to make decisions that will clear their desks for the next problem. Being prudent, they prefer to make minimum commitments and extremely cautious responses, to follow precedent closely, and to interpret their controlling directives as narrowly as possible. A harried official always prefers a "no" answer to a "yes," for the former not only spares him the responsibility for a decision that might later prove unwise but also obviates the necessity of opening up entirely new areas of analysis and decision for which he feels he lacks the time.

NATIONAL STYLE

Decision-makers in any nation are materially affected by what today is called "national style": the prevailing tradition and self-image of a society that predisposes its officials to perform their duties and make their decisions in a way considered unique and peculiarly appropriate. "Style" as a concept is much more useful—as well as being much easier to defend—than the once-popular idea of "national character." Although it is difficult to discover a character marking an entire people and expect all individuals to conform to it, it is obvious that the bulk of a given society will in their individual personalities reflect such a stereotype.

National style is important in shaping decisions because of its effect in setting the analytical pattern of the decision-maker himself. He is usually unconscious of the extent to which he partakes of a larger code of appropriate and socially sanctioned behavior as he grapples with his special problems, but only a hopelessly alienated (and therefore largely ineffective) public servant could dissociate himself completely from his society. A common style of analysis and decision forms one of the real elements of cohesiveness in all reasonably well-integrated government structures.

The relevance of notions of style to decisions may perhaps be best suggested by some examples. In Great Britain, for instance, the idea of "muddling through"—a conspicuous reluctance overtly to relate immediate choices to long-range purposes—gives British policy a remarkable resilience and adaptability that has long been the envy of other nations. Russia's obsession with secrecy is a stylistic trait that long antedates the Bolshevik Revolution. The French concern with "honor" and "glory" is far more than the mere symbolic and ritualistic matter it is for most other states; to France it is part of the national self-image and is taken very seriously. The style of the United States has long dictated casting international issues in moral terms and viewing foreign policy as a series of crises broken by random intervals of relaxation.

These tricks of national style—and the many others we might cite to epitomize virtually all other states—cannot help but modify the decisional dynamic each demonstrates. The ubiquity of considerations of style helps explain both deep animosities and close associations between pairs of states, as well as many otherwise perplexing patterns of interaction. We cannot expect the United States to act with a Russian concern for secrecy, nor can the Soviet Union conceive policy along any crisis-relaxation continuum. Nor would we expect that the maintenance of close and satisfactory relations between two such different styles would be any easy matter, completely independent of any differences in ideology and forms of government that might exist.

COMMITMENTS AND PRECEDENTS

Last in our list of the factors influencing decision, but frequently of controlling importance to the policy-maker, is the structure of already existing commitments and precedents within which the decision-maker must act. No policy decision is ever made *in vacuo* at a given moment in time; each is to a great degree affected by many earlier decisions and directed by the national interest. The state as a whole, the policy-making apparatus, and the individual decision-maker are all, in different ways, bound by the hand of the remote or the immediate past.

One important type of commitment that affects decisions is that made to a state's own mass opinion. We have noted its effect in our discussion of consensus. A second includes all the understandings, arrangements, alliances, and other fixed relationships a state has developed with its fellows. A decision violating any of these, or even changing one in any significant degree, would cause a perceptible response and open many new problems. Ordinarily, therefore, any such initiative is avoided except in clearly unavoidable cases. A third type of commitment is perhaps less obvious: longstanding hostilities and disagreements with other states also function as fixed factors and materially affect decisions.

This latter category merits a final word. Since major policy undertakings today require extensive "programming" and long-term implementation, a deep-seated conflict among states (such as the Cold War, the India-Pakistan dispute, or the Arab-Israeli imbroglio) rapidly assimilates an unspoken institutional character. Any radical improvement in relations would, in strict decisional terms, present almost as critical a problem as would a major crisis. Having become one of the "givens" of a state's international position, that government's decision-makers naturally assume the indefinite prolongation of the controversy to be preferable to almost any modification in its conditions.

Bibliography

* Almond, Gabriel, *American People and Foreign Policy*. New York: Frederick A. Praeger, 1960.
* Armstrong, John A., *Ideology, Politics and Government in the Soviet Union*. New York: Frederick A. Praeger, 1962.
 Dallin, Alexander, *Soviet Conduct in World Affairs*. New York: Columbia University Press, 1960.
* De Conde, Alexander, *American Secretary of State*. New York: Frederick A. Praeger, 1960.
* Farnsworth, D. N., *Senate Committee on Foreign Relations*. Urbana, Illinois: The University of Illinois Press, 1961.
 Hilsman, Roger, *Strategic Intelligence and National Decisions*. New York: The Free Press of Glencoe, 1956.
 Lerche, Charles O. Jr., *Foreign Policy of the American People*, Second edition. Englewood Cliffs, New Jersey: Prentice-Hall, Inc., 1961.
 Marshall, C. B., *The Limits of Foreign Policy*. New York: Holt, Rinehart, and Winston, 1954.

* Millis, Walter, (et al.), *Foreign Policy and the Free Society*. New York: Oceana Publications, 1958.

* Pentony, De Vere, *Soviet Foreign Policy*. San Francisco: Howard Chandler Publishing Company, 1961.

* Price, Don K. (ed.), *The Secretary of State*. Englewood Cliffs, New Jersey: Prentice-Hall, Inc., 1960.

  Robinson, James A., *Congress and Foreign Policy-Making*. Homewood, Illinois: The Dorsey Press, 1962.

* Rosenau, James N., *Public Opinion and Foreign Policy*. New York: Random House, 1961.

* Snyder, Richard and H. W. Bruck, *Foreign Policy and Decision Making: An Approach to the Study of International Politics*. New York: The Free Press of Glencoe, 1962.

* Spanier, John W., *American Foreign Policy Since World War II*. New York: Frederick A. Praeger, 1960.

---

* Indicates paperback edition.

Three

Capability
in Action

An old saw that says a great deal about the nature of foreign policy and the dynamics of interstate relations alleges that "a state does what it can and suffers what it must." A state's range of action is limited both by definition and in fact. The objectives it selects and the tactics it adopts for their achievement can never be any more than functions of its over-all capacity for action within the situation in which it is placed. The tension inherent in the contrast of absolute ends and sharply circumscribed means, as we noted earlier, makes policy-making a constant process of compromise and adjustment.

The nature and extent of the state's capacity to achieve its ends is obviously the other side of the coin of state purpose. We have said that a state in any situation attempts to get as much as it can of what it wants. At this point we are therefore interested in how a state estimates how much it can get in a given context; how these estimates find their way into policy decisions; and what factors and elements in a state's position contribute positively or negatively to its ability to achieve at least minimum satisfaction. Such matters as these we shall discuss in this chapter under the rubric of "state capability."

47

The Concept of "Capability"

DEFINITION

We begin with the broadest and most useful definition: a state's capability is its capacity to affect changes in the international environment in its own interest. This definition does not, of course, include all the actions a state may be in a position to take, but only those deemed advantageous to itself. The capacity to change the environment in a way inimical to or irrelevant to state purposes is simply disregarded as exterior to capability. The concept draws its validity from certain operating assumptions about the nature of foreign policy and therefore is meaningless except with reference to already-postulated purposes.

Change in environmental conditions is obviously the core of the concept's rationale. It is by means of its capability that a state "does what it can"; it "suffers what it must" under circumstances beyond its capability to affect. Change, furthermore, is to be understood in the broadest sense as situational relationships that are different than they would have been without the application of the state's capability. It therefore includes the neutralization of forces as well as the affirmative realignment of factors by the state concerned. It is by means of its capability that a state makes its intentions effective in the real world.

Capability is thus a summary way of referring to the "means" aspect of the ends-means continuum in foreign policy. It symbolizes the effective resources a state has at its command for the implementation and fulfillment of its objectives. However generally the notion may be conceived and discussed in the abstract, capability judgments in foreign policy are useful only when made in highly concrete, specific, and immediate terms. The policy-maker cannot afford vagueness; faced with an action decision, he must coldly canvass the several lines of action he can follow and select that one or those several that in his judgment are appropriate and adequate to the end he has in mind.

THE FUNCTION OF CAPABILITY

Capability redefines itself to some extent when it is actively committed to the service of state objectives. In the international political system, a state can achieve its purposes only by gaining the assent of its fellows to its designs. Lacking as it does an elaborate and effective institutional mechanism, international politics depends for the ratification of state decision upon an informal and unstable mechanism of consensus. The entire structure of state interaction stems from this basic operating requirement.

The assent of other states may be stated or only tacit. It may be voluntary, uninvolved, or grudging. It may be extended after a relatively simple process of explanation and persuasion, or only after a deep and direct struggle of will and power. Yet regardless of its source, nature, extent, or durability, it is this consensus alone that makes possible the accomplishment of a national objective. It is to the winning of this consent that a nation's foreign policy is directed and to which it commits its capability.

We may thus consider the operational function of state capability to be the engineering of an adequate international consensus. Almost any aspect of the policy process can be usefully viewed in these terms. An "open course of action" is actually a series of moves a state feels it can make without running into an effective international veto. The achievement of an objective is really the creation of a favorable state of affairs that other states are willing to accept. Policy-making is really a judgment about how much effort the state will need to make to gain sufficient assent or acquiescence from those other states that are involved in the situation. Conceiving capability as the measure of a state's ability to command and win agreement with its purposes gives focus and point to the concept and highlights the way in which it is actually used in policy-making.

INFLUENCE AND COERCION IN CAPABILITY

A moment's reflection will lead us to the conclusion that a state's ability to persuade other states to agree to its designs—that is, its capability—is demonstrated in two different ways. Faced with what he feels is the necessity to win the consent of another government, a policy-maker may be able to obtain such assent in an atmosphere of agreement. Consent may be given freely for any of a broad variety of reasons: the other state may itself approve of the projected action; it may be neutral or uninvolved in the question; or its disagreement may be so small as to be negligible. More commonly, the desired approval may be forthcoming after some measure of positive inducement: the promise of direct benefit, a modification of policy in another area, or some other *quid pro quo*. In any of these instances, however, the significant dimension is the absence of open conflict and the mutual adjustment of positions. The aspect of capability here involved is obviously that of "influence": the state is able to gain adequate consensus by various persuasive and/or harmonizing devices without ever calling into question issues of force or power.

When consent must be won for policy purposes in a context of conflict and disagreement between states, another dimension of capability becomes operative—that of *coercion*. This is the province of the "power struggle" pure and simple, as each state involved attempts to bend the other to its will. The forms of coercion are almost infinite in number, ranging from the mildest of argumentation through a long threat-pressure continuum on to the ultimate coercive method, that of physical force. At whatever level coercion is employed, however, its purpose is always the same. In the words of the classic definition of war, it is "to break the enemy's will to resist" so as to secure his agreement.

Influence and coercion are equally genuine and efficacious manifestations of state capability. Since conflict is always a much more exciting and newsworthy climate of human relationships than is harmony, the coercive aspect of capability usually receives greater attention and is often mistaken for the entirety of the phenomenon. Yet, operationally, statesmen spend a vast majority of their time and effort manipulating such influence as they may possess and resorting to coercion only as a last resort for matters permitting no lesser level of prosecution. It costs less to win consensus by influence. Fewer undesirable after effects are produced, and the results tend to be more lasting. The statesman who finds himself with no increments of capability available except coercive ones is indeed unfortunate. His choice of policies is sharply limited by the relatively high cost that any coercive procedure will entail.

CAPABILITY AND "POWER"

It is this danger of magnifying unduly the operational role of coercion that has led to the substantial discrediting of the once widely-held concept of "power." Although it is possible to define and use the term "power" much as we are using the term "capability" in this chapter, in common and journalistic usage power has come to symbolize the capacity of a state to coerce others or to avoid coercion by them. Such an emphasis on coercion leads naturally to a concentration on the most obvious and final form of coercive capacity—military force. Thus a construct of international politics grounded on something called "power" runs the risk of overemphasizing a victor and a vanquished in every international clash and confrontation of will and strength. In the vocabulary of the mathematical *theory of games*, international politics is thus conceived as a "zero-sum" game: one player can win only to the extent that other players lose.

This is simply not the way international politics proceeds most of the time. The values states seek may be and often are mutually exclusive and their prosecution possible only in an atmosphere of conflict. However, even this admission does not make all relationships coercive. The values may instead overlap or coincide. In such a situation, conflict and disagreement are irrelevant to the establishment of necessary equilibrium. A simplistic "power theory" of international politics ignores far too many aspects of the actual relations of states to be a reliable guide.

The concept of "power" contains another built-in conceptual trap. Capability is always the ability to do something; to act purposefully in an actual situation. Power should mean this also; in popular political discourse, however, power often becomes a status to which states aspire and which a chosen few achieve. Unsophisticated observers speak of a "powerful" state in the abstract as if they were saying something meaningful about it, regardless of how much or how little that state can actually do in immediate action situations. Capability preserves the necessary nexus with policy and action that a careless use of "power" often overlooks. It is for that reason that we use the former term in this book to refer to the over-all action competence of states.

Capability Judgments In Foreign Policy

Having outlined some of the ingredients in the concept itself, we turn next to a brief analysis of how capability is used in policy-making.

WHAT IS A CAPABILITY JUDGMENT?

It is important that we be quite percise about what we mean by a capability judgment. A capability judgment made in a policy context is no more than an analysis of the opportunities and limitations implicit in the operational environment of the state concerned. Its end result is the formulation of a range of possible action by the state—insofar as the analyzing statesmen can identify it. The key idea in any capability judgment is *possibility:* capability provides the state with the resources of action, but in no way predisposes the state to act in one way rather than another among those alternatives possible. The choice among alternatives is a value choice; capability judgments do no more than spell out the viable alternatives themselves.

Thus a capability judgment is a special form of situational analysis. The policy context dictates the specific elements of capability that enter into the analysis; the capability judgment establishes the parameters within which the operational decision will eventually be made. It is obvious that no sane statesman will attempt a policy that requires an effort beyond his state's capability.

JUDGING THE STATE'S OWN CAPABILITY

The policy-maker, therefore, must be as informed as possible of the several things he can do in the situation before he adopts a course of action. He must know what part of his nation's total resources are available to him in the particular situation; he may be and is usually restricted by the fact that much of the state's capability is already invested in other commitments and also by policy decisions that limit him to certain forms of action and prohibit others to him (for example, he may be told that military power is not available but that he may use all the propaganda and economic measures he wishes). He must also have made the most serious attempt to foretell the consequences of applying any of the available forms of capability.

This process, carried out to whatever level of detail is necessary and appropriate, leads to an appreciation of the span of meaningful choices he enjoys. It is on the basis of this judgment that he proceeds in applying the criterion of desirability to the several courses of action he has formulated and in selecting one of them as policy.

Of course, modern governments are acutely sensitive to the concept of capability and make a massive effort to keep up to date on the choices they have open at any time. It is only rarely that a policy-maker finds it necessary to go through the entire analytical operation sketched above. Usually he has at his fingertips generalized formulations of state capability applicable to detailed situations. The essentials of the process remain the same, regardless of how extensively it may become institutionalized.

CAPABILITY JUDGMENTS OF OTHER STATES

Capability judgments, as we shall discover in a moment, are really exercises in the determination of relationships. No capability judgment is of real use except in comparison with the capability of another state. Governments spend at least as much time and effort in attempting to judge the capability of other states as they do their own.

It is obviously critical to a strategist to have an appreciation of the range of action open to other states, particularly the ones with which he is directly involved at the moment. If he can sense the parameters of action his opposite number in the other government accepts, he will have a great advantage in developing his own policy. He will appreciate the conditions in which he will be able to operate freely as well as those in which he suffers serious inhibition. As a result, the major focus of political or "strategic" intelligence work in contemporary international politics is devoted to the development of elaborate formulations of the capabilities of all other states.

The method of reaching a capability judgment about another state is not radically different in nature from that used on one's own, but it is of course a more difficult task. The information on which the judgment is based is much more fragmentary and elusive. Its crucial ingredients must be normally wrenched away by guile or force since no state is usually eager to have any other gain complete insight into its own capabilities. Even more perplexing is the problem posed by differences in analytical points of view. Capability analysis, in spite of its purely possibilist focus, still requires the interpretation and evaluation of data, and no two states interpret facts in quite the same way. For capability judgments to be of maximum usefulness in devising strategy and tactics, a state must somehow make its analyses of the positions of other states more realistic by modifying its own possibilist formulations of the situation with empathetic consideration of how the other policy-maker views his own situation.

Factors In Capability Analysis

Capability analysis, we have concluded, is a crucial step in policy-making. We have also sketched out the essentials of the approach to reaching capability judgments. It is now appropriate for us to review the factors that enter into these analyses.

ANALYTICAL POINT OF VIEW

Perhaps the most important element in capability analysis is the point of view adopted by the analyst himself. A capability judgment is, as we have indicated, an estimate of the opportunities and limitations intrinsic to the decisional milieu. There immediately arises a gap between the environment as the analyst apperceives it and as it exists in reality. The policy-maker, subject to all the perceptive and behavioral limitations of any human being, must act on the milieu as he sees it and make the best estimate he can. He must do so, however, in full knowledge that many factors of the situation are unknown to him and will serve to modify and possibly upset whatever capability judgments he may make. We have already noted the impact of this generous element of unpredictability on

policy-making as leading to caution and tentativeness in commitment and to a strong preference for a sizable margin of error in
any decision.

Any "outside" capability analyst—anyone who makes estimates
without bearing responsibility for official action—necessarily has a
different point of view from that of an official. He may know many
things that the official does not. In addition, he may be free from
the institutional and social biases that complicate the decision-making process. Lastly, his freedom from the crushing burden of facing consequences of his decision may well induce a greater measure of optimism and a willingness to bear greater risk than is
normally characteristic of an insider. The "grandstand quarterback"
of foreign policy, be he student, journalist, electoral politician, or
concerned citizen, can never more than approximate the special analytical point of view of the responsible decision-maker wrestling
with questions of capability.

THE POLICY CONTEXT

The next factor in capability analysis that merits attention has
been alluded to several times previously. Here we need only make
the point emphatic. Capability is a useful concept and capability
judgments can be made meaningfully only in terms of a set of policies under analysis and evaluation. It is nonsense to speak of "capability" in the abstract as long as we grant that states move and act
in international politics to some purpose. Frequently, the policy
assumptions underlying a capability analysis may be left implicit
or phrased as contingencies; this in no way frees the analysis from
its policy roots. Even the "iffiest" of policy assumptions may serve
as the base for capability analysis.

Capability judgments made without reference to a policy context lend themselves easily to semi-mystical deterministic manipulation. The various deterministically-oriented "theories" or "laws" of
international politics tend to find their empiric root in one or another
of the physical "foundations" of national strength. Geographers,
demographers, military scholars, experts on raw materials, industrial and agricultural economists, and other specialists have all at
one time or another developed a single-factor theory of capability
and politics that purported to forecast the future of international

relationships. None of these formulations, however, has been able to explain more than a fraction of the totality of interstate maneuvering, and none has been able to escape the necessity of allowing for the supremacy of the policy considerations of statesmen and governments.

THE SITUATIONAL BASE

If capability makes sense only in terms of a policy context, it is also true that the concept is useful only within a specific situation. This is partly because the "open courses of action" and the "opportunities and limitations" in terms of which capability is phrased exist only within a concrete context. Even more significantly, the measure of the state's ability to influence or coerce agreement is also a function of the particular situation in which it is operating.

Specifically, in any situation a state never has more than a fraction of its total theoretical or actual capability available for its immediate purposes. This means that an over-all "favorable" capability position—a relatively large sphere of freedom of action within its general policy—may not translate into an equivalently high range of capability in a particular situation. To put it bluntly, a small and ordinarily weak state may, in an appropriate situation, have greater capability not only to influence a larger one but also to coerce it.

Certain forms of capability, whether influential or coercive, are appropriate to the peculiarities of any situation, while others are irrelevant. The actual capability a state enjoys in a situation, therefore, is determined by what increments of action it has available that are effective in meeting the exigencies of the context in view of the policy the state is pursuing at the moment. In this way the actual outcome of most international confrontations—especially those cast in an atmosphere of disagreement and attempted coercion —tends to be less a reflection of any generalized "power" relationship than a function of time, place, and the policies being carried out by the respective states.

RELATIVITY OF CAPABILITY

Capability is, as we have also observed, a concept of relativity. A capability judgment is relative in two different ways: in the first instance, a judgment is made of the state's capacity to act in behalf of an already-selected objective; second, any capability judgment is actually the state's capacity to act in comparison with the capabilities of other states to act.

Capability measured with reference to the state's ability to achieve an objective produces only one rational answer to the question, "how much capability does a state need?": "Enough." The criterion of any contingency-planning is that of "adequacy"—sufficient capability to fulfill the foreseen and anticipated needs of policy. There is no advantage in compiling action capacity beyond what a state sees itself as likely to need—with a generous overallowance for analytical error and unpredictable quirks of fate. The development of capability which has no policy relevance is no more than an international political example of "conspicuous consumption."

Furthermore, with capability rooted as it is in policy and situational contexts, its manipulation clearly requires the comparison of relative ranges of choice and action open to whatever states are involved in the problem. Regardless of the many things a state may be able to do in a situation, its net capability is zero if other states can cancel or neutralize each of its moves. On the other hand, even a narrow range of action may be enough to give the state absolute capability to achieve its ends if other states are relatively less well-off. The significant dimension in capability analysis is less that of absolute levels of change in the environment than whatever margin of operational superiority one state may enjoy over another. This is particularly pertinent in questions of military confrontations today. Several states have the "capability" to destroy each other with thermonuclear weapons. Since neither is able to focus its absolute military strength to gain a strategic advantage, for operational and policy purposes, the massive military machines of contemporary great powers are without relevance to the functional capability of their possessors.

CAPABILITY: A DYNAMISM

Finally, capability is a highly dynamic concept. A capability judgment involves the correlation of a broad variety of factors within a state with an international situation, all elements of which are moving at different speeds. Any final conclusion about relative capabilities, no matter how up-to-date the information on which it is based, is obsolete by the time of its formulation. To make such an analysis applicable to an existing situation it is necessary for the statesman to project into the future whatever trends and variables he feels are controlling, both in his own state and with regard to all others involved.

Thus a capability judgment is like an excursion ticket, "good for this day and train only." In pure theory, any single capability analysis should serve as the basis for only one action decision. Any later consideration of the same situation would require a new calculation of the relative status of all the states concerned. Literal adherence to this principle would render decision-making almost impossible; most governments merely adjust and touch up a generalized capability formulation with such additional data as they may have available and then proceed to a new decision. But even this partial recalculation suggests the evanescent and slippery character of the ingredients of a capability comparison, and the constant necessity of keeping it up to date.

Elements and Factors of Capability

Even after stressing as we have throughout this discussion that capability is a relative rather than an absolute phenomenon, and that any absolute "objective" formulation of a nation's capability, irrespective of a situational and policy context, suffers from unreality and a lack of usefulness, we must now admit that it is necessary and desirable to make at least a rough catalogue of the elements and factors in a state's position that contribute to its capacity to act effectively. The list and discussion that follows may be thought of as a kind of checklist that indicates the disparate sources from which a state may in a particular situation draw resources with which to support its policy. It is by no means to be conceived as leading to absolute operational conclusions about the "strength" or "power" of any state.

THE MAJOR CATEGORIES

The "elements and factors" of capability are usually broken into two broad categories for convenience of discussion, although as will become obvious, the classification is a rough one. Any over-precise conclusions based on the difference between one category and the other will be questionable at best and possibly in error. With this warning in mind, we may generalize that the capability of a state comes partially from tangible sources and partially from intangible ones.

Tangible factors are listed in various ways; here we include five categories. These are: (1) geographic position; (2) population and manpower; (3) resource endowment; (4) industrial and agricultural productive capacity; and (5) military power. Each of these is obviously capable of further subdivision and indeed their use in an actual capability analysis requires that they be broken down into greater detail.

The intangible factors we use here are four in number: (1) political, economic, and social structure; (2) educational and technical level; (3) national morale; and (4) international strategic position. As was the case with those we called "tangible," these four factors as named are extremely broad and necessarily vague. They must be given specific content and applicability if they are to be meaningfully used.

A quick comparison of the two categories of factors leads to one conclusion: the so-called tangibles each have a generous measure of intangibility about them, while the intangibles all have certain aspects of tangibility. In other words, the major dimension used in the analysis of the tangible factors is that of *quantity*—as modified by such notions as availability, convertibility, and substitutability. The significant dimension in the intangibles is *quality*—estimated not only in terms of "excellence," but also by such criteria as appropriateness and relevance. The analyst, in a word, *measures* the tangible factors but *evaluates* the intangibles; the quality factor built into the intangibles has a great deal to say about the effectiveness with which the tangibles are employed.

Thus a capability analysis in logic begins with the most obvious physical factors, such as geography, that not only are the most easily measured, but that also have the slowest rates of change. It proceeds through the less manifestly concrete and thus more dynamic factors and ultimately comes to rest at the opposite pole of intangibility where there is little empiric data on which to rely but a rapid rate of change and evolution with which to cope.

THE TANGIBLES: 1. GEOGRAPHY

Geographic factors enter into state capability in a number of ways. Among the more immediately remarkable are such characteristics as the size of the state (which, be it noted, is either an advantage, a handicap, or a neutral factor depending on the policy being pursued), its shape, topography, location, and climate. More subtle geographic influences include the nature of the state's frontiers, its neighbors, its insular, peninsular, littoral, or landlocked condition, its internal penetrability, and the distribution of its population over the landscape. No two of these factors affect any state in the same way, nor indeed does any one affect all states alike. Yet any capability analysis, either over-all or specific, must take such geographic factors, being relatively fixed conditions of state existence, into account.

Various theories of geographic determinism have plagued students for many years. Meaningful political relationships of immutable and inexorable character have been "discovered" in certain geographic factors. An elaborate theory of civilization can be grounded on climatological data; an insular position is claimed to "destine" a nation (like Britain or Japan) for maritime greatness. The most inclusive deterministic interpretation of geography is found in the several theories of "geopolitics." This approach is built on perhaps the most fundamental geographic fact of all, the arrangement of land and water on the face of the globe. One nineteenth-century school of thought found mastery of the seas to be the key to world power because of the critical role of seaborne commerce and military power. This doctrine was replaced by the "heartland" theory identified with the British Sir Halford Mackinder and the Nazi German Karl Haushofer in the 1920's and 1930's. In the latter doctrine, land power was held to be supreme and the "heartland" of the "world island"—roughly coterminous with the territory of the U.S.S.R.—was declared to be the one unassailable power base for world conquest.

Both the sea power theory and the "heartland" theory demonstrate the danger of drawing conclusions of inevitability from geographic facts, since each in turn was outdated and invalidated by changing technology. Sea power was overtaken by land power with the advent of the internal combustion engine; the "heartland" lost its immunity with the appearance of inter-continental ballistic missiles and other sophisticated delivery systems that overcome historical geographic barriers. Geography is neutral in its basic effect on state policy; it may be a handicap or an advantage depending on the purposes to which the policy is committed.

THE TANGIBLES: 2. POPULATION AND MANPOWER

A second tangible factor of immediate relevance is that of population and manpower. The basic datum is the gross number of human beings the state incorporates. On the assumption that other things being equal, greater population means greater capability to perform more tasks at a higher level of effectiveness. But other things are only seldom equal: population data must be qualified by such factors as age distribution, sex distribution, and spatial dispersion. For military purposes, as an example, a population clustering heavily in the upper age groups or with an imbalance of females, may make less of a contribution than might be estimated from its sheer size alone.

Population is perhaps a less meaningful notion for purposes of capability analysis than is "manpower," defined as that portion of the population that is available for foreign-policy purposes as broadly defined. Thus from the gross total must be subtracted all individuals who are politically useless as well as those needed simply to keep the society functional (such as food producers). The result is the manpower quotient that with appropriate direction, leadership, and administration can be used to contribute to the military, productive, and political capability of the state.

Capability estimates involving manpower, especially involving any but the briefest time spans, must take into account trends of evolution and development within the population. A comparison of birth and death rates, for example, will suggest not only such insights as the net growth rate, but also trends in age levels and life expectancy. It is possible over a fairly long time for government action to bring about perceptible change in population trends by the encouragement of early marriage and large families. France is today the outstanding example of a state that has done this successfully.

THE TANGIBLES: 3. NATURAL RESOURCES

The third more or less quantifiable element of capability is that of natural resources. These include the state's natural endowment and those additional reserves it can control. Natural resources are both agricultural (mainly food and fiber), and mineral. The latter category has been crucial since the Industrial Revolution as industrial processes have contributed so many new forms of capability to states. In this sense, mineral resources include energy sources (coal, petroleum, wood, etc.), the metals of ferrous metallurgy (iron ore and the various metals involved in steelmaking), non-ferrous metals, and non-metallic minerals.

Resource endowments clearly are limiting factors on capability; no state can function at a level beyond that permitted by its resources. But the rigid raw-material theory of international politics, popular several decades ago, today has few adherents. The development of synthetics and other new industrial processes, the elaboration of stockpiling techniques, and the unexpectedly high capacity of embattled populations to endure chronic shortages have all served largely to liberate states from the more rigid absolutes of the theory. States have shown remarkable ingenuity at escaping from resource limitations, and today an analyst may draw only the most general capability conclusions (with only peripheral relevance to immediate policy situations) from resource data.

THE TANGIBLES: 4. INDUSTRIAL AND AGRICULTURAL PRODUCTIVITY

In one sense, industrial and agricultural productivity as a capability factor is a function of the two preceding factors of manpower and resources: production is the application of human effort to the transformation of resources from raw material into finished product. Thus the level of industrial and agricultural production is in part determined by the initial resource endowment and in part by the amount and quality of manpower committed to the task.

Production levels are obviously of more immediate relevance to capability than mere resource potentials; whatever is produced is available for utilization at once or at least with only a minor amount of conversion. Sheer amounts of production, however, or even a less specific concept such as "productivity," are of only limited relevance to immediate capability judgments. Production takes many forms, and only a portion of the total output has any but the most general political applicability. The crucial capability factor involved in production is best suggested by asking: "how much are we producing of what we need at the moment?" Thus once more we see the critical part played by the policy context of capability.

Particularly apposite in dealing with productivity are such modifying considerations as availability, convertibility of facilities, and "lead time." Since capability judgments, as we know, normally involve some attempt to estimate future requirements and capacities, these "quality" interpretations of the productivity of a state provide estimates of what the state involved might be doing at some point in the future. Such estimates of the ability of the state to increase its politically significant production must take into account the willingness of the population to undergo relative hardship, since a major share of increased productive capability comes by subtraction from the civilian-consumption sector of the economy. The development of new productive capacity is never more than a minor factor.

THE TANGIBLES: 5. MILITARY POWER

At once the most obvious, but at the same time the most relativistic, of the tangible factors of capability is military power-in-being. Capability judgments must of course pay deep attention to military factors and frequently are based on them. It is by military means, as we have discovered, that states take overt action at the highest level of intensity; it is by military means that final solutions are arrived at in international politics. The military element in capability is obviously central to all estimates.

Such being the case, it is no wonder that a great deal more effort has been lavished on the development of doctrines and techniques for the estimation of military factors than on any other elements of capability. The analysis and evaluation of the several variables that enter into a state's military capability has been raised to almost a fine art in almost all states.

As with all the other tangible factors, the initial consideration is one of size: how large is the military establishment in terms of manpower? A second criterion is that of equipment and arms with regard to modernity and sophistication as well as to the capacity to produce more. Third, inquiry is made into deployment, by which is meant both the relative allocation of men and material among the various arms and services, and the pattern of their placement within the state's territory and (sometimes) its overseas bases. Finally, the full military capability of a state is comprehensible only in terms of whatever strategic and tactical doctrines are controlling at the time of the analysis; these principles will govern the way in which the armed forces are actually used in support of state purposes.

As we shall see in later chapters, in no area is the danger of absolute capability judgment greater, and in no area is it easier to fall into. There is a consoling but deceptive objectivity and clarity about raw manpower and equipment figures that often leads analysts into unsound, absolute conclusions. This difficulty has become compounded by the development of modern weapons and military techniques. In military capability it is especially true that what really counts is the military margin of superiority that may exist as between two states, not whatever absolute level of military power either may have mobilized. Switzerland, it is sometimes said, is a pygmy to France but a giant to Liechtenstein.

THE INTANGIBLES: 1. POLITICAL, ECONOMIC, AND SOCIAL STRUCTURE

We have pointed out that the tangible elements of capability tend to be measured whereas the intangibles are evaluated. Thus the analyst's approach to the intangibles is quite different; he is not seeking for a quantitative finding as much as he is interested in establishing the extent to which the phenomena he is studying contribute to or detract from the state's effectiveness in a specific situation.

This is immediately obvious when we examine the first in our list of intangibles—the political, economic, and social structure of a state. To begin with, the efficient capability analyst should be free from any stereotyped prejudices as to the intrinsic superiority of one political, economic, or social system to any others. Capability judgments are no place for ideological predispositions. He is instead prone to apply the yardstick of efficiency: considering the mission the state under analysis has set for itself, do these three structures represent the best possible way of mobilizing the nation's effort? Does the political system, for example, provide both for efficient administration and for a workable rapport with mass consensus, or is there sufficient disaffection to constitute a drag on governmental effectiveness? Does the economic system reduce waste, lost motion, uneconomic production, and inefficiency to the practical minimum or are many opportunities for a rationalized productive system lost? Is the society integrated and coordinated and thus capable of unified effort, or is it split apart so that internal tensions dilute the nation's international effort? These and analogous questions ultimately produce an over-all verdict on the general subject of how the nation organizes itself for international action and obviously constitutes a significant if imprecise factor in its over-all capability.

THE INTANGIBLES: 2. EDUCATIONAL AND TECHNOLOGICAL LEVEL

In a technological and scientific age, another societal characteristic that bears directly upon capability is the educational and technological level of the nation. Industrial productivity, military effectiveness, and simple social cohesiveness are all to a major extent functions of the extent to which education and technical facility are dispersed within the society. The level of education is one of the major qualitative modifiers of any quantitative finding respecting manpower.

Most fundamental to the matter of educational and technological level is the simple question of literacy. No state can muster a significant national effort if reading and writing, the basic communication skills, are mysteries to the bulk of or even to a significant minority of its people. For reasons both of effective consensus-building and of efficient administration, a literate population is felt to be a necessity if a state is to play a meaningful international role; the massive efforts made by such nations as China and India to bring minimal literacy to their peoples underscores its importance.

A second, almost as crucial, basic element in capability is what we might call tool skill: an orientation toward and a facility in the employment of the tools and techniques of modern industrial civilization. This is as much a matter of emotional adjustment and acculturation as it is one of actually learning skills and procedures. Unless a people are familiar with the many subtle ramifications of an industrial system, they will waste a good deal of effort in making the machinery work. Extensive training and the inculcation of the necessary discipline are prerequisites to effective tool skill.

The first two factors of literacy and tool skill are characteristics of the mass of a population. The third, and in many ways equally as crucial element in a nation's educational and technological level, is the quality of the highest stratum of educated specialists. Does the nation have enough specialists of the right sort? Is their training and level of performance adequate to the demands the nation will make of them? Is the over-all standard of scholarly, scientific, and technological effort advancing, declining, or merely static? These and related questions may in even short-run situations (such as a "crash" program of weapons development) be the real determinant of the state's working range of capability.

THE INTANGIBLES: 3. NATIONAL MORALE

Among the difficult factors to measure, yet beyond doubt one of the few constant determinants of capability, is the elusive notion of national morale. We use this term here to describe the mass state of mind in a nation with particular reference to the extent to which the society feels itself committed to a policy the government is pursuing and for which people are willing to work and, if necessary, to sacrifice.

A state, in other words, has high morale when the government feels itself supported by an active, well-formed, articulate, and involved consensus. Such a condition requires that the politically self-conscious portion of the population constitute the bulk of the society, that these individuals be convinced that the foreign-policy enterprises in which the government is involved are in fact derived from the prevailing mass values of the society, and that the consensus include a favorable vote of confidence in the capacity of the policy-makers to meet and overcome the challenges implicit in the policy.

Thus national morale has a direct effect on the vigor and human dynamics with which officials mobilize and employ the tangible factors in capability. Widespread apathy toward foreign policy establishes restrictive parameters on decision and active disagreement within the body politic virtually paralyzes the government. In this sense, morale involves not only the affirmative characteristics of zest, dedication, and confidence, but also such negative elements as discipline and the capacity to endure stress, disappointment, and temporary failure.

If a government concludes that the state of national morale is sufficiently questionable as to raise doubts about the endurability of the consensus on which the decision-makers must rely, the improvement of morale becomes a primary charge on the government. What particular strategies the government may employ depends upon its judgment on the nature of the deficiencies and peculiar dynamics of the society and its controlling values. It may choose to frighten its people or it may instead seek to encourage them; it may become more generous with information and explanation or may take the opposite tack by tightly controlling the flow of communication to the public. It may increase the pace of stimulation of the public psyche, or it may deliberately minimize tension. Whatever the devices adopted, however, its policy must remain largely in suspension until and unless its morale goals are achieved.

THE INTANGIBLES: 4. INTERNATIONAL STRATEGIC POSITION

The final element of capability—the state's international strategic position—brings us almost full circle. It is the general strategic role played by a state in world politics that raises issues of capability in the first place. We have stressed that capability is comprehensible only in a specific policy context. Now we conclude that in the state's own policy and strategy are factors that contribute to its working capability.

This is most immediately apparent in terms of the state's need for the support of other states in the service of its own policy. Exactly to the extent to which it feels it needs allies, its effective capability *vis-à-vis* its actual or potential associates is reduced; it must so conduct itself as to establish or maintain the desired cooperative relationship. Were it following a different policy, however, it would not require this particular alliance pattern and would thus have a greater freedom of choice and action in these areas.

A second manifestation of the impact of the state's international strategic position upon capability is derived from its interpretation of the position it occupies in the world. If the state feels itself under great and constant danger, it will obviously devote a much greater share of its available capability to the simple defense of its home territory, thus having a much more restricted margin available for affirmative action on the world stage. Any revision in the estimate a state makes of the threats it faces, automatically affects its capability in other areas. If it feels the threat has grown less, it is by that judgment freed for more extensive action elsewhere. If the threat is deemed to have become greater, adequate responsive action normally will call for a contraction of effort at other points.

What we are saying here is that in a peculiar and paradoxical way, the very objectives a state selects for itself and the way it interprets the situation in which it must operate, to a large extent determine its capability to achieve those objectives and to function in the situation. A state's international strategic position is to a large measure determined by itself; a state is to a great extent the architect of its own capability.

No more graphic proof could be adduced of the relativistic and policy-grounded nature of the concept of capability than this. The universe of the policy-maker and the capability analyst is largely of their own making. The judgments they reach and the decisions they make are expressions of their interpretation of the reality of their world. It should not be surprising that their conclusions about the ability of their state to achieve its purposes are so directly derived from their formulations of the nature of the problems they face.

Bibliography

* Berle, Adolf A., *Twentieth Century Capitalist Revolution*. New York: Harcourt, Brace and Company, 1954.

* Campbell, Robert W., *Soviet Economic Power*. Boston: Houghton Mifflin Company, 1960.

* Cole, J. P., *Geography of World Affairs*. Baltimore: Penguin Books, 1959.

* De Jouvenel, Bertrand, *Power: Its Nature and History of Its Growth*. Boston: Beacon Press, 1962.

Huntington, Samuel P., *Common Defense: Strategic Programs in National Politics*. New York: Columbia University Press, 1961.

Lasswell, Harold D. (et al), *A Study of Power*. New York: The Free Press of Glencoe, 1950.

Mackinder, Halford J., *Democratic Ideals and Reality*. New York: Henry Holt and Company, 1942.

Mouzon, Olin T., *International Resources and National Policy*. New York: Harper and Brothers, 1959.

* Nove, Alec, *Soviet Economy*. New York: Frederick A. Praeger, 1961.

* Rostow, W. W., *Stages of Economic Growth*. New York: Cambridge University Press, 1960.

* Russell, Bertrand, *Power: New Analysis*. New York: Barnes and Noble, University Books, 1962.

Schermerhorn, Richard A., *Society and Power*. New York: Random House, 1960.

Selznick, Philip, *The Organizational Weapon: A Study of Bolshevik Strategy and Tactics*. New York: The Free Press of Glencoe, 1959.

* Triffin, Robert, *Gold and the Dollar Crisis: The Future of Convertibility*. New Haven: Yale University Press, 1961.

Wengert, Norman, *Natural Resources and the Political Struggle*. New York: Random House, 1955.

---

* Indicates paperback edition.

Four

The Implementing
of Decisions

The policy-maker, after he has stipulated the objective he will seek and determined his capabilities for action within the particular situation, next turns to the problem of selecting the appropriate means of implementing his decisions. We have already suggested that he has a considerable range of choice in selecting detailed procedures and that he attempts to develop a course of action that in his opinion will carry him to the goal he has adopted. In this chapter we shall examine the generalized categories of state techniques, the four general channels through which the statesman may act in world politics. Our analysis will of course be aimed at characterizing the various families of techniques available to states and at distinguishing them from each other. We shall not attempt to elaborate a complete catalogue of state procedures in policy implementation, since these in practice are infinite in number and largely dependent upon random and unique factors in the operative situation.

We ought first, however, to make one basic point that will be implicit in all our subsequent discussion. This chapter concentrates on the various ways states may act, and this is of course a topic that merits extensive treatment. But action of any sort is not a necessary consequence of a policy decision; the net result of the elaborate analytical process we outlined in Chapter Two may be instead a resolve not to act at all. It is true that inaction is a form

71

of action and proceeds (at any rate, it should proceed) from the same intellectual process as does action itself. The strategy of inaction, however, obviously raises fewer questions of implementation. For our purposes, in our consideration of state techniques we should keep always in mind that a state decision to act represents at some level a deliberate choice of action over inaction in the particular context.

If a state decides to act, however, the nature of the state system opens four possible channels for the application of its strength. These four are in the literal sense classic in that they are intrinsic to international politics and represent the totality of the *ways* states may act. Today, of course, the increased complexities of life have opened countless doors for state action on behalf of policy, but regardless of their sophistication or their ostensible exotic nature, in the last analysis all may be fitted into one of the four standard categories.

A state may employ any of four different sets of techniques. The first of these is political in nature, and has as its most conspicuous manifestation the device of diplomacy. The second is economic, probably the most varied and complex of the four in its richness of artifice and stratagem. Third in the list are psychological techniques, of which propaganda and its operational derivatives are examples. Finally there are military techniques including the non-violent use of armed force and scaling gradually up to open warfare.

In pure theory, a state may place its entire reliance in a particular situation upon any single one of these generalized techniques; that is, it may choose to use diplomacy or propaganda or either of the remaining techniques as its only instrument of achieving a particular end. More commonly, however, states develop an approach based on a "mix" of techniques, blended in such proportions as will, in the estimation of the policy-maker, produce the greatest effect. It is axiomatic that a statesman may develop combinations of techniques in perfect analytical and operational freedom. Here as elsewhere in foreign-policy matters, the only "correct" technique is that one that best achieves the purpose the state has in mind.

It is with the implementation of policy that a state attempts to preserve flexibility. Since its capability to act is a function of the exigencies of the situation, it is most important that any operational commitment be so made as to permit intensification, reduction, modification, or even abandonment if circumstances should dictate. The need for such flexibility has been redoubled in this generation as modern technology has led to the collapse of time. The action time available to a state has been drastically reduced and it is vitally necessary that operational techniques be of a sort permitting rapid change.

Political Techniques: Diplomacy

In one sense all foreign-policy techniques are—or at any rate ought to be—political. No matter what a state may do in the execution of its purposes, its orientation and its goal is always political in that it seeks the maximization of its value system. Yet in practice the word "political" is applied more narrowly to refer to those methods that involve direct government-to-government relations. The contacts that governments have with each other and the manner in which this intercourse is carried on are generally subsumed under the name of diplomacy.

THE NATURE OF DIPLOMACY

Diplomacy, considered as a technique of state action, is essentially a process whereby communications from one government go directly into the decision-making apparatus of another. This means that diplomacy is in the last analysis the one direct technique of state action in that it exerts its diplomatic power upon the crucial personnel of the other government or governments. If, as we have argued, the operational purpose of policy is to secure the agreement of other states to national designs, it is only by diplomatic means that such assent can be formally registered and communicated. In this as in several other senses, diplomacy is the central technique of foreign policy.

Diplomacy is both a full-fledged technique in its own right and also the instrument by which the other techniques are often transmitted. A state, in other words, can act diplomatically in a purely political context using only the methods and resources of the diplomatic instrument. It may, on the other hand, implement economic, psychological, or even military action by diplomatic maneuvering.

Although the operating requirements of pure diplomacy and what we might call "mixed" diplomacy differ to some extent, their fundamental rationale remains essentially the same.

The actual procedures of diplomacy are many. They range from highly formal devices such as notes, *aides-memoires*, and *communiqués* at one extreme to more informal and almost casual conversations at the other. At bottom, diplomacy is a method of negotiating between sovereignties, and although the elaborate ritual and protocol that surround the practice may sometimes seem pretentious and time-consuming, it has its roots in the nature of the task. By diplomatic means a state transmits its position on as issue to another state and receives the other state's response. Whatever changes may take place in the respective positions are registered diplomatically, and the eventual elaboration of whatever relationship develops also lies in the hands of diplomats.

THE FUNCTIONS OF DIPLOMACY

We can distinguish several distinct functions of diplomacy. Which one or ones the working diplomat may be called upon to perform depends of course on the nature of the policy his government is following.

In the first place, diplomacy is to a major extent a technique of *coercion*. Not only are coercive moves made by other means communicated diplomatically, but within the narrower framework are found significant resources of pressure. In many cases, the rupture of diplomatic relations has a coercive element, as does the exclusion of the target state from international conferences or organizations. Coercion may also be applied in negotiation by an ultimatum, by the establishment of a rigid time-limit for the conclusion of an arrangement, or by the registration of a formal or informal protest or complaint. In the past few decades, "pragmatic" dictators have added an element of psychological coercion to diplomacy by eliminating the courtesy and good manners traditional to the art and conducting relationships in an atmosphere of vilification, bad language, and intensive emotion. It is undeniable that this procedure has had its advantages.

Second, diplomacy is also a technique of *persuasion*. The advancement of arguments on the one hand and the proffer of a *quid pro quo* on the other, both persuasive devices, are within the exclusive province of diplomatic technique. Harking back to our discussion of the forms of capability, we may say that diplomacy is the more frequently used and the best suited of all state techniques for the application of the influence component of state capability. It is true, of course, that the actual line between coercion and persuasion is often fuzzy and that the two approaches frequently blend into one another. Yet there is a real difference both in motivation and atmosphere, and most diplomatic initiatives are cast at least initially in a persuasive form.

Third, diplomacy is uniquely a procedure of *adjustment*. It is admirably suited to the task of enabling two states adequately to modify their positions on an issue in order to reach a stable relationship. Its directness of communication, its potentially non-coercive nature, its subtlety and flexibility, all contribute to its usefulness. States may prosecute their differences and intensify their conflicts by a great variety of methods, but they may reduce tensions between themselves only by diplomatic means. It seems scarcely necessary to add, however, that the adjustment function of diplomacy is effective only if both parties are amenable to negotiation. There is no magic in the diplomatic instrument adequate to overcome a state's unwillingness to change a policy.

Finally, diplomacy is a technique for reaching *agreement;* indeed, it has been said that diplomacy is the art of negotiating written agreements. Formal written agreements are as binding an international commitment as world politics offers, and these can be brought into existence only by diplomatic procedures. Again, we must note that agreement may involve either coercion, persuasion, or adjustment, and that no agreement is possible unless both parties wish one. On the other hand, even a strong interest in formalizing an understanding would be pointless were there not available instruments and procedures for reaching one. Here diplomacy comes usefully into its own.

SUCCESS AND FAILURE IN DIPLOMACY

What are the characteristics of good diplomacy? More directly, what are the marks of the policy of a state that is making good use of the diplomatic technique in its policy? Conversely, what is wrong with the normal practice of diplomacy in the contemporary world that has given the diplomat such an apparently small role in the conduct of international politics?

There is little disagreement about the requirements for success in diplomacy. The essentials of the diplomatic art have been well known for centuries and the actual practice of its masters furnish us with clear guide lines. We may here reduce the vast literature into four basic operative requirements.

1. *The diplomat must have a clear understanding of the situation in which he is operating.* This means that he be sensitive to the forces at work in his problem area. He must also be quite clear about his own purposes and the ultimate implications of his policy with respect to long-range goals. Lastly, he must have a clear understanding of the points of view, interests, and goals of other states. Without such empathy he will be virtually powerless.

2. *The diplomat must be fully aware of his real action capability.* He must appreciate how much coercive capacity his government will support him with, and how much influence he may enjoy at that particular moment. He dare not attempt initiatives that lie beyond his capability, nor should he content himself with less than a full exploitation of those resources that are appropriate to his objectives.

3. *The diplomat's approach must be flexible.* He must be prepared for unforeseen developments or to withstand the consequences of analytical error. He prepares himself for this by having some alternate policies and approaches in reserve, by having an unpublicized "fall-back" position available, and by being consistently eclectic in methodology. He distinguishes as much as possible between abstract "principle" and concrete interest, and remains firmly committed to the latter while quite flexible on the former.

4. *The diplomat is eager to compromise within limits of non-essentiality.* A clear priority system is essential to a diplomat because only in this way can he determine what issues are subject to bargaining and what issues are not. Priorities also suggest quantitative criteria to guide him in determining how extensively he may compromise without giving away matters of importance in return for only lesser concessions. In theory, a good diplomat should be always willing to give up a position of lower priority in order to

secure one of higher rank; although subject to drastic modification in practice, this rule does indeed have great importance in diplomatic maneuvering. The criterion of a good diplomatic bargain, be it noted, is less how much is given up than how much is won, for only the prize can determine whether or not the price was too high.

Diplomacy in the contemporary era has not proved itself able to cope adequately with the dilemmas of politics. So obvious has been its inadequacy that some critics have been moved to speculate on "the end of traditional diplomacy." In practice, since the end of World War II, the four rules we have formulated have been honored much more often in the breach than in the observance. Situations are analyzed far too often in ideological and nationalistic terms and too seldom in realistic tones. It is currently unfashionable ever to admit that one's opponent has a point of view at all, let alone one meriting consideration. Capability factors are grossly misinterpreted, especially in the military realm. Flexibility, thanks to ideology and nationalism, is usually a lost cause. And compromise is normally rejected as striking up a bargain with sin.

In these circumstances, diplomacy cannot flourish. What has passed as "diplomacy" has been either ill-concealed and blatant attempts at coercion, or non-purposive propaganda. Real negotiation, persuasion, and adjustment of positions culminating in agreement have been accidental, almost random, phenomena instead of the normal procedures of states in the system. Deep popular involvement in foreign policy by means of absolutist and emotional sloganizing, common in large and small states alike, has seriously impeded the force of diplomacy by depriving it of the necessary "elbow room" in which to maneuver.

Some hopeful signs, however, have been recently noticed that augur a revival of diplomatic activity in the true sense. The cold war era has been one marked by a constant advocacy of absolute solution to problems. Nearly two decades of struggle has had its effect; absolutist positions are advanced somewhat less seriously, and responsible and increasingly prudent governments are showing themselves willing at least to entertain the possibility of partial solutions. With this frame of mind becoming more common, the opportunity for diplomacy again to work its harmonizing and adjusting effect becomes somewhat brighter. The future will undoubtedly see relatively greater reliance on diplomacy and possibly a much more favorable record of its success.

Economic Techniques: The Carrot and the Stick

Economic techniques of state action are as old as the state system itself, but their full flower dates only from the Industrial Revolution. The increasing complexity of modern economic and industrial life has gone far to knit the world into a set of mutually interdependent societies. The sheer fact of this reciprocal involvement serves to open a broad range of action possibilities to states. Various sorts of international economic action aimed at the achievement of political goals have become a part of foreign policy for all states.

THE RATIONALE OF ECONOMIC METHODS

Probably the most obvious characteristic of economic techniques is their bewildering diversity. Almost any aspect of economic life can, with sufficient ingenuity on the part of policy-makers, be turned into a tool of state action. Certain generalizations, however, can be made about the rationale of economic methods in foreign policy.

In the first place, economic techniques are indirect in their application in contrast to the directness intrinsic to diplomacy. That is, their immediate target is not the decision-making apparatus of the other state but rather the totality of that state's society. The sought-for consent is supposed to flow from internal pressures in that society upon its government rather than from any direct action by the initiating state. It can be thus said that economic techniques are in a small way designed to force the hand of the other government and to urge or coerce it to accede to the wishes of the first state.

Second, as the title of this section indicates, economic methods are two-sided, in that they may be either coercive or persuasive in intent. A coercive economic move is one that in general or specific terms threatens the target state with deprivation or impoverishment unless it submits. A persuasive move holds out the bait of economic reward or advantage in return for satisfactory modification of a target state's behavior. Frequently, a single economic maneuver may partake of both, in that it threatens economic damage if no agreement is forthcoming but simultaneously promises rewards for acquiescence. Such ambivalence in effect is usually thought of as ideal.

Third, economic techniques are almost entirely creatures of the particular situation. The effectiveness of any such device is completely dependent upon the nature of the economic relations between the states involved. A state with no economic leverage on another would simply be ignored or laughed at if it threatened an economic reprisal to an unacceptable policy. Thus it follows that the maximum use of economic instruments is reserved to those few states with widespread economic influence or to those controlling crucial economic goods or services. An otherwise weak state controlling huge oil reserves, for example, has a considerable range of capability made possible only by its atypical and accidental economic situation. Ordinarily, however, a strong international economic position is a prerequisite to the use of economic instruments in policy.

Fourth, economic techniques are productive of generous amounts of resentment, resistance, and retaliation by the target state. Coercive economic moves obviously create hostility since no people can stolidly accept either the threat or the actuality of economic deprivation. Peculiarly enough, even persuasive and advantageous economic policies engender almost as much enmity among recipient peoples of sensitive nationalism, on the ground that it is humiliating and status-destroying to submit to bribery and blackmail for policy reasons. Much of the agitation in the non-western world for "foreign aid without strings" flows from this orientation.

Fifth, as a result, economic techniques have a much more limited range of effectiveness by themselves than was suspected even fairly recently. Strategists have learned to take account of resistance to economic pressures and to discount accordingly the return expected from their use. They must today be employed with great tact and delicacy in order to inhibit undesirable after-effects or else must be coupled with generous commitments of other forms of capability. As a rule, therefore, economic techniques today are only rarely used alone. An economic policy, if persuasive, is usually linked with extensive propaganda and diplomatic initiatives, while coercive programs are accompanied by a strong diplomatic line and frequently by military pressures of various sorts.

PERSUASIVE ECONOMIC TECHNIQUES

Under the conditions of contemporary world politics, certain persuasive economic techniques have proved useful and appropriate.

Probably the best-known is "foreign aid": the direct grant or favorable loan of either cash, credits, or goods to other countries. These may be "economic" in nature, and consist of foodstuffs, capital goods, or consumer products. On the other hand, the cold-war atmosphere has placed a high premium on "military" aid, including all types of military materiel and what the United States calls "defense support" aid in the form of economic aid committed to military purposes.

A second type, of great importance since the non-western revolution has become a reality, is development assistance. Advanced industrial states engage themselves to assist unindustrialized states to develop productive plants and foster a higher standard of living for their people. Originally undertaken in a cold-war context, development assistance has proved to be so expensive, so long-lasting, and so unproductive of cold-war advantage that its leading practitioners are seeking a less intensive and therefore more rational climate for its application. Its full political effect can obviously be determined only over a very long time span.

Third, much effort has gone into the use of trade policy as a technique of state action. Bilateral or multilateral trade agreements are a familiar feature of international politics today; most of them clearly have their political overtones and some—particularly those between a large and powerful state and a smaller one—clearly formalize the exchange of economic advantage on the one hand for political rewards on the other. In recent years, another aspect of trade policy has appeared: the creation of trading blocs and the extension of an invitation to join such a group as a form of persuasion to political cooperation. So powerful has this lure been that some traditionally neutral European states have been sorely tempted to abandon political non-alignment in order to secure the economic rewards of membership.

Closely linked with trade agreements are the many kinds of

moves possible in the area of currency stabilization and control. This technique was quite common in the early postwar period when currencies throughout the world were unstable and in need of assistances from those few nations with adequate reserves. Today, widespread stability has served to minimize its effect, although one peculiar anomaly exists: the United States, once the financial pillar of the entire free world, has for several years been suffering a balance-of-payment deficit and a consequent outflow of gold. Today, the United States is to some extent subject to the policy influence of this currency-stabilization device as used by its erstwhile clients in Europe.

COERCIVE ECONOMIC TECHNIQUES

Coercive economic techniques, as we have suggested, are limited in their number and in their variety only by the imaginativeness of the implementing state within the particular political and economic situation. Here we do no more than attempt a rough classification.

The first type we may call restrictions on economic relations. These include the whole apparatus of currency control, export licenses and quotas, tariffs (selective and otherwise), foreign exchange blocking and control, freezing of credits, and so on. The intent of all of these is to permit economic relations to continue but to ensure that they go on in a way favorable to the dominant state. An implicit aspect of all of them is the suggestion that an improvement in political relations would have immediate economic consequences.

More overtly coercive is the outright interruption of economic relations, primarily international trade. Here naked pressure is involved. If the target state is sufficiently dependent upon trade with the dominant state, interruption will cause serious hardship and impel the victim toward the reestablishment of normal patterns at a political price. Interruption of relations may be effective when the powerful state is a critical supplier of certain categories of goods or when it is a major market for the product of a single-commodity agricultural economy. Such a "boycott" is perhaps the most infuriating of all economic practices and brings in its train strong pressures for retaliation. Therefore, it is employed only seldom, and then only under especially favorable circumstances. A special type of coercion stems from the cancellation or suspension of a program of economic aid. Recipient states normally accustom themselves rapidly to a steady flow of assistance once such a program is established. Their dependence upon a continuation of aid makes them peculiarly vulnerable to the pressures that develop if the regular supply of assistance is interrupted. Again, this technique is most valuable when the coerced state is completely at the mercy of the state extending aid. If the former can actually do without the assistance, or if it should develop another source of aid, then net results of the effort may well be zero or even a minus factor.

There remains a collection of coercive economic steps that do not so readily lend themselves to classification. These are in a marked fashion dependent for their effect on almost accidental situational elements and their impact tends to be random and almost unpredictable. They include such trading practices as dumping, such politico-economic moves as preemptive purchase of raw materials (sometimes for the purpose of depriving another country of these supplies), and such manipulative tricks as unilateral currency devaluation or barter trade agreements.

CONCLUSIONS ON ECONOMIC TECHNIQUES

We have already hinted at the most significant conclusion about economic techniques: they are of only limited and special usefulness by themselves both because of the unpredictability of their results and of their relations-worsening effect. "Economic man" is no more real in international life than in domestic affairs.

A second conclusion, however, is that under appropriate circumstances, economic techniques may have an effect at once devastating and controlling. Coercion in economic terms may indeed cause hostility, but it may also produce rapid and extensive policy revision on the part of its victim. At the persuasive end of the spectrum, an imaginatively conceived and skillfully presented program has often earned major political dividends in a non-controversial climate. Discrimination in the use of economic techniques, adequate understanding of the operative factors in a situation, and a refusal to become enamored of a particular technique all contribute largely to their over-all usefulness.

Third, economic techniques are of less value in short-term situations than over a longer period. To attempt to extract short-run political gain from the application of a single economic device is frequently to court disappointment; only seldom is a target state so tightly caught as to be obliged to respond politically in a single dimension to an economic initiative. Over longer time spans, however, economic policies of the correct sort may well develop a pool of consent (or at least reduce barriers of disagreement) that will ultimately prove of major value. This caution has been violated consistently by both major powers during the cold-war era, with predictable results in frustration and failure.

Psychological Techniques: Propaganda and Culture

Psychological techniques, aimed at the mass psyches of relatively large bodies of people, are also an indirect technique of state action. Thanks to the improvement in the art and science of mass communication, propaganda and culture have become major elements in state capability and constitute in themselves a significant area of political action.

THE NATURE OF PROPAGANDA

Propaganda has been defined in many ways, but all the definitions agree that operationally it consists of messages in a context of action; that is, the purpose of communication is to inspire the audience to act in a particular way. From the propagandist's point of view, however, this generalized concept breaks down into two subcategories; some propaganda is basically a problem in audience-conditioning designed to increase both its size and its sympathetic receptivity, while the remainder is directly action-centered with the goal of persuading the audience to act in certain specified ways. Both forms have an important place in policy implementation.

PROPAGANDA AS A FOREIGN-POLICY TOOL

We should initially distinguish the four distinct and different "audiences" that the foreign-policy propagandist speaks to. The first is the propagandist's own people, whose morale and dedication require that they be kept adequately informed, inspired, and indoc-trinated. The second is the populace of those states associated with or friendly and cooperative to the propandizing state. These also need to have policy explained in such a way as to impress them with the necessity of remaining true to their allegiance. The third is the audience formed by those people who are neutral toward the propagandist's policy. Newly-important today, they may be won to the state or at least they might be prevented from going into active opposition by a well-conceived program of information. Finally, there is an audience composed of the people of states hostile or in opposition to the propagandist. Here propaganda seeks initially to reduce their support of their official policy and perhaps to loosen their bonds of loyalty.

We have phrased "audiences" in terms of "people" because propa-ganda is largely a mass phenomenon. Decision-making personnel themselves are normally both too committed and too sophisticated to be particularly amenable to propaganda from abroad. Most mass communicators believe that they obtain the greatest results for a given effort by aiming at the broadest possible audience, and the record of their accomplishments in international politics confirms this judgment.

The great bulk of the propaganda messages put out by states are of the audience-conditioning, sympathy-building type. The focus of most propaganda, in other words, is what is today called "image projection": the state seeks to be viewed in a favorable light by its several audiences. Direct calls to action are relatively few, partly because of the remote likelihood of their being heeded except in special circumstances and partly because of the ease with which they are blacked out or neutralized by domestic counter-propaganda.

It follows, therefore, that most foreign-policy propaganda is auxiliary to diplomatic efforts and that propaganda is only seldom the single dimension in which a state acts. Effective propaganda may multiply the policy impact of diplomatic, economic, or even military moves, but it can only rarely accomplish a specific end by itself. It is crucial, therefore, that propaganda be rooted directly in the state's ongoing policy and that major efforts to maintain con-sistency of word with action be axiomatic.

A seriously inhibiting factor affecting propaganda today is the simple fact that virtually everybody is using it. With each audience bombarded by messages and appeals from every point of the compass, and with almost every policy point of view receiving eloquent and repeated expression, the listener has little in the way of a clear impression by which to guide himself. He is likely to select from the welter of propaganda those messages and appeals with which he is already familiar and simply to ignore the remainder. Thus the policy impact of propaganda is seriously reduced since it has relatively little effect in changing established patterns of behavior and response. This factor helps explain the great emphasis on audience-building displayed by so many propagandizing states.

THE ROLE OF SUBVERSION

Although subversion—the attempt of a state to overthrow or weaken another by means of internal agitation and conspiracy—is a direct-action technique in its own right, it is included in this discussion of psychological techniques for a special reason. Crucial to the establishment and implementation of a subversive activity by a state is the psychological problem of destroying the bonds of loyalty that bind a citizen to his government. Thereafter, his loyalty must be replaced by a willingness to follow the commands of an alien and hostile state.

Subversion is, of course, an old technique; but it has been raised to its highest peak in the contemporary era. In part, this has been due to the increasing militancy of modern ideologies—particularly communism, fascism, and anticolonialism—and in part to the improvements in communication that have made it possible for a government to control a subversive movement (or many subversive movements) from a great distance. Even more important than either of these, however, in explaining the rise of subversion as a technique is the fact that the present age is one of great social disaffection, change, and revolution. When any society develops substantial internal divisions and deep animosities, the potential for the recruiting of subversives is present. Aggressive and shrewd agitators can often capitalize on such internal cleavages by enlisting key leaders and groups to prosecute their own purposes under the sponsorship of a foreign government.

In theory, subversion is a technique of revolution. Its ultimate purpose is the complete overthrow of the government and its replacement by the revolutionary group. As a technique of foreign policy, however, it is valuable even if it occurs at a much more restrained level. Organized subversion can deepen divisions within a society to the extent that the government's integrity is compromised, its vitality weakened, and its attention diverted from vital questions of foreign policy. If, as was said about some European countries immediately following World War II, a government must validate each policy decision twice—once in the government structure and once in a street riot—it obviously cannot act with the despatch and firmness that important foreign policy questions demand.

The current importance of subversion—and its "counterinsurgent" handmaiden, guerrilla warfare—should not obscure the fact that it is a technique of opportunity, usable only in those special circumstances where social and political revolution is at least incipient. Societies in which disaffection is minimal may be annoyed but never inhibited by subversion. What is more, only states with frankly revolutionary policy can successfully exploit popular discontent since only they have adequate appeal to emotionally involved rebellious individuals and groups. Thus it is almost axiomatic that states pursuing a stabilizing and mollifying status quo policy must combat subversion but are not in a position to make much use of it themselves.

CULTURAL TECHNIQUES IN FOREIGN POLICY

A special development in the field of psychological action is the "cultural offensive." States, using the standardized techniques of public relations, have taken in recent years to the active international promotion of the more prominent manifestations of their indigenous culture patterns. Aided markedly by advances in mass communication, nearly every government today seeks to "put its best foot forward" culturally by a vigorous advertising campaign before a global audience.

Part of the purpose of the cultural attack on mass consciousness is found in the operational demands of propaganda. A favorable cultural image of a nation and its government might well conduce an audience to listen approvingly to policy positions expounded by that same government. But there is a more far-reaching rationale to cultural techniques. Culture patterns—whether economic, social, esthetic, or political—are manifestations of the basic value system of a society. Winning favorable international response to certain cultural symbols is at least a major first step toward winning acceptance of the fundamental values on which they are based. Since foreign policy is at bottom an exercise in value-maximization, it can be thus argued that in one sense cultural techniques are a form of direct state action on behalf of national objectives.

So powerful have become some cultural programs and so concerned have some governments become at the possibility that their people might be seduced by attractive but specious cultural manifestations from abroad that pejorative terms such as "cultural imperialism" have been often heard in recent years. It has seemed as if many newer non-western states have reserved their greatest anticolonialist tirades for certain symbolic epitomes of western culture, such as articles of clothing and items of diet. In some way they seem to feel as if a deliberate cultivation of their peculiar cultural traits will free them from an unhealthy dependence on western ways.

We should also note that many aspects of culture have a vitality of their own and work their effect virtually independently of overt government action. Jazz music, Coca-Cola, and television are only three symbolic representations of American culture that have spread abroad widely with obvious—if not always favorable—results. This effect of uncontrolled culture spread is more important to relatively free societies than to authoritarian ones that make a much greater effort to shape a consistent and integrated international cultural image.

Military Techniques: War and its Approximations

We come now to the fourth and final set of techniques of state action: military capability and the role of force. We should at the outset establish our logical base by pointing out something of a paradox. In logic and in the practice of statecraft, there is no substantive difference between military techniques and any others:

war is thus "normal" in interstate relations since the criterion of appropriateness governing the use of military power is exactly the same as is used in any other policy decision. Yet statesmen have always recognized that the use of military techniques has been predictably more costly and more dangerous than other ways of acting. Therefore, they have normally considered military techniques to be analytically a last resort, to be used only if lesser measures prove inadequate to attain a necessary objective. The great technological revolution in warfare has sharpened the impact of this dilemma. Today, one of the more hotly debated theoretical issues, as well as one of the most pressing practical problems of policy-making, is that of the utility of military techniques in foreign policy.

WAR IN FOREIGN-POLICY CALCULATIONS

When we speak of "military techniques," we are really speaking of war. Reconciling policy considerations to the initiation, conduct or avoidance of war has long been one of the major concerns of the statesman.

It is important that we keep in mind that war is a means to a policy end, not an end in itself. "Victory" is a technique and not a goal. The object of war is exactly the same as that of any other type of state action: the achievement of enough international consent to permit the attainment of the preselected objective. Thus the extent to which military power is used in the active pursuit of policy goals is determined initially by the value placed on the objective and by the amount of resistance the state expects to and actually does meet. The objective of combat is, as was said long ago, to "break the enemy's will to resist"—not necessarily, be it noted, his *capacity* to resist.

Thus the resort to war is derived from the same type of cost/risk calculation that precedes any policy decision. There is a significant difference in a decision for war, however; although less in quality than in quantity. Costs in war are obviously much higher, since they must to a great extent be measured in human life. The risk factor demands greater odds in favor of success because the price of failure in war is much higher than in any other policy enterprise. Thus cost factors demand that war be reserved for purposes great enough to justify the inevitable expenditure. The greater the probable magnitude of a war, in other words, the fewer the objectives that merit such a costly enterprise. Considerations of risk as well inhibit the easy use of military power, since even under a simpler technology the necessary margin of superiority to make war a good risk was greater than in any other type of action.

In principle, therefore, war as a policy tool demands that the magnitude of the force and violence be used in reasonably accurate relationship to the worth of the objective, and appropriate to the extent and nature of the resistance to be met. It is this concept of the role of violence—phrased by Montesquieu as doing no more damage to the enemy than is absolutely necessary to the attainment of one's purposes—upon which the state system is founded, and it is in this way that war figures in the policy judgments of states.

TECHNOLOGY, NATIONALISM, AND WAR

Two of the great historical forces of modern times have seriously complicated the role of war in statecraft. The first of these is technology, that has made possible entirely new horizons in weaponry, and incalculably expanded the ability of states to inflict damage on each other. The second is modern nationalism, that has involved entire populations in warfare and largely dissipated the ability of governments to carefully control the magnitude of the military effort they make. Technology and nationalism have made war a struggle between peoples rather than between states. The objectives of war have become the total submission of the enemy, or his utter destruction; rather than the lesser purpose of winning his assent to a particular policy.

The world has entered the era of "total war." Warfare today has become divorced from single policy objectives and has become instead a simple if desperate matter of survival. Under the contemporary conditions of combat, a major war cannot be considered as a rational application of capability to foreign policy. Instead, it represents a catastrophic breakdown in the international political process.

THE APPROPRIATENESS OF WAR

The statesman today, knowing that the use of military techniques will trigger off extremely powerful nationalist emotions in his people and open himself and his state to the possibility of attack by the most horrible of new weapons, is cruelly inhibited in his policy choices. In theory as free as ever to resort to war, the logic of the cost/risk continuum is inexorable and frustrating to him.

With war certain to cost far more than it has ever done before, the number of objectives for which such an expenditure is justifiable has shrunk alarmingly. For almost any state, the prolongation of a list of goals meriting the initiation of war past the initial entry of national survival has become extremely difficult. By the same token, if any war in which he becomes engaged is potentially a war of survival, risk factors assume a new relevance. The odds in his favor which he must have before risking combat have climbed almost to the absolute, for he appreciates that his enemy is as likely as he is to assume that the struggle is total, and will therefore commit his ultimate capacities in his own defense. Neat calculations of margins of superiority are therefore virtually irrelevant. Total war can knowingly be unleashed only by a state that has a "first-strike" capacity to destroy or cripple the enemy and an approximation of invulnerability to whatever retaliatory capacity the enemy may possess either before or after the initial onslaught. The attainment of such dominance in the contemporary world is effectively beyond the capacity of any state.

Thus war has not become impossible, since either an irrational distortion of reality or a serious analytical error could lead a government to take the risk. What has happened to war is that it has become inappropriate to foreign policy, conceived and implemented in a climate of calculation, prudence, and rationality. This situation, so disruptive of many operating assumptions of international politics, has engaged the attention of scholars and statesmen ever since the dawn of the nuclear age. A considerable body of speculation and doctrine has been built up about the implications of modern warfare for the future of foreign policy and international politics. We shall be examining these contentions in some detail in Chapter Nine. Here we may anticipate our conclusion there, at least in general terms: a persuasive case for the continued relevance of military considerations to world politics has been built up, but the ubiquitous factors of cost and risk have served to deter states both large and small from venturing into the dangerous waters of open warfare ever since the Korean War of 1950–53.

MILITARY TECHNIQUES SHORT OF WAR

It is sometimes overlooked that the role of military techniques in policy implementation has by no means been confined to actual warfare. As a matter of fact, military factors have long been an ingredient in the normal conduct of foreign policy by all states.

The relative military rank of states has been one of the fundamental structural elements in the state system. The relations of any two states in time of "peace" have long been materially affected and often dominated by their respective military postures. In part this was due to the direct impact of military differentials that always involved a subtle or blatant threat to the weaker state. As long as a state retained the right and the capability effectively to back its demands by military force, a weaker state was obliged to include this consideration in its situational context and to guide itself by a quantitative and qualitative evaluation of the likelihood of this threat becoming a reality. But even more importantly, military differentials had a crucial status-conferring effect. Something very much like a class system long gave form to the international scene as great military powers, medium military powers, and weak military powers developed standardized relations to each other with differing rank, role, and status in world affairs. It is impossible to overestimate the historic impact of this factor.

But both the element of threat and the element of status (perhaps most usefully conceived as the institutionalized reflection of the threat) depended for their energizing effect upon the credibility of the military means. The threat of military power could influence a weaker state only if that government believed that the more powerful state was in the first place willing to risk the commitment of force and was also in a position to use that force meaningfully. The status reward of military capability—by no means entirely inoperative today—likewise if indirectly flowed from the credibility of military superiority. As soon as smaller states came to realize this paradox: that the more military capability major states acquired in the nuclear age the less real opportunity they had to use it and the less interested they were in committing themselves to its use, credibility began to erode. Threats lost their compelling character, and status began to be dissipated as well.

So far has this reevaluation of the real role of military techniques in foreign policy gone that some analysts contend that the world has so tied its hands in a military sense that it has entered the era of the "tyranny of the weak." If the purpose of high capability is to broaden the era of freedom of choice enjoyed by a state, then it is argued that the greatest measure of such freedom is in fact enjoyed by states almost entirely devoid of military power, while those governments with the largest establishments discover that their real freedom is drastically circumscribed by the very existence of their military machines. In practice, therefore, the weaker the state in a military sense the more actively it can prosecute its policy.

If this dour conclusion on the place of military techniques reflects a fundamental change in the nature of international relationships rather than a temporary distortion of regular patterns, then the international political system will inevitably undergo great and far-reaching modification. The military channel of action is historically not only the *ultima ratio* of states, but is essential to the operation of orderly relationships within the traditional system. Any major alteration in the place occupied by military methods and procedures must inevitably find its institutional reflection. If, however, either technological or conceptual progress results in a recapture of the controlling place of military factors, the system will find it possible to stabilize itself again.

Bibliography

Barghoorn, Fredrick C., *Soviet Cultural Offensive*. Princeton: Princeton University Press, 1960.

Dyer, Murray, *Weapon on the Wall: Rethinking Psychological Warfare*. Baltimore: Johns Hopkins University Press, 1959.

George, Alexander L., *Propaganda Analysis: A Study of Inferences Made from Nazi Propaganda in World War II*. Evanston, Illinois: Row Peterson and Company, 1959.

* Graebner, Norman S., *Cold War Diplomacy: American Foreign Policy, 1945–1960*. Princeton: D. Van Nostrand, 1962.

Holt, Robert F. and Robert W. Van De Velde, *Strategic Psychological Operations and American Foreign Policy*. Chicago: The University of Chicago Press, 1960.

* Hsieh, Alice, *Communist China's Strategy in the Nuclear Era.* Englewood Cliffs, New Jersey: Prentice-Hall, Inc., 1962.

* Liddell Hart, Basil H., *Strategy.* New York: Frederick A. Praeger, 1954.

Mao Tse-tung, *Mao Tse-tung on Guerrilla Warfare.* New York: Frederick A. Praeger, 1961.

Martin, Leslie J., *International Propaganda: Its Legal and Diplomatic Control.* Minneapolis, Minnesota: University of Minnesota Press, 1958.

Paret, Peter and John W. Shy, *Guerrillas in the 1960's.* New York: Frederick A. Praeger, 1962.

* Pentony, De Vere E., *United States Foreign Aid: Readings in the Problem Area of Wealth.* San Francisco: Howard Chandler Publishing Company, 1960.

* Ropp, Theodore, *War in the Modern World.* Durham, North Carolina: Duke University Press, 1960.

Selznick, Philip, *The Organizational Weapon: A Study of Bolshevik Strategy and Tactics.* New York: The Free Press of Glencoe, 1959.

Tanham, George K., *Communist Revolutionary Warfare: The Viet Minh in Indochina.* New York: Frederick A. Praeger, 1961.

* Whitaker, Urban G., Jr., *Propaganda and International Relations.* San Francisco: Howard Chandler Publishing Company, 1960.

* Indicates paperback edition.

Five

Ideas and Patterns
of International Politics

As we indicated in Chapter One, the second part of this book is devoted to the international political system: those more or less regularized patterns of relationships formed by the contacts that states have with each other. Our focus here will continue to be political in that we are most concerned with those relationships of states that stem from their respective attempts at value maximization. International politics is what results from the reactions and interactions of the foreign policies of states. These initiative, responsive, ameliorative, combative, and compensatory forms of state behavior demonstrate sufficient regularity that they form what we call here the "international system."

The System of States

The international system is a special type of social system. A "social system" is created when a number of operating units—individuals or groups—so regularize and pattern their relationships with one another that system-centered behavior becomes to a large extent predictable. The relationships of states satisfy this definition almost perfectly. The states of the world are the operating units, and something like three centuries of experience has brought such a degree of regularity to the structure and dynamics of their relations that the general shape of international behavior is very regular. It is with this concept that we begin our discussion.

THE CHARACTERISTICS OF THE SYSTEM

Although undoubtedly included within the general definition of a social system, the international political system has a number of characteristics that mark it off as distinctive and unique. It is this measure of difference, furthermore, that lends international politics its distinguishing characteristics.

In the first place, international politics goes on within a *system*, and not within a *society* or a *community*. Although many writers from time to time are moved to discuss what they call the "community of nations," or the "society of states," such terms must be taken as literary hyperbole rather than accurate reflections of reality. An indispensable element in either a society or a community is the acceptance of a common set of goals for social action and a common value consensus. The international system has neither common values nor any mutual goal other than sheer survival within the system. Each state, as we shall see in a moment, feels no responsibility to anyone or to anything outside itself. No society or community feeling is possible without a common loyalty.

The international system therefore lacks the essential aspects of a more highly organized and articulated community: a controlling moral consensus, a socially-sanctioned code of behavior that prohibits certain lines of action as destructive of good order and demands others as socially necessary, and an institutional structure adequate to implement the moral consensus and enforce the behavior code. Instead, the system gains its form and energy from a much more rudimentary set of controls, most remarkably a calculating kind of prudence that we have already encountered and characterized as "strategic," and a thrust to maintain and preserve the system in its essentials as preferable to any other basis of organization either more or less restrictive.

The operating assumptions of the international system may be classified as a semi-organized anarchy. In logic the anarchic presumptions of the free will of the individual state, the right of the state to choose any goal it wishes and to take any appropriate implementing action, and the resolution of conflicts of interest in terms of the relative strength of the disputing parties, are absolutely controlling. The principle of sovereignty, if taken literally—as we shall see in a moment—permits none but an anarchic base for political action among states. It is true that state policy in world affairs is always rooted in the possible necessity of the state's being thrown entirely upon its own resources with every other state's hand turned against it. It is common for the rhetoric of statecraft to evoke images of the individual state bravely making its way against the active or passive opposition of the remainder of the system. Yet the logic of anarchy is surprisingly unreliable as a base for predicting the outcome of state relations in the real world. Statesmen have made considerable progress in softening and diverting the more onerous consequences of the relatively under-organized international system.

In part this is due to the strong tendency for policy-makers to prefer an expediential to an absolute formulation of both goals and tactics. We already know how willing statesmen are to settle for half a loaf in foreign policy, the more so as the consequences of failure in an all-out effort become more awful. But the regularities of international politics are also in large part due to the impact of habit and inertia; statesmen no less than ordinary individuals are prisoners of their own past action patterns. The influence of custom and standardized practice has almost uniformly been exerted on the side of stabilization and regularization in the relationships of sovereignties. Today, although the anarchy of international politics is conceptually as obvious as ever, the international system is more elaborately and tightly organized than is generally appreciated.

THE NATION-STATE IN THE SYSTEM

The individual nation-state, as it sees itself a functional unit within the international system, is a solitary, self-contained, and self-justifying entity. It draws its motivations for action from within itself, feels itself obligated to no other state, is prepared to devote its own resources to the satisfactions of its needs, and is ready to enjoy the rewards or suffer the consequences of its own actions. It judges all situations and the actions of all other states by the single criterion of its controlling version of interest. It acquires enemies or friends and acts cooperatively or controversially in response to its internal evaluation of the ebb and flow of political action.

This emphasis on the internalized mission and function of the state in the system reflects the dominant note in the reality of international politics. The state is in theory a completely free agent, and attempts in practice to achieve as close as possible an approximation of this freedom. It is this non-identification of the political unit with any larger community and the greater operational freedom from restraint enjoyed by the state that makes international politics differ so markedly from other forms of social action.

It has been argued, by Machiavelli and his later disciples, that so complete is the state's control over its own international role that it is the architect of its own moral code. In these terms the only "good" the state serves—the supreme value of foreign policy—is the accomplishment of its own ends. Although in one sense circular reasoning and not especially useful as a criterion for determining ultimate moral questions, the notion of "reason of state" is of undeniably great value in formulating and executing foreign policy. Whatever the state may decide to do in international politics is by the very fact of decision transformed into a moral goal. Conflicting moral values that might inhibit individual commitment to state purposes are simply relegated to an inferior role. Thus qualms of conscience need never trouble the working policy-maker, for whatever he may conclude is demanded by the national interest thus becomes automatically moral and good. Success in achieving an objective is—regardless of other factors—in itself a "good" thing. Failure, on the other hand, is intrinsically immoral and therefore reprehensible.

Thus the motive force of the international system does not flow from any centralized source but from the nation-states themselves. The "climate" of world politics—the general atmosphere within which relations are conducted and which is subject to change over time—is neither a cosmic force nor an accident of history, but stems rather from the prevailing patterns of assumptions and action accepted by the dominant states of the system. Any basic change in the system, furthermore, will of necessity find its initial expression in modifications in the way states conceive of their international roles.

THE INTERSTATE RELATIONSHIP

These operational postulates govern the approach of states to each other. We have already mentioned that states, lacking any agreed-upon consensual base, must develop their respective postures upon a purely *ad hoc* basis. Initial stages of any interstate relationship in a new situation are always tentative and probing, as each seeks to discover the nature and extent of the involvement of its own interest with those of all the others. Only after each has determined to its own satisfaction the essential ingredients of the evolving relationship does it feel free to elaborate and exploit a strategy.

The relations of any two states within any situation can be located somewhere along a continuum ranging from total agreement at one extreme to total hostility at the other. The determining factor is of course the extent to which the respective interests coincide or conflict. In one sense, therefore, the outcome of any particular collision between states can be termed inevitable. Each has a pre-set notion of interest and the forces liberated by the interaction of these notions of purpose determine the shape of the relationship with almost mathematical precision.

Two further points should be made in this connection. First, any inevitability in the relationship develops after the respective notions of interest are determined; each state has complete freedom to formulate its interest as it may please. Thus the relationship is under complete control at one stage although almost entirely beyond manipulation after the critical point of goal-setting. Second, the degree of clash of interests does not in any way dictate the level of hostility or tension at which this disagreement is prosecuted. The magnitude of an area of disagreement does no more than outline the arena of conflict; whether the conflict is fought at a high level, a low level, or is allowed to lie virtually dormant, depends upon further policy decisions by the governments involved.

We have already discovered that this primacy of interest in the calculations of statesmen has made strategy and policy a very cautious and restrained business. With no certain foreknowledge of how other states will react to a given stimulus, a government must be on the safe side and assume the worst. Each state accepts as controlling the caution that any or all other nations are capable of becoming its enemy at any time and for causes, in the last analysis, beyond its own control. The potentiality of total opposition in any interstate relationship materially affects the substance of policy and its formulation.

Since—as we have also remarked previously—the objectives of states tend toward verbalization in absolute terms, it follows that governments tend to view each other as at least potential competitors for larger slices of a pie of rewards that is of fixed size. This explains the powerful tendency to view the interstate relationship as a zero-sum or two-sided game, in which one state's gain is at least operationally assumed to be the other state's loss. Much of the dynamics of day-by-day international politics stems from this (highly simplistic) view of the basic posture of states *vis-à-vis* each other.

THE POLE OF ORDER AND THE POLE OF DISORDER

The state system thus at any time is torn between the attraction of what we might symbolically call the pole of order and the pole of disorder. Conceptually and logically, the system is one that postulates disorder—disorder so complete and controlling as to reduce world politics to a law-of-the-jungle war of all against all. Operationally, however, violent outbreaks of disorder and open physical conflict may be "normal"; but they are also relatively infrequent. States spend a much larger proportion of their effort and time in prosecuting their ends in a context of order and restraint than they do in any type of "no-holds-barred" conflict.

The order-disorder dichotomy tends to stabilize the norm of international political interaction somewhere between the poles because of dynamic equilibrium. At any time, pressures leading toward disorder may be relatively more powerful than countervailing tendencies, and the system may head toward breakdown. Twice within the twentieth century, disorder has taken over completely during World Wars I and II. Normally, however, the closer toward open disorder the system drifts, the more powerful becomes the urge toward the reestablishment of order and the more likely equilibrium is to be restored. In the same way, if less obviously, there is such a thing as too much order in the system; "too much" in the sense that many states tend to feel that an over-stabilized set of relationships might deprive them of the freedom of decision and action they feel is intrinsic to sovereign status. An excess of stability may well trigger disorderly forces within the system into deliberate attempts to gain elbow room.

Equality and Inequality in International Politics

One of the more puzzling and paradoxical aspects of international politics is the constant tension between the claims of states to substantial equality and the practical fact of their actual inequality. Both equality and inequality have concrete manifestations in the conduct of the relations of states; both affect the way peoples and governments view the world and the tasks they attempt to accomplish in their foreign policies. Because states do exist simultaneously on the two planes of conceptual equality and operational inequality, the student must fully understand the implications of either factor and the most significant relations between them if he is to gain a grasp of the realities of international politics.

THE LAW AND THE MYTH OF SOVEREIGNTY

Equality of states as a characteristic of international politics has its roots in one of the basic concepts of the entire discipline of political science: sovereignty. From both the legal and the mythical consequences of sovereignty flow many fundamentals of international politics.

Sovereignty is legally a key characteristic of a state: to be accepted as a state, a political society must have wtihin itself a supreme law-giving authority with the power to issue commands from which there is no rightful appeal. The concept itself was born during the formative era of the modern state and today is thought to do no more than state a truism. No one would quarrel with the necessity of having a central source of political and legal authority with a state.

The difficulty with sovereignty arose when what was an internalized idea of considerable utility was applied to interstate relations. What in law and in logic could be the appropriate relationship between two sovereign states, each incorporating an authority that alleged itself to be supreme and which recognized no superior? No relationship was conceivable except one of complete legal and status equality. It is on this basis that international law is built; this is the body of jurisprudence that regulates the relationships of sovereignties.

Accordingly, sovereignty in international relations and law has come to stipulate the absolute and perfect legal equality of all states. None may rightfully dictate to another; each is declared to be the equal of all others in status, dignity, and honor. All of the protocol and procedure of formal international intercourse pays great respect to this symbolism of sovereign equality; even the Charter of the United Nations alleges that "the Organization is based on the principle of the sovereign equality of all its Members."

Legal sovereignty was given an added dimension with the birth of modern nationalism. As popular self-consciousness evolved into intensive nationalist identification, the doctrine of sovereignty with its insistence that all states were equal and independent became of great value in molding nations. Nothing was more welcome to an aroused nationalism than the bold legal assertion that any state was the sovereign equal of all others. From this has developed the contemporary myth of sovereignty.

Nationalism demands that the nation-state be at least symbolically free from responsibility to any external authority. The "national will" is sacred and not to be tampered with; the symbols of national identity—the flag, the uniform, the historical monuments—acquire overtones of mystical sanctity. The watchword of national-state freedom of will is, of course, the cry of "sovereignty!" Any over-impairment of sovereignty is to be resisted as a major patriotic duty.

Thus the myth of sovereignty and the concept of nationalism, both grounded in a formalized concept of state equality, unite to reinforce the anarchistic tendencies of the state system. This insistence on the uncontrollability of the state by any larger community has contributed largely to the instability of world politics of which we have already taken note. Operationally, the incapacity of the state-as-concept to accept coercion (for to do so would deny both the equality and the independence of states) has made it necessary for all international arrangements to be ratified by the (free or forced) consent of the participating states. So long as states consent formally, the integrity of sovereign equality is preserved at least on a *pro forma* basis.

THE POLITICAL INEQUALITY OF STATES

Sovereignty as law and concept is a reality of contemporary political life. It does little good to argue (as many devoted protagonists of international organization and world government frequently do) that the doctrine of sovereignty is "invalid." States persist in acting as if sovereignty were a reality and by that fact the doctrine acquires great political significance. But another equally stark fact must be faced: the conceptual equality of states exists alongside an absolute inequality in political competence.

States are completely equal in their right and their capacity to develop ego-images, select goals, and adopt action strategies. Where they are inequal is in their competence to fulfill their purposes. We have already glanced at the various facets of state life that contribute to capability, and in our examination we noted that all of these elements are variables. Either in absolute terms or with reference to a particular situational setting, no two states are ever equal in capability and must adopt their behavior to the verdicts of comparative strength.

This political inequality has long been recognized as controlling within the state system. It is most clearly seen in the surprisingly formalized horizontal stratification of states into great powers, medium powers, and small powers. Great powers are those few states whose capabilities are sufficiently great to permit them to establish and implement a totality of interest; in other words, a great power asserts and acts upon the political right to interfere in and be consulted with regard to the resolution of any issue anywhere in the world at any time. A medium power is treated with a modest degree of formal deference by great powers but is expected to confine its concerns to matters geographically or politically closer to home. A small power is permitted to exist but cannot ordinarily maintain an interest in opposition to either larger type; the conditions of its political activity are imposed upon it by the decisions of more powerful states.

Thus in political terms we find an infinity of gradations and discriminations of rank, power, and status. One of the most trying tasks of statesmen is to conduct relationships so as to preserve the useful fictions of legal equality while at the same time making certain that political solutions are reached that accurately reflect the controlling inequality. We already know that the favored device for the accomplishment of this purpose is the technique of consent.

THE TREND TOWARD GREATER INEQUALITY

One of the agonizing issues gripping contemporary international politics is the obvious fact that the gap between the mystique of state equality and the reality of political inequality is not decreasing but is instead growing greater. The vastly augmented store of capability conferred by modern technology on industrial states on the one hand, and the birth of so many new, underdeveloped, and unstable states on the other, has vastly extended the spectrum of inequality. The powerful are far more powerful both absolutely and relatively than ever before; the weak are relatively much weaker than ever before. In such a general context, to speak of the "sovereign equality" of—for example—the members of the United Nations, is to compound fatuity.

To some extent, however, the growing disparity between equality and inequality has been mitigated by certain other factors. The politically relevant forms of capability have changed drastically under postwar conditions, and we have already demonstrated that military differentials are not so absolute an element of inequality as they formerly were. Such universally-relevant supranational entities as the United Nations have also to some extent provided a way in which aggregates of strength can be constructed by small states so that by the creation of a sufficiently impressive bloc they can go far to offset the political dominance of larger states.

But these can do no more than soften the inexorable tendency of inequality to become more and more glaring. There is ample evidence today that both popular leaders and professional policy-makers are beginning to question the rationale of a political system that posits equality among states and yet attempts to function with such almost laughable disparity among all members. Whether or not the familiar political system can long survive gripped by such a major contradiction is one of the major issues of the contemporary era.

Power Politics

The controlling dynamic of the state system is and has long been known as "power politics." This well-known term, brought into English as a translation of the German word *Machtpolitik*, has both a pejorative and a descriptive connotation. It may be, and frequently is, used to characterize the relationships of states as being governed almost entirely by force or threat, without any consideration of right and justice. This meaning is perhaps the closest to the sense of the original German word. Our purpose here, however, is less to condemn power politics than to understand a process. We shall therefore confine the term to a purely descriptive use. Power politics in the discussion that follows simply characterizes the way in which the international political process actually works.

THE ASSUMPTIONS OF POWER POLITICS

We have already sketched out, in our discussion of the state system and the respective roles of equality and inequality in the relations of states, the underpinnings of the doctrines of power politics. There is nothing either mysterious or sinister about them. Granted the doctrinal and operating fundamentals of the nation-state, a political system including all states can develop in only one way. Power politics rests on a set of assumptions that are consciously accepted and deliberately implemented by all governments.

1. *There are no absolutes of right or justice in the relations of states.* Each state is the judge of the correctness of its own actions, and international politics goes on in a climate of moral relativism.

2. *The only collective value shared by all participants is the desirability of the preservation of the system.* Except for the common concern not to destroy the system and its members, states are conceived as being entirely on their own.

3. *Self-help is the rule of action.* Lacking common values, the system cannot boast institutions and mechanisms of collective action. Individual states must therefore enforce their own rights and can count on support from no external source.

4. *Each state has only as many rights as it can enforce itself.* The state, thrust on its own resources, is obliged to content itself with such rewards as its strength and the wit of its leaders can extract from the system.

5. *The relations of states are determined not by the application of any general principles but by the expediential interaction of their respective capabilities.* This is the crux of "power politics": considerations of "power" (capability) govern the outcome of state contacts.

6. *Operationally, therefore, factors of power determine questions of right.* In this sense, might (broadly interpreted) actually makes right.

We can see the extent to which these organizing and operating assumptions flow logically from the postulates about the nature of the sovereign nation-state that we have already laid down. If the test of any institution is its appropriateness to the social situation in which it is placed and its efficacy in solving the problems to which it is set, we must admit that these assumptions—seldom verbalized by statesmen as baldly as we have stated them, but always sedulously adhered to in the practice of statecraft—establish an admirably effective institutional structure for the conduct of international politics.

We can see, of course, that the validity of these assumptions depends ultimately upon the extent to which the phenomenon of power or capability can be meaningfully quantified. Such a relativistic and purportedly value-free system of regulating a set of relationships demands the existence of an arbitral apparatus of complete objectivity and universal acceptance. Power has played this role for centuries. Part of the generally blurred appearance of the international political system today is due to the diminished skill of statesmen in clarifying and quantifying the several categories of power. As a result many of these assumptions are under serious fire.

POWER STATUS IN INTERNATIONAL POLITICS

We pointed out earlier that the political inequality of states is and has long been recognized by clear differences in status among various categories of power. The process of power politics became formalized as a basis for state interaction only as status configurations reflecting the power and strength (actual, potential, or formal) of states were crystallized into institutional form.

The social system of international politics has traditionally been a sharply stratified one. The three great "classes" of states—great powers, medium powers, and small powers—have structured the entire political process. Parenthetically, it is interesting to note that the names given the several types clearly reflect the crucial impact of something called "power" in determining social place and status. An essential to a working class system is of course a full appreciation by each class of its relative place in the system and a recognition of the peculiar roles of all other classes. In this regard the international political system also qualifies as a fully-developed class society.

To continue our analogy, the relatively small group of great powers occupied the place of the dominant aristocracy in a civil society. Because their power brought right in its train, the great powers have throughout history insisted on their right to regulate all matters within the system in their individual and group interest. For many years the study of international politics actually involved no more than the analysis of the relations among a cluster of major states whose number varied between four and eight. So great and controlling was their influence and so complete was their collective monopoly over the relevant instruments of coercion that these few states demonstrated repeatedly their capacity to police all international relationships.

Membership in the elite inner circle of states was not the result of any mathematical calculation of power components, but rather a function of international practice and consensus. Certain states "qualified" and were taken into the group by co-optation—frequently registered in a major international conference culminating in a reordering peace treaty such as the Peace of Westphalia (1848), the Treaty of Utrecht (1713), the work of the Congress of Vienna (1815), and the several peace treaties known as the Peace of Paris at the end of World War I (1919). Each of these epoch-making (and epoch-ending) instruments brought erstwhile outsiders into the group of great powers and also expelled certain states either temporarily or permanently.

We have already indicated the chief reward of great-power status: the implicit right (rooted in action capability) of a major state to extend its interest as far as it wishes and to act in support of this interest. Thus great powers have always asserted that no question is inherently none of their business and insist on being consulted on the ultimate disposition of any question in which they may care to involve themselves. The fact that in doing so they may override longer-lived and deeper-rooted interests of lesser states is simply regarded as irrelevant, although some doctrinal efforts have been made in the direction of formulating principles of an alleged "responsibility of power" that would authorize great-power intervention anywhere.

The consensual base of great-power status is clearly shown by the periodic appearance of what we might call great-powers-by-courtesy: states that are given membership in the circle for various political reasons but who in fact lack a large reservoir of action capability. Spain, for example, was kept in the great-power class long after its effective role had been extinguished in the seventeenth century. Italy was given courtesy membership after its unification in 1870. France and (Nationalist) China were included at United States insistence in the immediate aftermath of World War II. Such states may enjoy great prestige among lesser powers, but their actual influence on the deliberations of the inner circle is usually minimal.

The international system gives formal recognition to the controlling place of great-power status through the mechanism of the "concert of power": formal assemblies of leading states who attempt jointly to arrange a set of relationships to their mutual satisfaction. In the past this has been done most obviously at major peace conferences such as the Congress of Vienna and at periodic gatherings for the resolution of particular problems. Leading historic examples of the latter type are the Congress of Verona (1822) and the Congress of Berlin (1878). Since 1945, the "concert of power" has had a dual aspect; the conference of opportunity continues in the form of the so-called "Conference of Foreign Ministers" of the great powers, while permanent concert activity is made possible in the Security Council of the United Nations.

Less need be said of the lower two status groups. The values of great-power status tend to be automatically accepted by all states, so each smaller state seeks to act as much like a great power as it can. Each seeks as broad an international role as it can effectuate; each is active in augmenting its limited store of status and deference. Each class (medium or small powers) has an infinity

of gradations within itself, and something like an international peck-
ing order is the norm. So great is the role of the great powers, however, these distinctions flow less from analyses and judgments
made by the lesser powers themselves than by (sometimes almost
casual) discriminatory evaluations flowing from the elite states.

PATTERNS OF POWER POLITICS

Within the general characteristics of the power-political system as we have outlined them, we can distinguish four clear patterns of relationships that have recurred frequently and are operative today. Two of these patterns involve only the great powers,
two involve the small powers and each relates to the general area
of great power-small power relationships.

The first pattern develops when the great powers are in substantial agreement about the existing shape of relationships among
themselves within the entire spectrum of issues. Such a situation
occurs only when the entire group—or at least all but a fraction
of the membership—is in terms of the prevailing situation committed to a generalized status quo orientation. Great-power agreement results in the combined force of the concert being exerted
in a coordinated way upon the arena of world politics and the almost inevitable control of international politics by the leading
states. A notable historical example of this pattern is provided
by the course of affairs in Europe between 1815 and roughly
1848.

The second pattern is the converse of the first in that the great
powers, instead of agreeing on the preferable state of relationships,
splits into hostile and competing camps. This situation normally
develops when revisionist points of view take control of a sizable
slice of the total power represented by the group of major states
and the dominant dimension of struggle becomes that between
status quo and revisionist policies. When major states fall out, the
over-all control the elite group can exercise on world affairs inevitably diminishes since the very fact of a break in their common
front and the dynamism that characterizes a great power struggle
offers opportunities for small states and coalitions to act effectively.
The neatest example of such a pattern is also the most recent: the
contemporary Cold War that has split the great powers so irrevocably.

The third pattern arises when the smaller states of the world (including what we have called both medium and small powers) develop a common interest, point of view, and over-all strategy to govern their responses to major states. This is a relatively recent development in world affairs, made possible only by the appearance of the United Nations as a universal actor that derives its motive force from its many small members. Under appropriate conditions—notably the military balance of terror that inhibits great-power use of armed force—this pattern has surprisingly great scope. Contemporary world politics featured by the rise in importance of the General Assembly of the United Nations and the increasing militancy of the small-state anticolonialist bloc, is a clear demonstration of the pattern.

The fourth pattern is historically far more common, consisting as it does of small state disorganization, lack of communication, and incipient or actual mutual hostility. In this pattern each small state is subject to being isolated and pressured by predatory medium or great powers irrespective of the state of unanimity of the elite group itself. It has been this tendency of the more numerous but less well organized aggregation of medium and small powers to break into uncoordinated fragments that has made the controlling and dominating mission of the great powers much simpler than it would otherwise have been.

One final point about these patterns should be made. Either the first or the second may be controlling the relations of the great powers. Either the third or the fourth may be controlling the status of the remainder of the states of the world. Whichever pair (one *or* two, three *or* four) are simultaneously functional determines the general shape of international power relations at any particular moment in history.

The Regularities of International Politics

The anarchy of the international system, at least in concept, contains the constant potential of explosion. Managing the affairs of states in a lawless environment requires the development and the application of a variety of relatively unstructured but very pervasive principles of action. These regularities of international politics function to control the external manifestations of power in the international order and to regulate by limiting the effect of power differentials among states. The acceptance by the controlling consensus of states at any time of one or another of these patterns is reflected in their policies. Self-preservation in a context of change is the controlling motivation for the willingness of states to submit to a regularized structuring of their over-all responses.

PATTERNS OF EQUILIBRIUM OF POWER

If we assume that the normal tendency of state relationships is to seek equilibrium, we may classify the equilibrium patterns of politics and power in a threefold system. Our first type is characterized by a widespread dispersal of action capability among the states of the system; this pattern has long been known as the "multiple balance of power," and received its most explicit institutionalization in the classic European system of the seventeenth through the nineteenth centuries. The second pattern is marked by a concentration of power on a bipolar basis around two great powers. This is the predominant pattern of the post-1945 world and obviously enough is usually identified as a "simple balance of power." Finally, there is the pattern of integrated power radiating from a single central point like the spokes of a wheel. Although never realized since the decay of the Roman Empire, the League of Nations and the United Nations represent attempts at its achievement in the modern world.

The multiple balance system is based on a concentration of power in individual states and is uncentralized. The simple balance is in one sense a mid-point in that the number of poles of concentration is reduced to two. The integrated system does away—at least in theory—with dispersed power entirely and replaces it with an integrated power structure.

MULTIPLE BALANCE OF POWER

The multiple balance was the controlling pattern of interstate relations throughout the seventeenth, eighteenth, nineteenth, and early twentieth centuries. During these centuries the international system was consistently pluralistic in that a multiplicity of great powers—always at least five at any time—dominated the course of world politics.

In a multiple balance system the great powers act so as to complement each other and—sometimes intentionally but more often instinctively—maximize the prospects of their survival as individual states and the durability of the system. A multiple balance system demands an implicit agreement to respect each other's existence and sphere of interests and to confine disagreements to issues considered marginal. Coalition formation is normal, as also is the tendency for these action groupings to balance each other off. Any reduction in the number of great powers is considered undesirable, as also—although to a lesser extent and much less explicitly—is any increase. Either modification in the family runs the risk of seriously upsetting whatever hard-won stability the system may boast. No great power in a multiple system, therefore, should seriously plan to eliminate another.

World War I signalled the final breakdown of the multiple balance system. Several profound historic trends only imperfectly understood at the time had undermined the operative conditions essential to the perpetuation of the neat and tidy world of an earlier period. (1) The emergence of Germany and Italy dramatically increased the number of great powers, while the two new major states energetically pressed for the expansion of the system to include their own interests. (2) The end of imperialist expansion terminated the digressive effect of colonial conquest and again focused great-power interests on each other. (3) Britain lost the freedom of action it had once enjoyed as the self-conscious "holder of the balance" and found itself drifting into hard-and-fast opposition to Germany and a blurred but binding affiliation with the Franco-Russian alliance. (4) The ramshackle empire of Austria-Hungary could no longer function meaningfully as a great power. After 1907, the inner political world of the great powers had become almost bipolar as two rigid blocs confronted each other in a situation permitting no real maneuver. "Balance" had become an irrelevant concept.

SIMPLE BALANCE OF POWER

The bipolarization of power between the United States and the U.S.S.R., in part due to historical accident in the World War II era but also the result of deliberate policy choices by both sides, has characterized world politics since 1945. In this simple balance ("simple" only in its structure, but fantastically difficult and dangerous to operate), shifting of alignments takes place around the poles of the two major powers and all states draw their international orientation from the general configurations of strength. Movement and change in a tight bipolar system, however, is minimized, since the rationale of great-power policy is to reduce the pluralism of international politics to a monistic concentration on the single issue of the bipolar struggle. The simple balance, therefore, is reminiscent of a seesaw in contrast to the similarity of the multiple balance to a chandelier.

INTEGRATION OF POWER

Integration of power is best represented in political terms by the classic concept of collective security, best exemplified today by the United Nations. In simple terms collective security is a system to make real the idea of "one for all and all for one."

The obligations of collective security are spelled out in Articles 39 through 51 of the Charter of the United Nations. The "teeth" of these provisions are found in Article 42:

> "(The Security Council) may take such action by air, sea, or land forces as may be necessary to maintain or restore international peace and security. Such action may include demonstrations, blockades and other operations by air, sea or land forces of Members of the United Nations."

The "other operations" hinted at obviously include military action under United Nations direction, first implemented in Korea and later in the Suez Canal Zone and in the Congo.

Collective security and the integration of power in the contemporary world have never been real successes. Pending the transfer of state sovereignty to a single world government of some sort, collective security may function only upon the basis of a massive consensus among the world's leading powers. So long as the political world remains so hopelessly divided into hostile camps, collective security demands the impossible, for the system was never designed to restrain part of the community on behalf of the remainder. Its rationale rather demands that any potential aggressor be an outcast with every man's hand turned against him the moment he threatens to violate the peaceful climate of relationships. Thus it follows that collective security is a viable pattern of relationships only when the vast preponderance of action capability is in the hands of states with a deep interest in the preservation of at least the essentials of the status quo. A significant revisionist faction among the major states renders the idea irrelevant. It is in no sense pessimistic to insist that the contemporary world is propitious to the policies of revisionism and that therefore true integration of power is not a real prospect in the foreseeable future.

METHODS OF THE BALANCE OF POWER

There are seven different techniques employed by states to maintain or rectify a balance of power: intervention, compensation, buffer zones, divide and rule, spheres of influence, armaments and alliances.

1. *Intervention* is the interference by one state in the internal affairs of another and may assume either defensive or offensive forms. A defensive intervention aims at the preservation of a particular regime or system. An offensive intervention, on the another hand, is directed at altering such a system.

Defensive intervention is based on the assumption that a state, particularly a great power, cannot permit the balance of power to be materially changed to its disadvantage by a change of government or policy by another state. Examples of defensive intervention are numerous in contemporary international politics: the Allied intervention in Russia in 1918 to maintain the pre-Bolshevik regime; the Soviet's intervention in Hungary in 1956 to protect the Kadar government; the American intervention in Lebanon in 1958 in support of the Shamoun administration.

Offensive intervention is expansive and is primarily manifested by penetration. Its purpose is to bring about a change of policy or government in another state, or if necessary, completely to eliminate its independence. The manner in which Italy and Germany became united in the second half of the 19th century represents offensive intervention employed by Prussia and Piedmont respectively. The establishment of communist governments in Eastern Europe following World War II illustrates Russian offensive intervention. The old American diplomatic custom of "dollar diplomacy" is still another example of this form of intervention in Latin America.

2. *Compensation* involves giving a state the equivalent of that of which it is deprived or the equal of that given to other states. This usually applies only to victorious states and their allies; defeated states usually lose territory without compensation. Peace treaties normally result in territorial changes which reflect the principle of compensation in some form. This was the spirit of the territorial settlements embodied in the peace treaties that followed World War I and World War II.

The basic assumption underlying compensation is that one state cannot afford to see another state increase its power without obtaining a compensating aggrandizement of its own. It was this principle that characterized the approach of the great powers during the second half of the nineteenth century towards the partitioning of Africa and the Far East. It was an insistence on compensation that made Mussolini join actively in the war on the side of the Axis after the fall of France; he refused to permit Hitler to settle Europe's future without deriving benefits for Italy. The assignment of mandated areas to France and Great Britain following the First World War, and the authorization of United Nations trust territories following the Second World War are more recent examples.

3. A *buffer zone* is a small power situated between two or more great powers. It may also be a relatively weak state located between the spheres of interest of great powers.

The assumption underlying the principle of a buffer zone is that it is in the interests of each of the interested great powers to prevent the other from controlling the buffer zone. Thus the competing powers each seek to preserve the integrity of the small state in the middle as preferable to its falling prey to the other.

Switzerland and Belgium have long been considered buffer states between Germany and France. During the latter part of the nineteenth century, Afghanistan was a buffer state between the British Empire and Russia, and the Spanish colonies in Africa played the same role between the colonial empires of France and Britain. At present, we can classify Austria as a buffer state between the Eastern and Western spheres of influence in Europe and Nepal a buffer state between India and Communist China.

116   *Concepts of International Politics*

4. *"Divide and rule"* means that a great power follows the policy of either dividing its opponents and competitors into hostile camps or at least of heightening their disunity. The principal assumption underlying this principle is that disunity and partition will keep the competitor weak.

The principle of "divide and rule" has been the traditional policy of France towards Germany. The present policy of the Soviet Union towards Europe represents another example of the divide and rule formula.

5. The *sphere of influence* is a device by which competing great powers delineate their areas of hegemony. Each one of the great powers concerned undertakes to respect the other's power rights in its own zone.

The assumption behind this principle is that in this manner disputes between great powers can be minimized. North Africa, for example, was considered a French sphere of influence from the latter nineteenth century until only a few years ago, while Egypt and the Sudan in their turn became British spheres of influence after 1882. The Balkans are presently regarded as belonging to the Russian sphere of influence.

6. *Armaments* are the principal means by which a great power tries to maintain and re-establish a balance of power to its favor. The underlying assumption here is that a greater quality and quantity of armaments maximizes the capabilities of a state for attack and deterrence. Hence, the inevitable corollary of the armaments race is a spiraling burden of military preparedness consuming an ever greater portion of the budgets of states. We shall examine this point in detail in Chapter Ten.

7. *Alliances* are the most important manifestations of the methods of balancing power. An alliance is an agreement between two or more states for the defensive or aggressive purposes of its members against a state or states outside the alliance. Leading contemporary alliances include the North Atlantic Treaty, the Warsaw Pact, the Rio Pact, the Central Treaty Organization, and the South East Asia Collective Defense Treaty.

Alliances are an essential function of the balance of power operating within the international system. The basic assumption underlying alliances is that through alliances a state can increase its own power, either by adding increments from other states or by withholding the power of other states from its competitors.

Alliances are dynamic; their changing pattern is not stimulated by principle, but rather reflects the circumstances of expediency as viewed by the state concerned. Common interests are the primary considerations in the establishment of alliances between states. The alliances themselves define the general policies and concrete measures serving these interests. Although the typical interests which unite states in an alliance against an opponent are explicit, these interests are less precise regarding the policies to be pursued and the objectives to be sought.

Alliances may be regarded as essential methods in the regulatory process of international politics. They are important instruments in the adaptation of the nation-state to the international system. They help to fill the gap between the ideals of organization and the realities of quasi-anarchy in the international system.

Bibliography

* Adam, Thomas R., *Modern Colonial Policies*. New York: Random House, 1954.

Burns, Arthur Lee, *Power Politics and the Growing Nuclear Club*. Princeton: Princeton University Press, 1959.

Claude, Inis L. Jr., *Power and International Relations*. New York: Random House, 1962.

* Gareau, Fredrick H. (ed.), *Balance of Power and Nuclear Deterrence*. Boston: Houghton Mifflin and Company, 1962.

Gould, L. J. and E. W. Steel (eds.), *People, Power, and Politics*. New York: Random House, 1961.

* Graebner, N. S., *Cold War Diplomacy: American Foreign Policy, 1945–1960*. Princeton: D. Van Nostrand, 1962.

Gulick, Edward V., *Europe's Classical Balance of Power: A Case History of the Theory of European Statecraft*. Ithaca, New York: Cornell University Press, 1955.

Laski, Harold J., *Authority in the Modern State*. New Haven: Yale University Press, 1919.

————, *The Foundations of Sovereignty and Other Essays*. New York: Harcourt, Brace & World, Inc., 1921.

* ————, *Introduction to Politics*. New York: Barnes and Noble, 1962.

Liska, George, *International Equilibrium: A Theoretical Essay on the Politics and Organization of Security.* Cambridge: Harvard University Press, 1957.

Meriam, Charles E., *History of the Theory of Sovereignty Since Rousseau.* New York: Columbia University Press, 1928.

Moon, P. T., *Imperialism and World Politics.* New York: Macmillan and Company, 1926.

Morgenthau, Hans J., *Politics Among Nations*, 3d ed. New York: Alfred A. Knopf, 1960.

* Schumpeter, J., *Imperialism and Social Classes.* New York: The Meridian Books, 1955.

Wight, Martin, *Power Politics.* London: The Royal Institute of International Affairs, 1946.

* Indicates paperback edition.

Six

The Conditions of
International Politics Today

The international political system, incorporating the set of historically validated ideas and patterns that we have just examined, has in this generation come into an abrupt conjunction with modern technology. The several revolutions of the contemporary era—in transportation, in communication, in energy, in production, in weapons, and in space—have all had their direct effect on the relations of states. The conditions of international politics today are radically different from those of even half a century ago. A large part of the tensions of international politics in the nuclear era comes from the inevitably frustrating effort to fit the contemporary environment into the traditional political categories.

Today the states of the world function within a closed political system. In analytical terms, the frontier of international politics has disappeared. There is, in other words, "no place to hide." Every explosion of political, economic, or social force within this closed system inevitably radiates to all portions of the globe. No part of the earth's surface can be classified as politically undesirable or strategically unimportant. Every state is in some way relevant to every other state.

The States of the World

One manifestation of the new dimensions of international politics is the great change that has occurred in the number and the nature

119

of participants in the process. With the members of the international political system so different, it is no wonder that the process has been greatly modified.

THE CONTEMPORARY INTERNATIONAL SYSTEM

The total number of national actors (states) in international politics has almost doubled since the end of World War II. When the United Nations was established in 1945, its membership included fifty-one states. By 1962, United Nations membership had risen to 110. This increase in number is further highlighted by the current geographic distribution of the membership. In 1945, the United Nations had twenty members from Latin America, nineteen from Europe and other western areas, nine from Asia, and three from Africa. The number of Latin American states remained unchanged until Jamaica and Trinidad-Tobago became independent in 1962, while that of Europe and the West has increased by nine. In contrast, the number of African states has increased to thirty-three and that of Asia to twenty-five. Together, the non-western states of Africa and Asia constitute at present 54 per cent of the membership. Of the fifty-seven Afro-Asian states, no less than fifty-two have escaped from colonial status since the end of World War II.

Thus the system which was, as we shall see in a moment, once a purely western culture pattern has been invaded and bids fair to be taken over by non-western peoples and their value structures. This great shift in the background and general orientation of the bulk of participants in international politics has had a number of immediate consequences for the system.

(1) Consensus is much more difficult to develop on many issues than it was when all important states shared a common moral and historical orientation. The new states arrive at world politics with a point of view different from that of the older states, and apply different criteria of judgment and evaluation. The resulting communication between West and non-West has thus been marked by great suspicion, misunderstanding, and confusion of motivations.

(2) A new force—non-western nationalism expressing itself usually in the form of anticolonialism—has come to play a major determining force in the course of political life. Many of the new states look upon their former colonial masters as their natural ene-

mies and press their case against colonialism almost as a matter of principle. The older states with a history of rule over alien peoples have found themselves morally and intellectually almost powerless against this onslaught.

(3) The dawn of political consciousness in many once-somnolent peoples has brought home to them the startling contrast between the way of life with which they are familiar and the much higher standard long enjoyed by the older states. They have turned to their governments to win for them by international action what they feel to be their just share of the good things of life. This familiar "revolution of rising expectations" is a direct consequence of the broader membership in the international political system.

(4) On their own part, the older and better established members of the system have been obliged to broaden their own political horizons to take account of the new conditions of international life. Not only have they been required to extend their interests to include many once-neglected areas of the world, but they also have been constrained to deal with a broad range of substantive problems —economic development, human rights, and so on—that rest outside the traditional context of international politics.

THE ORIGINS OF THE SYSTEM

The world political order as we know it today emerged from the European state system that followed the collapse of feudalism.

The Renaissance and Reformation transformed the political conditions of the medieval period into a milieu that made possible the development of the modern European nation-state. The Renaissance laid the foundation for the secularization of European thought, whereas the Reformation set in motion the nationalization of the once-universal concept of Christendom. In addition, new means of communication and the so-called "commercial revolution" shook the foundations of feudalism. These forces led first to the modern idea of the state and subsequently to the European nation-state system that was formally institutionalized in the Peace of Westphalia in 1648. Prior to World War II, "international politics" was largely synonymous with the politics of Europe and European-rooted culture. The basic concepts which energize international politics today—sovereignty, nationalism, war, international law and organization, and many others—were thus systematized over three centuries ago.

The gradual development of a multiplicity of independent units that acknowledged no universal political superior and the establishment of continuous and organized relations among the western national states marked the beginning of what has come to be called power politics. Beginning with the fifteenth and sixteenth centuries, the newly-established European states began to reach out and circle the globe. Leaders in this effort were those maritime powers located on the circumference of Europe: Portugal and Spain initially, and later France, Great Britain, and Holland. Wherever they went they planted their flags in the non-European world and established outposts for what rapidly became empires. The western community of national states was thus extended to the rest of mankind. The Industrial Revolution accelerated the rate of European colonial expansion because many of the raw materials for nascent European industries were located outside Europe.

What originated in European institutions during the fifteenth century had by 1900 become a global system incorporating the political values and structures of the West. This cultural root of international politics points up a significant paradox. Today, the new states of Asia and Africa are admittedly in revolt against a system which they feel "enslaved" them, and yet they are at the same time seeking to join that system themselves and to use as their instrument of revolt a state form frankly borrowed from western models.

DIVERSITY AND INTEGRATION

As long as power in the international order was confined to a limited number of European and western states there was no need for—and consequently no movement toward—any supranational authority to regulate the relations of states. The balance of power as practiced by the statesmen of Europe served to keep the international political process adequately stabilized. Since the effective action of the balance of power depended on the configurations assumed by an unequal distribution of power among states, the services of Great Britain as the self-conscious holder and wielder of the balance were required most of the time.

The new dimensions of international politics have given rise to a drastic modification of the traditional patterns of distribution of power. The fundamental conditions upon which the old system were based have evaporated. The devolution of power apparent since the onset of the Industrial Revolution has created the entirely new situation in which states now find themselves. Three of these trends merit separate mention.

(1) The number of *national actors* in international politics has increased. We have seen that the number of states has more than doubled since World War II from about 60 to roughly 120 today. This increase has been almost entirely in the category of small states. By using the normal criteria of classification, the number of small powers increased from about 40 in 1945 to approximately 85 today. Middle powers increased from only 12 to less than 20—a one-third gain.

(2) The number of *essential national actors* has, on the other hand, actually decreased. During World War II there were eight essential national actors (great powers)—the United States, the Soviet Union, the United Kingdom, France, Italy, Germany, China, and Japan. Today the number has been reduced to two unmistakably essential states (the United States and the U.S.S.R.), a third near-essential state (the United Kingdom), and two aspirants to essentiality (India and China). If and when the process of European integration reaches fruition, it is probable that this listing will also include an entity called "Europe" as a new essential national actor. The number of great powers in the world today, however, is the smallest it has been since the beginning of the state system.

(3) The differentials between categories of national actors are becoming wider. Differences in industrial, political, and military conditions rooted in the newer aspects of technology have made "the rich richer and the poor poorer." Barring some reversal of trends, many experts fear the indefinite prolongation of this evolution with important consequences for the future of international politics.

These trends, operating as they do within the more intimate international environment created by technology, have had an interesting and significant dual effect. On the one hand they have led to the concentration of the visible forms of international power within the major political blocs that dominate contemporary world affairs. These rigid groupings, expressing in their most intense form the traditional values of the state system, emphasize the diversity on which the political approach of states to each other has long been based. On the other hand, the integration of power demanded by the newer questions with which the system is now seized has received its institutionalization in the form of a new phenomenon: the universal actor as epitomized by the United Nations and its subordinate and associated multilateral agencies. The struggle between diversity and integration, although as old as political life itself, has thus acquired a new and portentous dimension; the bipolar system and the United Nations system as ways of organizing power stand in direct confrontation today.

Nationalism: Old and Young

Nationalism is the common sentiment or feeling of solidarity which transforms a people into a nationality and which expresses itself in an attitude which ascribes to the collective activity of the nation a very high (frequently the highest) place in the hierarchy of social value. Nationalism converts a "state" into a "nation-state"; the latter is thus the political structure that reflects a people considering themselves a nation. As such, nationalism is one of the absolutely controlling phenomena of world politics today as it has been since the American and French Revolutions.

CHARACTERISTICS OF NATIONALISM

Nationalism grows from a variety of sources. Some of the more obvious factors that impel individuals to join with others in a national group include a common language, religion, historical background, cultural tradition, and racial background. Several of these may interact in subtle ways to reinforce a cohesive tendency in a people. The nationalist ethos is best expressed in the broadly-based and deeply-felt philosophy of political, economic, and social life that becomes the operational creed of the nation. It is also reflected in a complex variety of symbols: external enemies, myths, heroes, history, and folklore.

TRADITIONAL EUROPEAN NATIONALISM

Rudimentary forms of nationalism can be traced to the states of antiquity. Ancient peoples commonly considered themselves divinely chosen and believed that their gods were the sworn foes of other states. They regarded themselves as greatly superior in all aspects to the rest of mankind, viewing others as approaching excellence in proportion to their acceptance of the particular values of the state.

It was the development of the European state system and the expansion of Western civilization, however, that gradually brought to sharp focus the effect of nationalism in international politics. The Hundred Years War (1337–1451) between France and England may be considered the beginning of modern nationalism. In England during the twelfth and thirteenth centuries, the initial foundations for the union of Norman and Saxon into Englishmen were laid down, to be fully achieved by the middle of the fourteenth century. In France, an elementary form of French national consciousness first appeared during the Hundred Years War. The French, however, lacked the more elaborate political institutions of the English and the development of full national identity was thus slower in France than in Britain. By the seventeenth century, however, England and France had become nations in almost a contemporary sense, to be followed shortly by Sweden, Holland, Spain, and Denmark.

In these European societies, nationalism was originally directed at the centralization of government through the unity of law and administration. It gradually evolved, however, into a more liberal movement dedicated to the termination of royal absolutism by preaching the principle that the state belongs to the people. It thus became a condition of civilized life and functioned as a principle of political order and freedom. The European tended to turn to nationalism so as to discover a more meaningful relationship to his increasingly secularized environment. So powerful did it become that in many societies it acquired many of the characteristics of a secular religion, partially filling the gap left by the destruction of the medieval synthesis.

The unifying influence in nationalism which initially brought order and stability within the national state, however, ultimately promoted outside it a highly diverse community of sovereign states. Whereas nationalism during the early stages of its growth in Europe promised peace, order, and justice predicated on the fulfillment of national aspirations, the paradox of nationalist logic was highlighted after the middle of the eighteenth century. Since then it has functioned more as a force of disintegration and fragmentation than of unity.

In an important way nationalism is self-contradictory. Two principles make up its substance: the expression of aspirations for personal and civil liberty by the individual, and the thrust for political dignity and freedom for the society. In practice these two principles are inescapably antagonistic. Either can serve as the basis for political action but never both together, at least for any period of time.

THE IMPACT OF NATIONALISM

The development of international politics since the middle of the eighteenth century furnishes much evidence that the effective implementation of nationalism without aggravating the conditions of international politics is difficult if not impossible. A people's aspiration to create a nation-state has almost always conflicted with territorial claims of other states. Nationalists generally have not been satisfied with internal achievements, but tend rather to seek glory through expansion and empire, whether territorial, economic, or cultural. Intense nationalistic identification, furthermore, tends to undermine flexibility in policy and the capacity to compromise in interstate disputes.

The series of major wars that have been waged since 1815—especially World Wars I and II—embodied overt attempts in various ways to apply the principles of nationalism. Almost every one was fought by one or more belligerents in the name of national self-determination and the results of these wars were reflected in peace settlements allegedly predicated upon the same principles. Yet, in the final analysis, a victory of nationalism, instead of bringing peace and order to international politics, tended only to lead to an exchange of the roles of the oppressor and oppressed. Far from creating a more stable system, nationalism contributed to the "Balkanization" of the international order and exaggerated an already strong proclivity to tension.

NATIONALISM IN THE NON-WESTERN WORLD

Modern nationalism as it is manifesting itself in the emerging Asian and African states shares only one aspect with the principle of early European nationalism: the nation is held to be the ultimate point of reference for political loyalties and actions. Otherwise non-western nationalism is a special, almost exotic growth.

In the original phase of nationalism in Europe (sometimes called the "liberating" phase) the nation was conceived as the ultimate end of political action, although nationalisms with similar ends were recognized and tolerated. The goal of nationalism was in practice "one nation in one state" and nothing more. In twentieth-century western nationalism (known as "integrating" nationalism), the phenomenon of the nation-in-a-state is usually regarded as no more than the starting point of a universal mission of value dissemination whose ultimate objectives in some cases extend to the entire world. This "nationalistic universalism," a type of political Messianism, claims the right of one nation acting through a set of state institutions to impose its own values and institutions upon as many nations as it wishes.

The impact of both forms of western nationalism on the non-western world has been explosive. In large part this is due to the fact that the environment was peculiarly prepared to respond to the stimulus of these ideas. Since the middle of the nineteenth century, non-western peoples that impinged upon the expanding West have been searching for some orienting concept upon which to base an adequate response. With their old societal and personal values eroded by the technological transformation that is so obvious everywhere in the underdeveloped world, these peoples have found in nationalism a method of giving new meaning to their lives.

The non-western world is in the grip of a crushing necessity to reconcile tradition with the demands of modern thought and life. Success in this effort has been no more than minimal because of the peculiar dimensions of the problem: non-western leaders are seeking a sufficient mass revival to produce a political and cultural renaissance, but they fear massive social or political revolutionary change. Thus caught between the necessity of doing something and the reluctance to do too much, leadership in the non-western world faces the danger of fleeing from over contradiction into moral and intellectual skepticism. Old codes no longer meet the social and political need, but new principles of intellectual life from the West are unpalatable. Socio-political stasis has become the consequence.

Into this vacuum has moved the ambivalent concept of nationalism, imported originally as part of the baggage of colonialism but given peculiar twists by native spokesmen. Nationalism in most of the non-western world is difficult for the older and more settled societies in the West to comprehend. The emerging nations are not really purusing nationalist aspirations in any traditional sense. The operative goal of these states is no less than the rejuvenation and ultimate vindication of their respective civilizations, to be effected by the reconciliation of old aspirations with new values.

Although using the language of western political discourse, national arguments in Asia and Africa do not incorporate the familiar assumptions of the West. The veneer of western ideas is too thin; the full implications of the nation-state are not appreciated. Consequently, it has proved dangerously easy for ambitious and harried leaders of mass movements to use nationalist slogans as devices of apology and self-defense against past failures and present difficulties.

In much of the non-western world, a nation in the western sense cannot be found included within the boundaries of any present state. These states, after all, reflect not spontaneous political growth but rather the after-effects of the division of the world by European colonial powers. In many instances no concept of nationality exists; family and tribal loyalties still form the central core of the society. Government is minimal in organization and in effect, and the visible symbols of national identity are few and unimportant. The intelligentsia tends to be too sophisticated to respond to the call, while the masses are so insensitive that only the crudest and most obvious stimuli have any effect.

Thus nationalism in Asia and Africa is grandiose and almost dreamy in its expression. Incompatible ideas are conjoined in the same breath. The past grandeur of the various societies is lovingly evoked at the same time that the people are exhorted to slough off their old ways and to join the mainstream of modern life. Withdrawal and pervasive self-expression are equally prominent. The non-western world wants at the same time to escape from the "vulgarities" of western life, to emulate the comforts to be found there, and to reform the rest of the world in its own "spiritual" image. Nationalism in the new states is more of an expression of an attitude toward life and a reflection of culture shock than it is a formalized belief system and a base for governmental action. As such, its future is difficult to forecast.

The Technological Revolution

The technological revolution has accelerated the pace of history. Ideas covering all domains of human activity—political organization and institutions, economic and social organizations, religion, fine arts, science, and strategy and tactics—all radiate quickly from their respective sources of origin and penetrate the various parts of the world. This process has been rapidly breaking down ancient customs, introducing seeds of doubt and hope, initiating controversies between political groups within states, and giving rise to new concepts of ends and means. Social institutions everywhere are in flux. The technological revolution has ushered in revolution in many other phases of life as well.

The increased pace of history and the conquest of time have had a curious double effect. On the one hand, men everywhere are involved in international affairs to an extent undreamed of only a generation and a half ago. World politics "is on everyone's breakfast table" every day. In this sense, the technological changes of this era have gone far to make men members of one global community of interest. On the other hand, however, technology and the pace of change have helped to consolidate human organization and loyalty behind the one familiar institution in an age of transition: the nation-state. Thus technology both simplifies and complicates the formulation and the resolution of the problems of international politics.

THE REVOLUTION IN COMMUNICATION AND TRANSPORTATION

The new revolutionary means of communication and transportation are making it possible to travel to any point in the world in a matter of hours and to communicate with any part of the world within a few minutes. These developments have obvious consequences both for the conduct of interstate relations and for the substance of the questions that concern states.

Operationally, the revolution in transportation and communication has affected all the instrumentalities of foreign policy. Diplomacy has been heavily invaded by "back seat driving" from the foreign office and the role of resident ambassadors markedly reduced in importance. Electronic and printing media have completely changed the rationale of propaganda and other methods of psychological warfare. Economic measures now permit much more rapid application to specific situations. By far the most obvious effect of transportation and communication, however, is in the field of military methods. A ballistic missile, for example, is both a vehicle and an unmistakable message; delivery systems are means of transportation while guidance systems reflect the application of modern communications science.

Substantively, the technology of transportation and communication have made the world smaller and much more constrictive. The tension between diversity and integration of which we earlier took note is heightened by the impact of the shrunken arena of world politics. On the one hand, a greater sense of unity and common destiny is sensed by men everywhere; men are in a much greater variety of ways mutually interdependent and their conduct reflects this realization. On the other hand, states as organizational units have all become much more vulnerable to a greater range of pressures and actual or potential attack. As individuals, men are increasingly driven together by modern transportation and communication; as political groups, they are further driven apart by fears and suspicions.

THE ENERGY REVOLUTION

Probably the most spectacular of the several aspects of the new technology is that suggested by the successful attempt to release the energy of the atom and its nucleus. Modern political power since 1750 has had its roots in industrial power, and industrial power is no more than a function of its energy base. The industrial establishments of modern states are built on the technology of steel with familiar sources of energy such as coal (by far the most important), water power, petroleum, and—as a derivative—electricity.

If (or when) the theoretical potential of nuclear energy is realized in practice, many of the relatively fixed assumptions about the relative power positions of states will be invalidated. At present the energy released by nuclear fission (to say nothing of the vastly greater energy potential in thermonuclear fusion) is expensive to produce and of little industrial significance. But any significant lowering of the cost level would raise a host of tantalizing possibilities.

States presently debarred from effective industrialization because of poor resource endowments of energy sources could acquire the potential of large-scale industry overnight. Already-industrialized states that lagged behind in the conversion might find themselves hopelessly outstripped by relative newcomers. The ranks of the great powers could suddenly be increased and the classification of "small power" might require extensive redefinition. Like almost all aspects of the new technology, however, the energy revolution might cut two ways; at first blush—as we have been suggesting—its effect might be to exaggerate differences and potential conflicts. Ultimately, however, its logic might well demand its effective implementation on the broadest possible international base.

THE PRODUCTION REVOLUTION

Even within the context of the coal-iron technology, a revolution in production methods is occurring and has already had its major effects. The most notorious aspect of the new production is of course automation—the performance by computer-programmed machines of incredibly complex processes of manufacture—but its political ramifications are almost endless.

The states of western Europe, for example, were forced to rebuild their war-ravaged industrial plants almost from scratch after 1945. Today they find that their new factories, incorporating the latest theories and techniques of production, are able to gain competitive advantages over the older and less rationalized establishments in the United States and Great Britain. When modern industrialization takes a firm root in the non-western world, it will almost certainly be able to skip the earlier evolutionary steps and move quickly into equally revolutionary methods of manufacture and distribution. Thus, coupled with the new horizons opened by the energy revolution, the possibility arises that the future will see relatively small but superlatively efficient productive plants located in the new-underdeveloped parts of the world. What this might mean for the economic dimension of international relations would seem to be self-evident.

THE WEAPONS REVOLUTION

Modern technology, using both the energy potential of nucleonics and radical innovations in transportation and communication, has consummated a frightening revolution in the weapons of warfare. We speak of the present era as "the nuclear age." Here, of course, we are becoming aware of the awful consequences to the entire fabric of human life should the application of advanced technology develop only new methods of killing people.

Weaponry has been drastically expanded in at least two major dimensions: the "projectile" that does the damage to the target and is in one sense the weapon itself, and the "delivery system" that moves the projectile from its point of launching to the target. In the Roman empire, the spearhead or the edge of the sword was the projectile, and the delivery system included the remainder of the spear or sword and the soldier himself who carried the weapon into combat and launched it against its target. Today the logic remains the same, but technology—which has progressed through bows and arrows, muskets, rifled artillery, and engine-driven aircraft—has now improved both the projectile and the delivery system to the extent that entirely new concepts are needed to encompass the requirements of warfare.

So damaging have become the new weapons and so long-range and speedy have become modern delivery systems that the new weapons [epitomized by the intercontinental ballistic missile (ICBM) with its hydrogen-bomb warhead] have almost priced war out of the international political market. In every nuclear state and in many non-nuclear ones as well, military scholars and strategists are seeking a rationale that will make the employment of these weapons of unparalleled destruction efficient instruments of national policy. Their failure to break through conceptually as clearly as the scientists have broken through technologically has made war an exceptionally hazardous gamble for states and given international conflict since 1945 a frustrating and inconclusive character.

THE SPACE REVOLUTION

In recent years the "nuclear age" has also become the "age of space" as both the U.S.S.R. and the United States have made successful initial forays into the nearer reaches of outer space. The venture is so vast and its possible consequences so awesome that the international system and the political consciousness of men have not yet discovered any viable basis of adjustment to the phenomenon. All governments realize somehow that the penetration of space by man is fraught with consequences for the relations of states on the face of the earth, but none is yet certain that it appreciates either their significance or even the direction that the space revolution will lead them. There is little doubt, however, that space technology strengthens some of the assumptions of international politics and utterly invalidates others. Coming to terms with space in all its implications is a task that statesmen must take on with no delay.

THE HUMAN REVOLUTION

Technology, finally, has had its way with man as a biological entity. Both medical research and public health techniques have produced revolutionary effects on the human condition. Massive research campaigns to combat the more prevalent diseases hold out the prospect of the "conquest" of tuberculosis, cardiac disease, malaria, cancer, and other widespread causes of death. The application of even rudimentary measures of sanitation and preventive medicine have had spectacular results on epidemic diseases that breed in squalor and filth. The prospect is increased longevity and the possibility of relative immunity to the ordinary ills of the body.

Western morality teaches that this is a noble cause; to preserve human life is the highest calling of a man of good will. And yet, western statesmen have recently been brought to face with the operational consequences of this effort. The question is being asked more and more openly: what advantage is it really to a society to have its people spared death by malaria only to have them starve to death, die in mob riots, or be killed in a war? Ecologists raise questions about the ultimate danger involved in upsetting the natural balance of life on the planet; demographers warn us of the already-frightening "population explosion" and its future political consequences.

Yet the effort to conquer disease and early or unnecessary death goes on. Men are living longer and more and more human beings inhabit our planet. The challenging problem of over-population may require a massive technological effort by the combined forces of governments everywhere. We shall return to this subject and other aspects of the technological revolution in more detail in Chapter Eleven.

The New Institutions of International Politics

Institutions usually develop in a functional response to the needs of the times. Hence the satisfaction of unprecedented needs generated by the technological revolution has given rise to new institutions with new functions in international politics. The experience of two world wars accelerated their development. Thus the need to regulate new conditions in the international system has resulted in the institutionalization of novel international action units, supranational actors which we may classify as bloc actors, universal actors, and regional actors.

THE SUPRANATIONAL ACTORS

The term supranational actors designates a class of international actors whose structure, composition, and interests transcend national boundaries. There are three major types. *Bloc actors* are groups of states that share certain controlling security interests and a common orientation in their foreign policy objectives. The *universal actor* comprises within its structure almost all the existing members of the international system, and takes the form of a general international organization. Its interests incorporate all aspects of international life. *Regional actors* are associations of states sharing common interests that are more inclusive than the mere security interests and less comprehensive than the interests of the universal actor. Membership usually follows a geographic rationale.

BLOC ACTORS

Bloc actors are not completely new phenomena in international politics. By virtue of the technological revolution, however, they have become more common and cohesive. Today most of the essential national actors in international politics are bound into two blocs by means of alliances. Each bloc is led by a dominant essential national actor, the United States and the Soviet Union respectively, and comprises a number of middle and small powers who act in conjunction with their respective leaders on many issues.

The identity and integrity of each bloc depends in practice on its ability to preserve the capacity of the dominant essential actor to be the leading producer of all those things—materials, money, moral stimulus, and leadership—thought necessary to the vital interest of all other members of the bloc. This is not, however, a simple matter of the bloc leader exercising internal hegemony over its minor associates. Each of the essential actors makes great commitments to the other members, but this protection is reciprocal in nature. Even though relatively small and weak, bloc members each contribute in some measure directly to the over-all viability of the grouping.

Thus the foreign-policy tasks of the United States and the Soviet Union have become ever more complex as the range of their bloc interests has expanded. Each bloc has attempted to extend its span of effective action to embrace whatever area of the world in which it might wish to operate. Interbloc conflict, a phenomenon familiar to the history and logic of the traditionally structured western state system, has in this era come forcibly into contact with the emerging and newly sensitive and operationally viable non-western world.

The new nations, most of them coming on the international scene after the major blocs had been institutionalized, have reacted by resisting affiliation with either and by developing a variety of workable definitions of "neutralism." This idea, although admittedly imprecise and laden with emotion, unquestionably reflects both the instinctive leanings of many non-western states and the practical range of possibilities open to them in the pattern of interbloc relations.

So consistent has been the reaction of the bulk of the emerging nations to the massive confrontation of the two great groupings that today it is common to speak of a "neutral bloc." While on the one hand this is an overstatement (as also is the popular term "Afro-Asian bloc"), since the neutral group displays neither the relatively high degree of integration nor the policy consensus that mark a genuine bloc actor, it is undeniable that on cold-war issues the otherwise incongruous neutral states have frequently been able to form a common front in opposition to the attempt of the bloc leaders to universalize their dispute.

On other sorts of issues, however, and especially on questions subsumed under the energizing but vague issue of "anticolonialism," the neutral bloc demonstrates clear fissiparous tendencies. Sub-blocs are often formed, frequently on a geographical basis (an African bloc, and Arab bloc, a South Asian bloc, and so on), and these smaller—but often tighter—groupings function as independent combining units in the process of developing a viable systemic consensus on a particular issue.

THE UNIVERSAL ACTOR

The same pressures toward supranational (or suprastate) organization that have given rise to the evolution of blocs have also contributed to the creation of the most inclusive institutional form: the universal actor, represented between the two World Wars by the League of Nations and today by the United Nations system. The essence of the universal actor in international politics is that it acts on the international system in the name of all members of the system. It is armed at any moment with whatever measure of effective systemwide consensus is available, and performs functions restrictive, ameliorative, or affirmative as the case may dictate.

THE LEAGUE OF NATIONS

The League of Nations, founded as part of the peace settlement after World War I, was the first serious attempt to create a universal actor. Although the total membership ultimately included the majority of national actors then active, significant failures to assume membership virtually doomed it to ineffectiveness. The United

States never became a member, and never during the League's brief history were all the other great powers members at the same time. After a hectic noonday of prosperity in the mid-1920's, the League fell apart under the successive shocks of the depression of 1929, the Japanese invasion of Manchuria in 1931, the rise of Hitler, Italy's aggression in Ethiopia, the Spanish civil war, and the Russo-Finnish war of 1939–40. It went out of formal existence in 1946 when its property and personnel were transferred to the United Nations.

THE UNITED NATIONS

World War II stimulated the establishment of the United Nations. The real history of the UN begins with the London Declaration of January 1941, the Atlantic Charter of August 1941, the United Nations Declaration of January 1942, and the Moscow Conference of October 1943. Churchill, Roosevelt, and Stalin during the Tehran Conference of 1943 strongly supported the movement. In the Dumbarton Oaks Conference between August and October 1944, the governments of the United States, Great Britain, the Soviet Union, and China drew up the blueprint for what later became the Charter of the United Nations. At the Yalta Conference in February 1945, the United States, Britain, and the U.S.S.R. agreed that a conference (the United Nations Conference on International Organization) designed to draft the Charter of the United Nations should meet in San Francisco on April 25, 1945. The San Francisco Conference met between April 25 and June 26, 1945, with fifty-one states attending. On October 24, 1945, the United Nations was officially established.

The declared purposes of the United Nations are to maintain international peace and security, to develop friendly relations among states based on respect, equal rights, and self-determination of peoples, to cooperate in solving economic, social, cultural, and humanitarian international problems, and to promote respect for fundamental freedoms and human rights.

The United Nations has a number of operational principles set forth in its Charter:

(1) The sovereign equality of all its members is assumed, at least theoretically.

(2) Members are to fulfill in good faith the obligations they have assumed under the Charter.

(3) Members are to settle their disputes by peaceful means and refrain from the threat or the use of force.

(4) Members are to give every assistance to the United Nations and refrain from giving assistance to belligerent states.

(5) The United Nations is not to intervene in matters essentially within the domestic jurisdiction of member states.

The United Nations is different from the League of Nations in a number of respects. Above all, the essential national actors of the international system are all members of the United Nations. The United Nations places a greater emphasis upon social and economic problems, while the League was primarily a security organization. The United Nations has developed a more elaborate organizational structure and hence is better equipped than the League to carry out its functions. Finally, the failure of the League itself has made international society more willing to adapt itself to the United Nations.

THE SPECIALIZED AGENCIES

The development of the United Nations has stimulated the growth of non-state actors operating in the form of the specialized agencies: multilateral institutions to assist the United Nations in carrying out the economic and social stipulations of the Charter. The specialized agencies have emerged in functional response to the new technical, economic, social, and humanitarian conditions of the international system. The Economic and Social Council (a "principal organ" of the United Nations) is responsible for their coordination.

There are now fourteen specialized agencies. Three were established before World War II: the International Telecommunication Union (ITU) and the Universal Postal Union (UPU) were originally founded in the latter parts of the nineteenth century, whereas the International Labor Organization (ILO) developed with the League of Nations. The remaining eleven agencies are products of the Second World War and the United Nations. These agencies are: The International Bank for Reconstruction and Development (IBRD), the International Monetary Fund (IMF), the International Finance Corporation (IFC), the International Development Association (IDA), the Food and Agriculture Organization (FAO), the United Nations Educational, Social, and Cultural Organization (UNESCO), the World Health Organization (WHO), the International Civil Aviation Organization (UCAO), the World Meteorological Organization (WMO), the Inter-Governmental Maritime Consultative Organization (IGMCO), and the International Trade Organization (ITO). This last remains only a charter with insufficient adherents; the actual work of expediting international trade is done through the General Agreement on Tariffs and Trade (GATT), established in 1948.

THE ROLE OF THE UNITED NATIONS IN THE INTERNATIONAL SYSTEM

Since its inception in 1945 the United Nations has modified the international milieu in a number of significant respects.

(1) The United Nations provides the international system with channels for cooperation and negotiation between national actors. The mere fact that contending states are members of the same organization often facilitates the prospects of peaceful settlement of their disputes.

(2) The United Nations furnishes states with an opportunity to express their interests and policies before a global audience. Thus it increases each state's appreciation of the views of other states and makes them all more aware of the importance of world opinion.

(3) The United Nations provides states with an interest in preventing or avoiding conflict within the system with a forum within which to make their influence felt. Thus the organization increases the capability of each national actor to influence other national actors. By combining its votes with those of other states, a small state has the opportunity to increase its bargaining power. A great power, by lining up small states in its support, may give the moral sanction of a majority vote to what could otherwise be purely an act of force.

(4) The United Nations provides the international system with a forum for the mobilization of world public opinion. Small states may use this forum to embarrass the great powers that could easily overpower them but may prefer not to do so in the full light of international publicity.

(5) The United Nations contributes to the development of a feeling of belonging to a world community. This often concretely reflects the evolving integrative trends of world affairs.

(6) Finally, the United Nations equips the international system with the means to improve economic and social conditions in the international system. This broadening of the bases of cooperation between states is inevitably a force toward greater order and stability.

REGIONAL ACTORS

There are two types of regional actors (regional organizations) operating in the international system: general regional actors and regional actors dealing with specific economic and technical cooperation. The distinction between the two categories of regional actors is determined by differences in the character of their membership, their purposes, and their range of interests.

General regional actors are more inclusive in membership. Their range of interests tends to be broader and less defined than the regional actors for specific technical and economic cooperation. They are associations of states with a community of historical interests. Some examples of general regional actors are the Organization of American States comprising the United States and the Latin American republics, the Commonwealth of Nations composed of Great Britain and fifteen states once forming part of the British Empire, and the French Community which includes France and six states formerly units of the French Empire.

Regional actors for specific technical and economic cooperation are more exclusive in membership. Their interests are limited to economic, social, and technical matters. Examples of this type of regional actor are the Organization of Economic Cooperation and Development (OECD), composed of seventeen European states, Canada, and the United States; the Council for Mutual Economic Assistance (CEMA), comprising the Soviet Union and the communist states of Eastern Europe; and the Colombo plan, consisting of Great Britain and twenty-one other states mostly in South and Southeast Asia.

Regional actors have appeared in response to the need for units of action larger than the nation-state but falling short of the full range of universalism. Their usefulness depends in great measure upon whether or not the problems they face can actually be solved on a regional basis. Because of their smaller and generally more cohesive membership, by and large, regional actors have proved to be more effective action organizations than has the United Nations.

Bibliography

Barghoorn, Fredrick C., *Soviet Russian Nationalism*. New York: Oxford University Press, Inc., 1956.

* Bloomfield, Lincoln, (ed.), *Outer Space: Prospects for Man and Society*. Englewood Cliffs, N. J.: Prentice-Hall, Inc., Spectrum Books, 1962.

* Coyle, David C., *United Nations and How it Works*. New York: Mentor Books, 1961.

* Dean, Vera Micheles, *The Nature of the Non-Western World*. New York: Mentor Books, 1957.

Hayes, Carlton J., *Historical Evolution of Modern Nationalism*. New York: Macmillan and Company, 1931.

* Kedourie, Elie, *Nationalism*. New York: Frederick A. Praeger, 1960.

* Kohn, Hans, *American Nationalism*. New York: Collier Books, 1961.

————, *Nationalism*. Princeton: D. Van Nostrand and Company, 1955.

Mangone, Gerald, *Short History of International Organizations*. New York: McGraw-Hill and Company, 1954.

* Martin, Laurence W., *Neutralism and Nonalignment*. New York: Frederick A. Praeger, 1962.

* McClelland, Charles A., *United Nations: The Continuing Debate*. San Francisco: Howard Chandler Publishing Company, 1960.

Northrop. F. S. C., *Meeting of East and West: An Inquiry Concerning World Understanding*. New York: Macmillan and Company, 1946.

Toynbee, Arnold J., *World and the West*. New York: Oxford University Press, 1953.

Walters, Francis Paul, *History of the League of Nations*. New York: Oxford University Press, 1952.

Wolfers, Arnold, *Alliance Policy in the Cold War*. Baltimore: Johns Hopkins Press, 1959.

---

* Indicates paperback edition.

Seven

Conflict
and Adjustment

Politics, as we have already learned, is the pursuit of the common good as understood by a given community. This idea underlies the conduct of the relationships of states. The controlling idea of the common good energizes the formulation of aims and objectives which, for all their shifting and changing qualities, nevertheless mark evolving stages in the pursuit of the ideal. Every attempt to organize the international system is in this sense a response to the urge to attain the common good.

In international politics, however, states are concerned with practicalities. Absolute ends are less immediately germane than relative means. The conscious search for the common good is thus reduced to a secondary place in the international system. The unequal distribution of power and the mystique of sovereignty make the international order relatively unresponsive to ideas of the public weal on any basis transcending the nation-state.

This emphasis on state-centered common good has immediate consequences for the process of dynamics and change in the international system. No community of interest sufficient to control all members exists. Any change in relationships is thus at least as likely to be the result of conflict as of peaceful adjustment; in fact, conflict of some form is quantitatively the more usual atmosphere of change and realignment in world politics.

The Nature of Conflict

Competition, actual, seeming, or potential, is a normal relation between states. This fundamental fact is an historical result of the growth of the nation-state system. International conflict has become an intermittent but inevitable feature of world politics.

THE SOURCES OF CONFLICT

The nation-state system is inherently competitive. Its natural fruit is an ego-centered concept of state destiny: an aspiration to preserve and increase the power and stature of a state relative to those of any and all of its fellows. When a state insists upon the universal recognition of its political independence and its freedom of choice and action, it finds itself in a dilemma. It must grant every other state the same freedom and independence, yet it cannot really trust anyone but itself. It must seek salvation by its own efforts and maintain a very guarded attitude toward every other state. Its absolute security is possible only if it controls more power than the remainder of the world combined. When one state makes even slight progress toward this objective, however, all other states in their turn feel less secure toward it, and all are impelled to seek some corresponding advantage to again rectify the balance.

The logic of this paradox derives from the fact that a political decision on the part of a state always comprehends an expression of the relative priority that its government assigns to certain objectives and interests as against others. The interdependence of states exercises a pacifying influence in international politics only so far as political conflicts remain limited; the needs of interdependence are virtually powerless to disarm political antagonisms that are already consolidated.

The absolute character of interests and objectives inherent in the national policies of states reinforces the tendency toward interstate conflict. While a limited objective that is spelled out in concrete terms is capable of achievement, an absolute objective tends instead to involve the state seeking it in continuous struggle. The enhancement of prestige, the aggrandizement of power, and the promotion of ideology are common examples of absolute objectives. They attract opposition and conflict because of their lack of rational content and clearly defined limits. On the other hand, the unilateral defense of territorial integrity and of political independence, even though they are themselves concrete, have been on occasion conceived in such absolute terms as to bring on intense conflict.

TYPES OF CONFLICT

There are two broad categories of international conflict, with the criterion of classification being the principal techniques utilized. Non-violent conflict, the first type, involves the use of diplomacy, pacific methods of settlement, or forcible procedures short of war as means of prosecuting national purposes in a climate of disagreement. In violent conflict, on the other hand, major reliance by contending parties is placed upon military measures and wars.

VIOLENT CONFLICT IN INTERNATIONAL POLITICS

War is the most common form of violent international conflict: a condition in which two or more states carry on a conflict by armed force. War is, of course, a legal status as well as a means of executing policy, but its policy relevance is much greater.

Since the sixteenth century war has become ever more devastating as weapons have increased in effectiveness and new theories of warfare have been developed. Today entire populations are personally involved and identified with war. All people now participate directly in military operations as combatants, targets, or producers. The objectives of war are now usually formulated in terms of one nation gaining an absolute triumph over another. The once-limited conduct of warfare has become universal in scale, and great powers, forces, and ideas are hopelessly caught up in it.

Wars do not usually arise out of disputes concerning the respective rights of the belligerents, but spring instead from conflicts of interest. State motives in war are entirely political even though a legal discussion of "right" and "justice" often furnishes the pretext for violence. Many causes of war have been isolated by scholars, but rather than enumerating them here we may simply generalize that since war is rooted in the international system, any specific war is more a product of the general dynamic of that system than it is of the unique circumstances out of which the conflict has grown.

NON-VIOLENT CONFLICT IN INTERNATIONAL POLITICS

In its essence, the difference between non-violent and violent conflict is one of degree rather than kind. Non-violent conflict has the same rationale as war with the single exception that the states involved conclude that cost and risk factors as related to the worth of the objective in dispute demand that the struggle be prosecuted at a lower level of intensity and commitment. Otherwise both the purpose and the conduct of the conflict is governed by the same principles of strategy and tactics that control the most violent warfare.

As a rule, states accept non-violent conflict as routine but look on violent conflict as exceptional. The over-all costs of non-violent conflict are always less than those of a war, at least within a given time span. By the same token, the penalty for defeat in a non-violent struggle is almost always less than that demanded by a military victor.

OBJECTIVES OF CONFLICT

Analytically we can distinguish between two major categories of conflict objectives. The first, *balancing-objective* conflict, is endemic to a relatively fluid international situation characterized by a wide dispersal of power and the operations of a multiple balance system. Under such circumstances, the purpose motivating the participants in an interstate conflict is more than anything the restoration of a disturbed equilibrium. The range of choice that all parties enjoy is accepted as narrow, and their efforts tend to be concentrated upon a single object of controversy substantially independent of their relations in other policy areas. *Hegemonic-objective* conflict, on the other hand, has domination rather than balance as its goal. The disputing parties are less concerned with the specific objectives they may be pursuing than with the establishment of a clear margin of superiority over the other in a very broad —perhaps universal—range of issues. Balancing-objective conflict, in other words, concerns itself primarily with a particular set of relationships in the real world, while in hegemonic-objective conflict, the controversy over details is no more than a pallid reflection of much deeper maladjustments in the political approach of the involved states reacting to each other.

Balancing-objective conflicts assume many forms, stemming as they do from the essential requirements of the international system for simultaneous dynamism and equilibrium. Among the broadest categories are the clash of expansionist politics, the revisionist-status quo confrontation, disputes between aroused nationalisms, conflicts growing out of history, and a variety of racial, religious, social, and cultural involvements. Hegemonic-objective conflict, on the other hand, has only one real form although it is almost infinite in its manifestations.

BALANCING-OBJECTIVE CONFLICT: EXPANSIONIST POLICIES

The form of conflict that arises from a collision between two or more states following policies of expansion or revision is the most dynamic and potentially dangerous. Such states are usually driven by strong motivations: prestige, the acquisition of raw materials, new markets, cheap labor, military bases, or various internal pressures. When a revisionist policy encounters resistance, there is a tendency for the government to increase its own pressure. When two such states conflict, the dispute becomes marked by the rapid increase in the power each commits to the objective it is seeking and a rapid development of crises. Furthermore, revisionist states find it difficult to reverse policies short of their ultimate objective because of the internal and international pressure developing.

Imperialism and the type of colonial methods in which it is expressed are a common historical example of conflict of expanding policies. The traditional methods of expansion underwent steady decline beginning with the first half of the twentieth century; half a century later the great colonial empires were dissolving. But new types of expansionism are developing in the forms of economic dependencies and satellite states. Economic dependencies are nominally independent states whose major economic activities are heavily under the control or influence of a great power. Satellite states, on the other hand, are nominally independent states whose political life and foreign policies are in varying degrees under the control or direct influence of a more powerful state. Conflicts growing from these relationships are prone to be both intense and prolonged.

BALANCING-OBJECTIVE CONFLICT: REVISIONISM VERSUS STATUS QUO

A frequently recurring form of conflict arises from a situation in which an expanding policy collides with the interests of a passive, status quo state. The distinction between this type of conflict and the first is important. In expansionism, the motives of the contending states are basically identical. Both are seeking to reach the same general objective of an expansion in their span of control. In the type we discuss here, the objectives of the contending states are complementary. The revisionist state seeks to take away from the passive state a particular object of advantage. The latter, seeking nothing, tries to retain what it already has.

In this form of conflict, the revisionist state always takes the initiative. It seeks through any appropriate means to detach the passive state from its control of the dispute. The status quo state restrains its actions in a strategic sense to defensive measures, countering each affirmative step of the revisionist state as it is taken. It may on occasion, however, assume a tactical initiative.

BALANCING-OBJECTIVE CONFLICT: CONFLICT OF NATIONALISM

Many of the areas of tension in contemporary international politics are characterized by a battle of embittered or exaggerated nationalist attitudes. When aroused, a nationalistic group becomes heedless of the regularities of international politics and uninformed about the subtler details of the policy either its own government or the government of its enemy is following. As such, it becomes impatient and demands outlets. When mass emotions are aroused in a particular state great pressures are brought upon the government demanding that forceful measures be taken against the offender. The other state is impelled to react in a similar manner. In this way a web of conflict is woven from which both states find it difficult to extricate themselves.

Another example of nationalist conflict is furnished by colonial revolutions and their aftermath. No subject people can become free of alien control without first developing a keen sense of nationalistic particularism and making the achievement of independence a primary objective. When independence is achieved, the hatreds that evolved through the struggle for self-determination continue and form a significant part of the policy of the new state toward their former colonial masters.

Still another source out of which nationalist conflict grows is the clash of expanding great-power nationalisms. When a people with a "universalist" outlook on the world live in a state having great power resources, a powerful dynamic element is injected into international politics. When two such states exist simultaneously, a serious and long lasting conflict develops. This was the case of French and British nationalism in the Napoleonic era. Today, the rival nationalisms, each with its universal overtones, are the Russian and the American.

BALANCING-OBJECTIVE CONFLICT: CONFLICT OF HISTORICAL EXPERIENCE

The foreign policies of many states are characterized by nationalist animosities nourished by a long history. Despite the fact that the origins of these hatreds are often veiled in obscurity, they have become to the concerned people a familiar and expected part of the way their government formulates its foreign policies. While these animosities lie dormant for long periods, they often flare up at critical moments. Familiar examples of such historical animosities are the Russo-German, the Franco-German, and the Greco-Turkish nationalist hatreds. Some of these, of course, slowly recede in the face of changed circumstances.

BALANCING-OBJECTIVE CONFLICT: CONFLICT OF RACIAL, RELIGIOUS, SOCIAL, AND CULTURAL ISSUES

In these forms of conflict the issues are often trivial in themselves. The specific objects of controversy tend to be symbolic of deeper ideological differences. Compromise is usually difficult, since in the minds of the people it would involve making concessions upon points of fundamental moral significance. Examples of such conflicts are the racial issue in the Union of South Africa and the religious split between Muslims and Hindus in India and Pakistan.

HEGEMONIC-OBJECTIVE CONFLICT

This form of conflict has become synonomous with the "Cold War" and the bipolarization of power between the United States and the Soviet Union. A single broad purpose illuminates an entire family of conflict issues. It has its crisis points along what has been called "the international shatter zone" where the main opposing forces are in direct contact. In its military aspect it takes the form of a tireless race for allies, raw materials, bases, and armaments. In political terms it requires a constant search for "victory." In psychic terms it calls for the pursuit of absolute hegemony over the adversary.

At present, on the periphery of the eastern and western camps, the Cold War multiplies the zones of possible friction. Calculated pressures are heightened or relaxed according to circumstances and are aimed less at winning a premature decision than at testing resistance and asserting the prestige and image of either party.

On the ideological plane, hegemonic-objective struggle gives rise to an enterprise of subversion that has found a reply in a call for a crusade by zealots. The mobilization of minds and psychological warfare support the politico-military effort. This form of tension gives rise to the centralization of governmental power in both major states and thrives on what becomes a conventionally high level of mass emotional stress. It produces a generalized anxiety, is prolific of myths, and generates self-justifying theorems that identify national objectives with the imperatives of an absolute ideology. The themes of provocation and inequality developed with a rhythm of increasing "power" energize continued action and reaction in a climate of crisis.

Hegemonic-objective conflict requires long-term planning and must reckon with time. Given the present balances of forces, the more sensitive both sides are to the risk of total war the greater the corresponding tendency for the cold war to establish itself as a way of life and to develop fixed patterns and practices.

THE TACTICS OF CONFLICT

Certain elements of the intellectual process involved in conducting international conflict can usefully be reviewed here. At bottom, there are three sorts of decisions a policy-maker must make in the course of a struggle with another state: (1) when to begin the active phase of the conflict; (2) how to conduct his own part of the dispute; (3) when to break off the controversy and resume normal relations.

The first decision concerning the moment of beginning the active struggle is usually made by the state with the greater involvement of interest or the greater pressure for action. Once the crucial overt act has been taken, a certain power of decision yet remains with the second state since it is not obliged to respond unless it wishes to. If the original provocation was above the threshold of tolerability, some conflict-oriented response is almost automatic. Lesser initiatives may often be ignored unless escalated or repeated. This general principle is, however, more applicable to non-violent moves than to military attack, since modern nationalistic states react without hesitation to direct military onslaught.

Once launched on an open conflict, each side has further tactical decisions to make depending on whether its approach is basically balancing or hegemonic. If initial considerations of intensity become relevant, how deeply will either side commit itself to this particular quarrel? Next, various operational decisions must be made. Will the state attempt to work changes in the general situational environment, or will its effort be expanded in attempting to preserve the status quo? Will neutralizing policies—if they are the ones adopted —be in the form of direct head-to-head counters to initiatives from the other state or will they be indirect counter offensives? Will a defensive strategy remain defensive throughout the struggle or will success lead to a magnification of objectives and the acceptance of an unforeshadowed offensive program? All these and many other similar questions relate directly to how the state chooses to formulate policy and doctrine for the conflict.

Ending a conflict is frequently much more difficult than beginning one. In principle, a state may escape from a dispute on any of four grounds: (1) the achievement of its objective; (2) the negotiation of an acceptable compromise that gives it adequate if incomplete satisfaction in return for its effort and involvement; (3) the abandonment of the conflict as inevitably inconclusive; (4) complete defeat. The first and fourth of these reasons are self-evident if the objective is explicit and the cost/risk factors are kept well in mind. An acceptable compromise is often the most useful avenue of escape, but it is feasible only if both sides are fully aware of their respective notions of acceptability and if their minimum requirements coincide. An inconclusive breakoff, occurring usually only if both sides decide that their objectives are beyond reach at a bearable cost and risk, is only seldom made explicit; usually a broken-off conflict quietly lapses without fanfare or formal registry.

The Adjustment of Conflict

The existence of conflict in the international system requires that states develop techniques for the adjustment and settlement of their disputes. While states have established and in some cases perfected these techniques, the choice of a particular method and its ultimate success or failure depends upon the purpose, skill, and interests of the contending parties.

Not every conflict or disagreement that arises between states needs to be formally adjusted or settled. Many disputes in essence settle themselves, particularly if they are left alone. It is, however, when popular passions become increasingly inflamed, and especially where the object of the conflict is a matter of great importance to the disputing states, that a formal adjustment may become the only viable alternative to violence. Usually the more pressing and important the dispute is thought to be, the more difficult it is to discover an acceptable solution, because of the danger that both sides may have hopelessly involved their prestige. Unless both sides are able adequately to preserve their self-respect, the substantive core of the problem may be beyond reach.

The methods developed over the centuries for the adjustment and settlement of international conflict may be classified into three general categories: methods of pacific settlement, coercive procedures short of war, and forcible procedures through war. Each of these has its strengths and weaknesses.

PACIFIC SETTLEMENT

The methods of pacific settlement make available a variety of peaceful substitutes for violence. In general terms they may be classified as diplomatic-political or judicial.

DIPLOMATIC AND POLITICAL METHODS

Diplomatic and political methods of adjusting conflict do not result in any final judgments which the disputing states are obligated to accept. Hence diplomatic methods are described as non-decisional or non-binding. Settlement thus rests on mutual agreement usually based on substantive compromise. Political disputes involving value judgments of environmental factors are particularly susceptible to diplomatic procedures.

Diplomatic methods of settlement can be attempted through direct negotiations, good offices, mediation, inquiry, and conciliation.

Direct negotiation may take the form of bilateral or multilateral diplomacy. Such negotiations may be conducted between heads of state (as in the case of the presently common personal or summit diplomacy), directly through ambassadors and other accredited diplomats of the concerned parties, or through an international conference.

Good Offices is the name given to a semi-diplomatic contact through the intervention of a third party (a state, an international organization, or a prominent individual). It is frequently resorted to when the disputing parties have become deadlocked in their diplomatic negotiations. A third state offers its services to act as a go-between and to expedite contacts between the disputants. Negotiations proceed through the third party. The third party, however, is not empowered to suggest a solution nor does it participate directly in the negotiations. Good offices, once accepted, usually lead to mediation. A famous example of good offices was the role played by President Theodore Roosevelt at the conclusion of the Russo-Japanese war in 1905.

Mediation is a procedure by which, in addition to good offices, a third party participates actively in the negotiations. It tries aggressively to reconcile the opposite claims and to appease mutual resentments the contending parties have developed. The mediator may not impose its own solutions on the dispute, but is expected to take a strong initiative in proposing formulas. The role of Dr. Ralph Bunche as United Nations mediator during the Arab-Israeli war in 1948 is a famous modern instance of the use of this technique.

Inquiry designates the settlement of a dispute through the establishment of a commission of inquiry. Such a group, consisting of an equal number of members from each of the disputing parties plus one or more from a third state or states, acts to facilitate solution of the conflict. Article 33 of the Charter of the United Nations authorized the organization to create such a commission when appropriate.

The commission of inquiry does no more than elicit the facts of a dispute by means of impartial investigation. The theory of inquiry is based upon two assumptions: first, a basic obstacle to amicable settlement derives from the initial difficulty of establishing a statement of the facts to which both parties agree. Second, this difficulty perpetuates itself by allowing passions to be aroused which obstruct agreement between the parties on points of principle.

An example of this form of settlement was the Commission of Inquiry which convened in Paris in 1905 to deal with the Anglo-Russian dispute over the action of a Russian fleet firing on English fishermen in the North Sea. The Commission's report of the facts led to a speedy liquidation of the controversy.

Conciliation is a procedure that combines inquiry and mediation. An individual or a commission (structured much like a commission of inquiry) may perform the functions of conciliation. Its functions thus extend both to the determination of the facts and to the presentation of formal recommendations for settlement.

The procedure of conciliation becomes appropriate because inquiry itself makes only a minimal contribution to the resolution of many conflicts. Conciliation, by combining mediation and inquiry, multiplies the pacifying effects of both in the settlement of troublesome disputes. It is the most formalized of the diplomatic and political methods of settling international conflicts. It is peculiarly useful for serious political disputes. Its flexibility makes it more adaptable to varying circumstances than would be more rigid judicial or legislative procedures. Its object is always peace by compromise, not justice by law. The United Nations, for example, has used several conciliation commissions since 1945; perhaps the most famous is that for Palestine that oversees the truce arranged by Dr. Bunche.

It must be pointed out that neither inquiry nor conciliation provides a means of settling conflict unless a solution is worked out that is acceptable to the disputing parties. Usually it will command the assent of the contending parties only when it offers them terms sufficiently attractive to persuade all involved that they have gained in rewards enough to justify breaking off the struggle.

JUDICIAL METHODS

Judicial methods of settlement are an attempt to regularize the terms and procedures on the basis of which disputes are disposed of. The two judicial procedures are arbitration and adjudication. Solutions are reached on the basis of law—and in some cases equity —but they explicitly exclude political compromise, since only legal (justiciable) disputes can be judicially resolved. The awards of arbitration and the decisions of an international court are binding on the disputing parties and hence these procedures are described as decisional or binding.

Arbitration is accomplished either by an *ad hoc* tribunal or by the Permanent Court of Arbitration at the Hague. Adjudication today is the exclusive province of the International Court of Justice, an organ of the United Nations system. With few relatively unimportant exceptions, submission of a dispute to either judicial procedure is a voluntary act of the states involved.

Judicial methods of settling disputes have certain advantages over any diplomatic method. Probably most important is the fact that the conflict is taken almost entirely out of the hands of the disputing parties. Prestige problems which might impede a settlement are thus largely avoided. The conflict is disposed of by reference to standards common to both parties and external to the dispute. Thus judicial settlement may depoliticize a dispute more completely than diplomatic methods of settlement, since it implies the voluntary renunciation by the parties of their individual powers of decision and submission to the impersonal criteria of law.

On the other hand, judicial settlement of disputes presents certain disadvantages. Relatively few of the important issues of international politics can be usefully cast in terms of a justiciable controversy. The more crucial the conflict is held to be by the parties, the greater the likelihood that neither will be anxious for a settlement by any outside agency.

Arbitration may be defined as the settlement of international disputes through judges chosen by the parties. The first Hague Conference in 1899 established the Permanent Court of Arbitration. Since that date this court became the principal instrument of international arbitration. The Permanent Court consists of a panel of judges, four appointed for six-year terms by each member state.

Disputing parties wishing to use the Permanent Court of Arbitration must first negotiate an instrument called the *compromis d'arbitrage*. In this agreement, the procedures which the tribunal will follow and the rules of law to be applied are stipulated. Each party then selects two judges from the panel, only one of whom can be its own national. These four judges choose a fifth member, called the "umpire." In their deliberations, the arbitrators can only utilize whatever rules of law the contending states have agreed on in the *compromis* for the settlement of that particular dispute.

Adjudication has come to designate the settlement of an international dispute by the International Court of Justice of the United Nations. The court was established in 1945 as a successor to the Permanent Court of International Justice which was set up by the League of Nations. Its headquarters is also at the Hague. It consists of fifteen judges elected concurrently by the Security Council and the General Assembly of the United Nations for a term of nine years. The decisions of the court can be based on either law or the principle of *ex aequo et bono* (equity and justice).

All members of the United Nations are automatically parties to the Statute of the ICJ. In practice, however, states are not compelled to submit their disputes to the court, particularly since each state may qualify its adherence to the Court's Statute. A state not belonging to the United Nations may separately adhere to the court on conditions to be determined by the General Assembly on recommendations of the Security Council.

Those states which are parties to the Court's Statute may at any time declare that they recognize as compulsory, *ipso facto*, and without special agreement, in relation to any state accepting the same obligation, the jurisdiction of the court in all legal disputes concerning (1) interpretations of a treaty, (2) any question of international law, (3) the existence of any fact, which, if established, would constitute a breach of international obligation, and (4) the nature or extent of the reparation to be made for the breach of an international obligation. States which thus choose to accept this compulsory jurisdiction may do so either unconditionally, on a basis of reciprocity, or for only a certain time.

However, the functions of arbitration and adjudication as methods of settling international conflict are narrow. Obstacles to the broadening of these functions spring directly from the nature of the state system and the eminently political character of the relations it engenders. The settlement of disputes between states is never comparable to the settlement of disputes between individual persons.

For individuals, judicial settlement is the impersonal application of law, an expression of inculcated discipline embracing virtually the whole of social relations. This predisposes individuals to limit their claims to what is legally defensible and to formulate them in legal terms. The international system incorporates neither a hierarchic order embracing the totality of state interests and values, nor a single central power system that can effectively control the play of competing forces. Law therefore is only peripheral to the real disputes of states and can have no more than a random effect on their settlement.

COERCIVE PROCEDURES SHORT OF WAR

States turn to coercive but non-violent methods of settling a dispute if pacific procedures fail to produce satisfaction. Most of these devices, although finding their expression in the mechanics of the diplomatic process, have their ultimate coercive effect in the psychological realm.

Among the leading non-violent coercive techniques we may mention the recall of diplomats, the expulsion of the diplomats of the other state, a denial of recognition, a rupture of diplomatic relations, and a suspension of treaty obligations. Somewhat more obviously "unfriendly" (in the legal sense) is the class of actions involving "force short of war": blockade, boycott, embargo, reprisal, and retorsion (a technically complex form of retaliation).

FORCIBLE PROCEDURES: THE ROLE OF WAR

The *ultima ratio* of international politics, the final and unanswerable device for producing solutions to conflict, has always been the organized application of violence in the form of war. A non-regulatory social structure like the international system can have no final arbiter of a clash of wills except violence. The maturation of the international political process has resulted in a well-defined place for the institution of war.

War is a distinct way of prosecuting conflict, not a special category of conflict. The disagreement between states that gives rise to armed combat lies in the policies or the nationalist identifications of the adversaries, and the decision to fight the issue to a decision is an expediential one. The principles of tactics that govern other types of conflict apply to war as well, perhaps even more sharply. It is, for example, especially important to know when to initiate war, how to fight it, and when to stop.

Wars also partake of the general characteristics of conflict in that they may be either balancing-objective or hegemonic-objective. Another way of putting the same point is that a war may either be fought by tacit agreement within the terms of reference and restraint laid down by the international system and thus be related to the controlling equilibrium of forces, or it may be potentially destructive of the system by threatening to alter relationships drastically, dysfunctionally, and permanently. The balancing-objective form of war is known today as "limited" war, while the hegemonic-objective type is the familiar "total" war.

Limited war—the form of war made classic by centuries of successful prosecution—is conceptually a method within the family of familiar policy techniques, a single enterprise aimed at achieving a single objective. The amount of violence employed is supposed to be calculated finely with no more damage done than is necessary to gain "victory" in the form of the postulated goal. The end of such a war in theory is marked by the reestablishment of normal relations between the former enemies after the political readjustments made necessary by the war have been consummated.

Such wars are supposed to culminate in a negotiated peace. Both sides, having fought their campaigns with partial commitments of power, thus retain bargaining capability when the struggle ends. The terms of peace reflect the continuing power relationship between them as modified by the verdict of the battlefield.

Nationalism and technology—the two forces that have had so devastating an effect on so much of international politics—have transformed this sophisticated notion of war as a regulating and adjusting device into a much simpler yet much more deadly form of action. Previously defined as the establishment of a balance, nationalism redefined war as the attainment of hegemony. Technology made it possible for wars to become struggles of annihilation between peoples rather than the resolution of single-issue disputes between states.

In total war, discrimination in the use of violence has become extremely difficult. Greater military efficiency may be achieved by the new weapons of wholesale slaughter. Thus victory to be real must be total. The only acceptable forms of defeat conceivable are either utter destruction or abject submission in order to avoid such pulverization. No lesser margin of superiority will be sufficient to induce a people to surrender to a loathed enemy as long as they possess the capacity to fight on.

In logic, therefore, the only possible solutions that total war can render are absolute verdicts of dominance and submission. In the traditional course of international politics, questions demanding absolute answers have been relatively uncommon and long recognized as dangerous in that the consequences of a hegemonic decision are unpredictable. The so-called military dilemma of the contemporary era flows from the difficulty statesmen are having in developing a clear political (dispute-settling or objective-gaining) role for modern warfare.

It is incorrect to argue that total war cannot render a political decision. Decisions are possible even in a thermonuclear war. But what total war cannot do is to provide the broad spectrum of possible outcomes that simpler warfare was able to make available. It is inconceivable, for example, that anything resembling the traditional form of negotiated peace could ever emerge from a war initiated by a massive nuclear exchange. Solutions by total war are inevitably extreme; only two political outcomes are possible today to an all-out struggle between nuclear powers. Such a war will either run its full course and result in the collapse, capitulation, or obliteration of one belligerent and a claim of victory for the other, or it will be abandoned by both as inconclusive and mutually devastating. An expensive and dangerous method that can produce only absolute answers or none at all is of only limited political usefulness. War is in no sense a widely applicable method of resolving conflict today.

Regulating Mechanisms of International Politics

The fact that international politics is not conducted through legalistic methods has necessitated states to establish regulating mechanisms to pursue their programs of action in the international system. Hence, the growth of the nation-state system has been accompanied by the development of mechanisms to facilitate representation and negotiation between states and to enable them to communicate their interests, views, offers, and demands. These regulating mechanisms have become crystallized in the process of growth of the nation-state system and include international agreements, the organization of foreign representation, and international conferences.

INTERNATIONAL AGREEMENTS

Treaties are the principal form of international agreements. A treaty is no more than a formal agreement in writing between two or more states. As such, the treaty is the principal regulator of international politics, reflecting as it does stabilized relationships and an adaptation to law. Since sovereignty commands that a state consider itself bound only by an undeniable manifestation of its own will, a treaty is a singularly appropriate instrument of state interaction.

Treaties owe much of their special sanctity to the moral and practical influence of the old Roman doctrine of *pacta sunt servanda:*

"treaties (contracts) must be observed." The expectation that states ordinarily will honor their treaty obligations serves to temper the play of political forces. Any political relationship that states may wish to regularize may appropriately be written into a treaty. Much of international law, for example, is treaty law.

MAKING A TREATY

A treaty comes into existence as the culmination of a process involving several steps. We may perhaps most usefully list them in order:

(1) Representation: each concerned state delegates authority to its accredited agents to represent its interests.
(2) Negotiation: the agents bargain their way to a mutually acceptable text.
(3) Agreement: on a final form of the treaty.
(4) Signature: by the chiefs of delegations.
(5) Ratification: by the governments concerned.
(6) Exchange of ratifications: among all signatories.
(7) Promulgation and publication: of the terms of the treaty within each signatory state and registration of the document with the United Nations.

TERMINATION OF TREATIES

Treaties are terminated by various means. Dissolution of an agreement by fulfilling the objectives of the treaty automatically terminates a treaty obligation. A treaty containing a time limit expires at the end of the stipulated period (unless renewed). If a treaty is violated by one party, the other party or parties may consider their obligation discharged. A treaty is also terminated should a party to the treaty lose its international personality through annexation or other means.

Whether a state is released from its treaty obligation by reason of an essential change of the circumstances under which the treaty was concluded remains a delicate problem in international law. Every contract, according to Roman law, carried the clause *rebus sic stantibus*, meaning that substantial change in circumstances would render the contract void. Such a doctrine in international law would be a great convenience to many states embarrassed by awkward treaty obligations, but would clearly be destructive to the principle of binding agreements. Accordingly, *rebus sic stantibus* has never been fully accepted in treaty law, although many states assert the principle and on occasion may successfully act upon it.

CLASSIFICATION OF TREATIES

Several methods of classifying treaties exist. The first divides treaties into bilateral or multilateral depending upon the number of participating states. A second identifies treaties as simple or conditional depending on whether the obligation incurred is absolute or qualified. A third marks treaties as executed or executionary depending on whether the document is dispositive or continuous. Finally, treaties may be characterized by their subject matter, such as treaties of alliance, of commerce, and so on.

OTHER FORMS OF INTERNATIONAL AGREEMENTS

Other forms of international agreements are common in world politics. The leading types include: (1) executive agreements: understandings between sovereigns that—except in the United States and a few other states—are legally identical with treaties; (2) conventions: multilateral treaties, often of a legislative character; (3) protocols: less formal and less binding memoranda of agreement among states; (4) cartels: agreements between belligerent states in time of war for various humanitarian purposes such as the exchange of prisoners; (5) concordats: agreements between the Papacy and a state.

FOREIGN REPRESENTATION

The diplomatic apparatus for foreign representation has its origins shrouded in antiquity, but attained its first modern form during the Renaissance when the Italian city-states began the custom of appointing permanent ambassadors. Reaching fuller development during the formative stages of the nation-state system, diplomatic procedures were stabilized at the Peace of Westphalia in 1648 and were brought up to date at the Conference of Aix-la-Chappelle in

1818. The most recent amendments were made at a multilateral conference in Vienna in 1961.

Diplomats today are organized into a rank system that is accepted by all states. Heads of missions constitute one major classification. The highest-ranking mission heads are ambassadors, papal nuncios, and papal legates. Below this group are, in order, envoys extraordinary and ministers plenipotentiary, ministers resident, and chargés d'affaires (*ad hoc, en titre*, or *ad interim*). An *ad hoc* or *en titre* chargé is assigned as such by his government if such government for its own reasons does not wish to designate a head of mission. An *ad interim* chargé substitutes for the mission chief during the latter's temporary absence.

Within each mission the chief is in charge. His second in command usually carries the title of counselor of embassy or some similar title. Below this level are first, second, and third secretaries of embassy and a variety of special officials covering a range of duties (cultural and press officers, military and labor attachés, and the like).

DIPLOMATIC FUNCTIONS

Diplomats resident abroad have innumerable special functions, but generally they may be grouped under three major heads and a newly-emerging fourth. First in the list of tasks is that of representation. The diplomat symbolizes his own country in all its dealings with his host. Second, the diplomat is charged to a major—although declining—extent with negotiation of all manner of questions. Third, the diplomat is *par excellence* a medium of communication between his own government and that of his host. Finally, and of major importance only in comparatively recent times, diplomats have developed a real public relations mission in explaining and interpreting their own culture to the citizens of the state to which they are accredited.

The functions of diplomats have been steadily modified during the past century. Diplomats were once the personal representatives of monarchs, but obviously cannot adopt such a personalized role today when they so often represent mass democracies and huge bureaucratic structures. Improvements in communication have deprived diplomatic negotiators of their former freedom to work out their own compromises. Foreign offices insist on controlling the finest details of an ongoing negotiation. Transportation has been raised to such a level of speed and reliability as to permit much diplomatic intercourse to go on in an atmosphere of multilateral conference rather than the intimate head-to-head sessions of an earlier era.

INTERNATIONAL CONFERENCES

Any multilateral diplomatic exchange is in the strict sense an international conference. Conferences are of many sorts. The best-known is of course the inter-governmental conference at which delegates are the official represenatives of their governments and which deal with questions in an atmosphere of public policy. Here is where law-making or law-codifying treaties may be drafted or where major international issues may be resolved by multilateral decision.

Semi-governmental conferences, at which delegates are not official government representatives but nevertheless are spokesmen for national positions, form a second type. Naturally such conferences cannot deal with political issues; but often—as at meetings of the International Olympic Committee—make decisions on non-political problems that have strong political implications.

Conferences may also be classified by subject matter, although a complete list would be extremely long. Among the most significant are, of course, peace conferences to work out the details of the settlement that follows a war. Since 1945, a number of conferences to deal with new international questions such as international civil aviation, the law of the sea, or outer space, have been convened. In the past, epoch-making decisions on the legalization of certain aspects of state practice (such as the mitigation of the horrors of war) have been made at such conferences.

Conference procedures have reached their apogee in the United Nations, which has sometimes been called a permanent conference. Not only do the regular sessions of the various Councils and the General Assembly constitute conference activity but many specialized conferences are convened under the sponsorship of the organization. Suiting so well the technological requirements of international action in the contemporary era, conference procedures, especially as employed by the United Nations, will be certain to expand in elaborateness and in frequency of use. It is, for example, noteworthy that the "summit conference" is often suggested as a possibly efficacious technique for liquidating all or part of the Cold War.

Bibliography

Bloomfield, Lincoln P., *Evolution or Revolution: The United Nations and the Problem of Peaceful Territorial Change.* Cambridge: Harvard University Press, 1957.

Corbett, Percy E., *Law in Diplomacy.* Princeton: Princeton University Press, 1959.

Dunn, Fredrick S., *War and the Minds of Men.* New York: Macmillan and Company, 1944.

Langer, William L., *Diplomacy of Imperialism.* New York: Alfred A. Knopf, 1935.

* MacBridge, Roger Lea, *Treaties Versus the Constitution.* Caldwell, Idaho: The Caxton Printers, 1955.

* McFarquhar, Rodrick, *The Sino-Soviet Dispute.* New York: Frederick A. Praeger, 1962.

Nicolson, Harold, *The Evolution of the Diplomatic Method.* New York: Macmillan and Company, 1955.

————, *Diplomacy,* Second edition. London: Oxford University Press, 1950.

* Plischke, Elmer, *Summit Diplomacy.* College Park: University of Maryland, 1958.

* Roberts, H. L., *Russia and America, Dangers and Prospects.* New York: New American Library of World Literature, 1956.

Satow, Ernest M., *Guide to Diplomatic Practice.* London: Longmans Green & Co., 1957.

Schelling, Thomas C., *Strategy of Conflict.* Cambridge: Harvard University Press, 1960.

Stone, Julius, *Legal Control of International Conflict.* New York: Holt, Rinehart, and Winston, 1954.

Thayer, Charles W., *Diplomat.* New York: Harper & Brothers, 1959.

---

* Indicates paperback edition.

Eight

Limitations
on State Action

In spite of the deceptively simple logic of sovereignty that derives complete freedom of state choice from the postulate of absolute power, the international system could not survive unless states accepted and acted upon a well-understood set of restraints. The limitations on state action that all governments acknowledge to be the price they pay for the continued viability of the international system are only partially formulated. To a large extent they rest upon tacit agreement and the force of practice. To ignore these almost amorphous and illogical considerations, or to deduce an over-rigorous mechanistic doctrine of blind power as the energizing factor in international politics, is to condemn oneself to system-building in a vacuum. The limitations on the freedom of the state to act in international politics are not only as intrinsically important as that freedom itself, but also serve to give it form and direction.

In this chapter we shall examine three great families of restraints that all in some measure inhibit the choices that states make. We shall initially consider the extent to which states are restrained by the teachings of morality. We shall next examine the impact of international law as it performs its peculiar role of narrowing human choice in foreign policy to those actions that are legally sanctioned. Finally, we shall briefly review the effect of the statesman's code of prudence in international politics. This three-category list is by

no means exhaustive. Each restraint, however, acts in its own
fashion to reduce the effective range of state action to something
much smaller and less impressive than pure theory might indicate.

Morality As a Limitation: What Is a Moral Consensus?

The state is composed of human beings, all of whom accept and
act upon a set of moral principles. All human action may be judged
with varying degrees of accuracy and relevance in moral terms.
These two factors—the moral base of government action in the international order, and the application of norms of morality to the
behavior of states—constitute the basic elements of any discussion
of morality as a limitation on international political action.

THE MORAL PROBLEM IN INTERNATIONAL POLITICS

Central to this perplexing issue is the intrinsic morality of the
state and the relative claims of public purpose and private morality
on the consciences of individuals. It has long been obvious, for example, that the foreign policy of any national state has no necessary
nexus with any absolute or universal moral code. Whether the state
is viewed as an amoral agent destined to function in an order beyond
and irrelevant to moral codes, or whether it is judged as the architect of its own moral principles that are higher and more binding
on individuals than private ethics, the result is the same. Individuals
—particularly those subscribing to the Judeo-Christian code—are
generally held to be disqualified from passing meaningful moral
judgments on state action.

As long as the political sphere of human action does not impinge
on private morality, such a duality raises few problems other than
abstract ones. The moral issue becomes poignant, however, when
the commands of the state to the individual represent a direct contradiction of what he has been taught to regard as right and good.
The classic instance is, of course, the taking of human life. The Ten
Commandments stipulate that "Thou shalt not kill," but killing
enemies of the state on command of one's government is an act of
the highest patriotism.

Modern states have not felt themselves seriously inhibited by this contradiction. Nationalist codes of all types either emphasize that ordinary moral scruples do not apply to public purposes or else assert that killing, stealing, or lying on behalf of the state are in themselves moral acts. Somewhat more sophisticated versions of these arguments suggest that moral principles might apply in ordinary circumstances, but the demonic nature of the enemy (be he fascist, communist, Japanese, or whatever), and the special sacredness of the national mission, are ample reasons for individuals to suppress any qualms they might have.

Theologians, philosophers, and psychologists of all schools of thought and methods of analysis have grappled with the problem of reconciling the requirements of foreign policy with the absolutes of personal morality, or at least of reducing the clash between them to a bearable level. The public is sometimes told, for example, that since man is inherently sinful he should not worry overmuch about committing what he might consider to be immoral acts for public reasons. It is argued that a sufficiently worthy end justifies any expedient means. Morality and conscience are no more than semi-suppressed guilt feelings, runs another argument, and "mental health" is attained by a cheerful support of political leadership and performance of whatever tasks are assigned to the citizen.

The ingenuity of these arguments has in no way relieved many adherents of western cultural values from the dilemma in which they feel they are placed. Traditional morality at many points contradicts the pretensions of the state and no completely satisfying rationale of reconciliation can be found. The enormity of the world crisis and the cataclysmic strategies many states have adopted have sharpened this acute sense of moral crisis.

THE RUPTURE OF THE MORAL CONSENSUS

The problem, always inherent in international politics itself, has been exaggerated by the trends of development of the state system in the past two centuries. Modern international politics was born in Europe in the aftermath of the universal moral code of the Middle Ages. The monarchs who played the game in its early stages operated within a clear moral consensus and a fully understood set of principles of action. Czar Alexander's "Holy Alliance" of 1815 that proposed joint action by the rulers of Europe in a spirit of Christian brotherhood was startlingly inappropriate for its age; but in another sense was no more than a platitudinous evocation of the implicit assumptions of international politics a century earlier.

The moral consensus that served to restrain international politics in the seventeenth and eighteenth century no longer exists. Its disappearance is due to two related historic forces, nationalism and universal ideology. Nationalism of the modern sort, born in the era of the French Revolution, replaced "mankind" or "Christendom" as the supreme moral unit, with the concept of the "nation." The national group became invested with the special moral superiority and sacred mission that had formerly been much more widely dispersed. From this atomization of a once-universal moral code came a congeries of differing political moralities, all phrased in absolute terms but each incorporating a distinct national point of view on questions of good and evil. Universal ideologies of the contemporary type stem from a particular world view unique to each, and develop much more sweeping interpretations of human action than do nationalist exegeses; but their effect is even more divisive. Nationalism proceeds from a moral base but has a generous admixture of crass and concrete calculation; modern ideologies, however, fit all human experience within a moralistic framework and deduce action programs rigidly from postulates about the moral nature of man.

Today, therefore, two additional sets of moral codes vie with traditional western morality for the allegiance of individuals. Nationalist morality and ideological morality often join forces—as in the case of communist states—but as often conflict. Judeo-Christian principles with clear universalist implications are commonly modified, stretched, or even perverted to serve one or the other newer moralities. The political consequences of this moral pluralism are obvious.

No state admits publicly today that its policy has any other but a moral base. Political conflict between mature states has an inescapable moral dimension as both sets of participants insist that their goals are no less than the achievement of the highest good. The inescapability of such moral disputation is equalled by its futility. Only very occasionally does a moral argument advanced by one side even receive a hearing, let alone acceptance, by the other. The international order today is not suffering from too few moral referents, but rather from far too many.

MORALITY AND FOREIGN POLICY

The ubiquity of moral discourse has an immediate and important effect on the choices states make. Decision-making, as we pointed out earlier, goes on in a social context, and a large portion of this milieu flows from the moral orientation of the society. The objectives of policy are derived from social values the moral basis of which is self-evident. A moral code generates a world view, a way of observing, classifying, and giving meaning to phenomena in the real world. Thus what we have called situational analysis by any government is obviously limited by the prevailing moral predispositions of the society. The tactics of policy are again in their turn clearly affected by social considerations of what is right and permissible and what is wrong and prohibited in public action. At every turn, internal morality guides and inhibits the policy-maker.

If a policy is developed by men who partake of the consensus themselves and if it is commensurable with public interpretations of absolute good, its implementation is greatly strengthened. Any contradiction or ignoring of mass moral expectations, on the other hand, raises the prospect of internal divisions or at the least of reduced public vigor and zeal. Such matters as nuclear testing, espionage, strategic bombardment, and compromise bargaining with communists have, for example, spawned serious moral problems for Americans in the past few years.

MORALITY, INTEREST, AND POWER

Two questionable dichotomies have plagued the discussion and analysis of moral issues in international politics, especially within the orbit of western culture. The first draws a distinction between morality and national interest; the second between morality and power. Although these conflicts are far too complex either to detail or to solve here, some observations would seem to be in point.

The alleged clash between morality and national interest would seem to be false on its face. There is no necessary reason why the teachings of any moral code and the formulation of national interest by any state should conflict. National interest is based on a controlling value system. If a state chooses to make the advancement of moral principles its highest political value, its national interest is no less a valid criterion for that reason. In many states those who profess to discover such a contradiction are in reality pressing a particular policy in the face of opposition and—especially in the United States—are convinced that their case is strengthened by casting aspersions on "idealists" who advance moral principles in support of different policy prescriptions.

Morality and power constitute a more formidable contrast. Power in this sense is, of course, understood to be brute force, alleged often to be a manifestation of man's inherent sinfulness. Thus power is deprived of moral neutrality and instrumental character and is elevated to a positive factor in a moral equation. A state, it is alleged, can be either moral and therefore ineffective in a power-dominated world, or it can be powerful and effective. Such an embrace of power is a compromise with strict morality, to be justified only on the basis of the duality of man's nature. Absolute moral solutions cannot be found in an amoral (often immoral) system, so men are urged, albeit sometimes regretfully, to eschew strict moral principles in the interest of the effective use of power.

Analytically, this position is illogical and indefensible. There is no reason to equate power with force or to strip it of moral content. A state is concerned with winning consensus in the international order in support of its purposes. It is not difficult either to imagine or to cite many examples of cases in which moral principles have proved to be important to the achievement of that necessary consent. In this sense, morality becomes itself a part of power—or, more accurately, of capability. The role of morality in strengthening or weakening a state's international competence is therefore a function of particular situations and is not subject to any generalizations in advance of action in a concrete context.

Neither as a basis for calculating capability nor as a pretext for suspending individual moral scruples is the distinction between morality and power a meaningful one. Power may be used for immoral purposes or for moral ones. Morality may be exterior to capability or one of its key components. The lack of absolute moral

solutions to international problems does not free man from his responsibility to remain a moral being, even when considering questions of foreign policy. Power and morality are concepts that belong in different analytical frames of reference and cannot be joined
in any prescriptive way.

THE RISE OF INTERNATIONAL MORALITY

One of the dreams that has energized the efforts of many would-
be reformers of international politics is that of a rebirth of an international moral consensus. If some way could be discovered to re-
create the common moral ground rules that had governed the course
of international politics prior to the birth of modern nationalism,
the political system and mankind itself would be enormously better
off. The danger that differing but equally deeply-felt moral out-
looks might precipitate catastrophe would be sharply reduced, and
the possibilities for finding common ground for mutually acceptable
solutions to important problems would be correspondingly increased. It is some such idea of what was called in the nineteenth
century a "natural harmony of interest" among all men that motivated a large part of the effort that culminated first in the League
of Nations and later in the United Nations.

An international moral consensus is a crucial prerequisite to an
orderly and stabilized world. Both more efficient international organization and safer international politics must remain illusory hopes
so long as the human species, bound increasingly into one tightly-
packed political space by an inexorable technology, continues to
break up into quarrelsome and mutually exclusive factions on moral
issues. Any significant improvement in the tension climate of world
affairs will require that men reach some agreement on their basic
moral terms of reference.

Put this way, the proposition has traditionally been felt to be self-
cancelling; a world divided into a set of sovereign states each of
which is busily perfecting and promoting its own nationalistic morality has long been held to be incapable of mustering adequate
agreement on any set of propositions broad enough to permit the
formulation of "international morality." Ideologies, cutting across
national and ethical lines as they do, provide a broader base of moral

action than state morality, but ideological conflict represents movement away from consensus rather than toward it. The failure of Woodrow Wilson's dream of the "Parliament of Man" as epitomized in the League of Nations and the deep and bitter divisions of the cold-war era seem conclusive proof of the unattainability of international moral consensus short of a divine miracle or a destructive cataclysm.

But the patterns of contemporary international politics are developing in such a way as to throw doubt on this long-standing generalization. The technology that has made war so destructive has also brought nations physically into closer contact with each other. In the United Nations especially, but generally in all manner of conferences, meetings, and assemblies, men and governments are jointly exploring the larger issues of the age and discovering, often to their surprise, that the moral judgments they make are astonishingly similar. From this nascent awareness of a common interest in a single destiny has emerged the beginnings of a true international morality.

Its root is, of course, expediential: the deeply sensed urge to survive in a world of great danger. No moral code makes a senseless death a morally justifiable act, and sanity argues that the continued existence of the human species is itself a highly desirable goal. Sheer biological survival is not, however, the crux of this new moral outlook. It is not so much that men deny that there are things worth dying for but rather that they insist that they die *for* something rather than merely expire in a Wagnerian immolation. Dying for a cause is frivolous unless the cause is in some way advanced or defended by death. Beyond this fundamental moral judgment, the new morality is slowly proceeding to develop a more elaborate rationale on which to base state behavior in a less political world.

Inevitably, any international morality must weaken the monistic bonds of nationalism. Although ours is still a highly nationalistic age, the character of mass national identifications is perceptibly changing. In some areas a clear decline has set in, in others nationalism is still seeking a new direction, and in still others it is seeking larger units of loyalty. Only a few states espouse the old, militant, integrating impact of nationalism. In like fashion, the signs of a relaxation in the impact of ideologies on the behavior patterns of mass man, detectable only in very recent years, is a hopeful sign.

THE RESTRAINING EFFECT OF MORAL CONSENSUS

The new, and as yet peripheral, force of international morality is given such form as it may assume by means of an international consensus. Whether expressed formally in the General Assembly of the United Nations or informally by the intangible of "world opinion," collective moral judgment is now a situational factor with which policy-makers in all states must reckon.

International moral restraint is, of course, powerless to prevent a great power from taking a single overt step or even from launching a particular policy. It is not, and probably never will be, an instrument for casting an effective veto on a unique event. Its role up to the present has been to help condition the climate of decision for large and small states alike, developing ever clearer and more restrictive parameters within which the state system can move. Nor is it likely that its negative restraining function will ever be overtaken in importance by a positive and goal-postulating role. Morality may define the permissible for states but will never define the mandatory.

But the logic of technology and the evolving mutual awareness of more and more men have combined to make moral judgments again relevant to the course of international politics. There is now being born a supranational and suprastate criterion of evaluation available to men everywhere. On balance, its usefulness to this point, although admittedly limited, argues for its continued and more extensive application. Morality, international as well as internal, is and will continue to be a limitation on state action, difficult to define but impossible to ignore.

International Law

International law consists of that body of rules and principles of action intended to regulate relations among states. This definition applies to what is known as "public" international law. Private international law, otherwise called "conflict of laws," consists of the rules governing the disposal of cases involving litigants claiming rights under different legal systems. Our study here is primarily concerned with public international law.

NATURAL LAW

Law and its political institutions reflect the ideological and normative order of the society in which they operate. Law can exist only in a society. There is no law in a community without norms. Law is effective in a society only when its positive laws (commands issued by officials) correspond to its "living" laws: customs, traditions, and experience.

During medieval and early modern times many jurists advanced a theory of natural law which was intrinsic in God and nature and was discoverable by human reason. We see today, however, that the idea of natural law which was advanced in their writings was almost entirely an historical development with origins in Greco-Roman philosophy and jurisprudence, and in Christian ethics. It was influential in the era of the "medieval synthesis," helping to provide a common moral, religious, and philosophical basis for a unified society. The increasing extension of international contacts to non-European cultures has made this concept of natural law, rooted as it was in European philosophical, legal and religious principles, no longer valid as a basis for the evolution of an universal international law.

THE NATURE OF INTERNATIONAL LAW

Whether international law is "law" in the true sense has been a subject of long and constant debate among jurists. Certain theoretical aspects of the nature of law must be understood in order to grasp the significance of this problem.

Law in the abstract suggests a fixed relationship between or among certain entities. Two types of law may be distinguished in terms of their subjects: natural law (in the technical sense) and human law. Natural law is the law of natural causes of human or non-human phenomena and thus contains no element of volition. In human relations, however, volition is omnipresent. Human law covers the relations among persons or groups governed by rules which the subjects admit to be binding upon themselves in that they have explicitly or tacitly agreed to conform their actions to its terms and to be subject to official demands for obedience. Human law rests ultimately on agreement.

International law is a branch of human law. In spite of the implications of sovereignty to the international behavior of states, the international system is generally regarded by all its members as having a legal base. Such a base is deemed to rest on the consent (in theory explicit) of all states bound by the law.

International law is a product of the operation of the international system itself. Its growth is almost accidental in that it seldom is the result of deliberate planning. Instead it develops slowly from international practice and often a particular rule has attained near-maturity before statesmen appreciate that there has been an addition to the total corpus of the law.

Probably the greatest inspiration for the continued growth of international law throughout history has been the demands of states for reciprocity, uniformity, and equality of treatment by all of their fellows. In international practice this demand approximates the ideal of "justice" in that each state expects the law to give it its due. The legal rights a state may enjoy (as apart from the freedom of action they may have to influence or coerce other states) depend upon the willingness of other states to recognize them in practice. The divergence that may and usually does exist between this idea of justice and the working principles of international intercourse may be bridged only by the effective application of the rule of consent.

THE SOURCES OF INTERNATIONAL LAW

The sources of international law are treaties, custom and usage, the general principles of law, judicial precedents, text-writers, and pure reason.

International agreements that become the basis for lasting international law are usually the multilateral instruments concluded among a sizable number of states; bilateral agreements are usually regarded as a possible "evidence" of law. Custom is not in itself law, but becomes so when enough states feel that the custom reflects a legal rule. The "general principles of law" include those rules, principles and procedures recognized by courts of "civilized nations." Judicial precedents consist of the decisions of international courts. Text-writers, on the other hand, provide useful evidence of what the law is; their speculations, furthermore, provide a frequently relevant judgment of what the law ought to be. Finally, reason as a source of law refers to the judicial function of discovering a principle to cover a new situation by applying legal logic in a way that lawyers accept as valid.

DEVELOPMENT OF INTERNATIONAL LAW

Elements of what is known as international law can be traced to ancient times, when treaties gradually appeared among the ancient city-states of Mesopotamia, Egypt, India, and China. During the Greek era, a complex web of agreements were signed among the Hellenic city-states establishing the personal and property rights of their respective citizens resident in a city-state other than their own. The Greeks entered into alliances, promoted the right of asylum, the practices of arbitration, and established federal leagues.

During the period of the Roman Empire occasional precepts were laid down on the treatment of ambassadors, the conclusion of treaties, and the extradition of criminals. The famous *jurisconsuls* gave their attention to the reasons justifying war and the preliminaries to its declaration. In addition, the Romans developed the concept of *jus gentium:* the customs and laws common to all peoples. The great contribution of Greece and Rome to international law was the philosophical and juristic concept of a universal society of mankind governed by natural law.

The fragmentary international institutions of ancient times were further developed in medieval Europe. Codes of universal rules for the regulation of trade and the acts of merchants on land and sea were added. In addition, medieval theologians such as Saint Augustine and others elaborated on the precepts of natural law and the doctrines of just and unjust war.

The beginnings of modern international law, however, are generally traced to the establishment of nation-states and more precisely to the Peace of Westphalia in 1648. Beginning with the sixteenth century, a number of jurists produced various treatises which became the foundations for modern international law. Francisco de Vittoria presented legal justifications for the Spanish conquest in

America; the Italian Perino Belli and Spaniard Balthasar Ayala published treatises on war and military tactics; Alberico Gentile, an Italian, wrote a thesis on just and unjust war; Francisco Suarez, another Spaniard, made differentiations between *jus naturale* and *jus gentium*. All these writers were anxious to reduce the frequency of war and to mitigate its cruelties.

In 1625, Hugo Grotius, a native of the Netherlands, wrote the first comprehensive treatise on international law that has remained a classic, *De Juri Belli ac Pacis* (Law of War and Peace). This work set forth a general system of law to govern the relations of states. Grotius' writings dealt mostly with war and the circumstances which make war just and lawful; his discussions on the law of peace were much less elaborate. He discoursed at length on the laws of the Romans and Hebrews and discussed the relationship between law of nature and *jus gentium*.

SCHOOLS OF THOUGHT OF INTERNATIONAL LAW

Beginning with the sixteenth century, various schools of thought regarding the nature of international law gradually developed and are yet discernible today.

The *naturalists* hold that natural law is the one and only legal system governing states. They argue that natural law comes to humanity through human reason and the nature of man. Law in this way cannot be derived from the consent of its subjects, but rather is the supreme command of a superhuman authority, often explicitly divine in nature. Custom has thus no legal force and treaties are binding only because of their basis in natural law. Samuel Pufendorf is generally regarded as the classic exponent of this school; his views were presented in the *Law of Nature and Nations* (1672).

The *positivists* originated in the eighteenth century but did not become conspicuous until the nineteenth. The positivists emphasize the role of consent as the source of international law. They believe that dictates of the law of nature not incorporated in practice by the overt consent of men are binding only upon their individual consciences. "Natural law" to them is no more than a set of moral principles external to real law. Cornelis Bynkershoek was an early positivist whose views were expressed in a major work, *Forum of Ambassadors and Question of Public Law* (1773).

The *eclectics* contend that the sources of international law are both natural law and consent. The school appeared as early as the seventeenth century and is probably the dominant group today. Its great early exponent was Hugo Grotius; he was followed by Emerich Vattel in his *Droit des Gens* (the Law of Nations), (1758), and many others.

THE SUBJECT MATTER OF INTERNATIONAL LAW

The considerable dimensions of international law can be reduced to three general areas of subject matter. These are the acquisition and meaning of statehood, the rules and procedures of peaceful international intercourse, and the rules and procedures of war.

The law of statehood deals with the legal personality of the state and its rights, duties and privileges. It covers such subjects as the assumption of statehood through recognition, state succession, and the loss of international personality. It delineates the methods of acquiring and losing territory. It defines the status of equality of states and the responsibility of a state for events on its territory and actions by its nationals abroad. It distinguishes the territorial jurisdiction of states over air, land, and sea. It also covers state jurisdiction over persons, including the broad ground of nationality, citizenship, and the rights of resident or transitory aliens in its territory.

The rules and procedures of peaceful international intercourse include the law of diplomacy, the law of treaties, and the law of pacific settlement of international disputes. The law of diplomacy prescribes the powers and privileges of diplomats and establishes the protocol affecting the way in which diplomatic business is carried on. The law of treaties is one of the most important aspects of all international law. It designates the methods of negotiation, the tests of validity, the rules of interpretation, and the processes of termination of a treaty. The law regulating the pacific settlement of international disputes controls the various procedures utilized to settle international conflicts short of war and the rights of parties to such procedures.

The law of war deals initially with the legal concepts of belligerency and neutrality. In traditional international law, belligerency grants a state many legal rights it does not enjoy while at peace and deprives it of others. It also requires a state to obey the laws governing the conduct of warfare. On the other hand, neutrality confers certain special rights upon a neutral state, such as the maximum immunity practicable from the effects of the war. In return, it imposes certain obligations on the neutral state, such as the abstention from specific unneutral acts and the preservation of strict impartiality. In addition, the law of war covers the rules for the conduct of warfare relating to population, prisoners of war, the prohibition of certain weapons, and similar matters.

INTERNATIONAL LAW AS A REGULATORY MECHANISM

International law undoubtedly functions as a regulatory and limiting mechanism in international politics, but only in an intermittent and partially effective fashion. In large measure this incomplete effect is due to certain key characteristics of international law as a legal system.

First, its exact content is still and will probably always be indeterminate, since states define their legal rights and duties themselves with a sharp eye to their own interests. Second, international law is still largely a self-help system and is thus not enforced in the fashion of municipal law by a socially sanctioned international institution. Third, obedience to law is in legal theory a voluntary act on the part of any state, for any lesser doctrine would do irreparable damage to the foundationstone of sovereignty. Fourth, international law is an incomplete system with many aspects of interstate life clearly beyond the scope of the law. The political judgments of states are generally regarded as beyond legal restraint.

In spite of these shortcomings, however, the great bulk of normal and routine international and intergovernmental relations takes place within the framework of principles of international law. Such key notions as the rights and duties of states, the conduct of diplomacy, and the negotiation, ratification, and application of treaties have been all brought solidly under legal control. In general we may conclude that procedural law is very well established in the relations of states, but that substantive law (that gives concrete content to abstract matters of right) is still amorphous. It is at the latter point that law begins most obviously to fail as a regulatory technique.

THE SANCTIONS OF INTERNATIONAL LAW

International law, like international politics, emphasizes self-help and the unilateral enforcement of legal rights. The international order does not provide automatic and effective social sanctions for the principles of law which it identifies. Yet it is a mistake to conclude that there are no sanctions at all to contribute to the enforcement of the legal rights of states.

The greatest sanction of all, the one that led to the birth of the legal order in the first place and has constantly stimulated its growth, is expediency. An international legal code exists because states find it more rewarding to develop and apply generalized legal rules to their relations than to live always in a condition of unregulated anarchy. States, in other words, are impelled toward obedience to the law because the positive advantages of obedience are usually considered to be relatively greater than those arising from disobedience.

A second category of sanction is inertia, or habit. Long-standing legal procedures have become so well established in state practice that conformity to them is usually a matter of unthinking but conditioned response. The possibility of disobedience simply does not become one of the realistic action alternatives considered by the policy-maker.

Finally, as at least a semi-coercive sanction today we may cite here the international consensual apparatus to which we made reference earlier in this chapter. We must of course be on our guard not to overestimate the effect or the extent of world public opinion, but we must also be most careful not to underestimate it. A legal sanction, after all, is primarily a method of securing obedience to law rather than of punishing disobedience, and it is undeniable today that the only occasionally articulated demand of much of mankind for greater order in world relations has resulted in much greater attention to legal niceties by all types of governments. State decisions to "bow" to world opinion on legal issues may be expediential rather than principled, but the effect is the same: a greater conformity of state behavior with the rule of law. This is in essence the function of all sanctions.

RECENT TRENDS IN INTERNATIONAL LAW

Contemporary trends in international law demonstate a closer nexus with international politics. It has proved impossible to adjust life to law, so today the controlling emphasis is upon the adjustment of law to life. The international law of the nineteenth and earlier centuries assumed the sovereignty of states. Its object was not to eliminate war, but rather to restrict it in time, place, and method, and hence to establish an equilibrium of power. In the twentieth century international law has acquired instead the goal of establishing an equilibrium of justice, and assumes the interdependence of states and the integration of power.

The technological revolution has produced both a positive and a negative effect on international law. The progressive development of the positivist view secularized the entire concept of international law and weakened its moral foundations. This development heightened the role of power by making it more difficult to subject states to rules of law. In a power-oriented society law maintains the supremacy of force and hierarchies established on the basis of power, and gives legal respectability and sanctity to the system. In recent years many new states have joined the international system that do not share in the historic tradition of international law. Hence, they are not at all sympathetically inclined to limit their claims to what is legally defensible under the old system, a system that they feel is biased in favor of older, more developed, and more powerful states. In this sense, modern trends already have begun to weaken the universality of law.

On the other hand, the logic of the technological revolution and its by-products compels states to establish a better balance between law and politics. It has driven into the minds of statesmen the need for a more cohesive international system. International law today is formulating these demands in terms of new standards of justice. The relationship between international law and the dynamics of the international political system is more apparent today than at any previous moment in history. Law and social organization, after all, operate upon each other reciprocally: law sets limits to the structure, functions, and effectiveness of a social system, while the organizational dynamics of a society control the development, formulation, and application of legal rules. Modern technology, by making this two-way relationship obvious and by demonstrating the necessity for much greater cohesiveness in the international order, thus emerges as a positive force for the elaboration of international law. A more effective legal system in interstate relations will be an automatic function of an increasingly interdependent world society.

The Calculus of Prudence In Statecraft

In Part I, our analysis of the foreign-policy process pointed out that strategy in foreign policy or in war is a very conservative enterprise. The inexorabilities of cost and risk in an intrinsically unstable system of action combine to inhibit decision and to limit implementation. When all is said and done, perhaps the most powerful and certainly the most widely applicable restraint on state freedom of choice is the code of prudence that governs rational policy-making.

RATIONALITY AND PRUDENCE IN STATECRAFT

Operationally, there is no reason why all statesmen should be sane; a lunatic, provided only that he were capable of issuing coherent orders, is as qualified to operate the controls of government as is a philosopher-king. But sanity and rationality are ordinarily assumed to be requisite qualities in a foreign-policy-maker because only men marked by these traits are able to anticipate the probable results of their several actions and to govern their decisions in response to these calculations. The rational statesman is the prudent statesman.

An analytical and rational approach to foreign policy must be marked by caution because of a number of factors to which we have alluded earlier, among them the incompleteness of information, the possibility of accident or pure chance, and the perverseness of the human personality. If every decision takes due account of these limitations on the accuracy and validity of choice, a generous margin of error is inevitably built into policy. Game theory teaches that the primary responsibility of the player is to ensure his continued participation in the game; no more graphic summary could be made of the task of the statesman who invests his nation's survival in his ability to match strategies with his fellow policy-makers.

THE ROLE OF PROBABILITY

Policy-making requires the application of probability theory. Every statesman accepts as a primary postulate that nothing in international politics is either inevitable or impossible—or at least that the determination of inevitabilities or impossibilities is beyond the scope of his analytical techniques. He therefore is forced back to the determination of the relative probability of the various possible outcomes he can discern to each problem he faces. He must base his action decisions upon the greater probability of one outcome rather than another, with the necessary margin for error being determined by his conclusion as to how much more probable one alternative is than others.

One psychiatric interpretation of this situation asserts that to ignore relative probabilities in favor of a fixation on the possibilities inherent in a situation is a mark of paranoia. A statesman may on occasion—as did Adolf Hitler in trusting to his "intuition" that the Nazi armies would defeat the Soviet forces in World War II—conclude that a certain eventuality is cosmically inevitable, and pay for his error with his head. Much more common, however, is the opposite failure: to conclude that a wished-for result is impossible and thereby to miss a real opportunity for meaningful action. Whether statesmen who commit these blunders are in sober fact paranoid or not, they certainly are performing at a level far below the optimum and their respective nations bear the cost of their failures.

THE VIRTUES OF HALF A LOAF

A further manifestation of the ubiquity of prudential calculation is the strong preference statesmen demonstrate for partial successes achieved at minimum risk over all-or-nothing choices. With continued survival as the prime consideration in statecraft, rational policy-makers strive to gain such prizes as can be won without endangering their major preoccupation. This has contributed to what we have already remarked to be a characteristic pattern of interstate conflict: the struggle for small victories with only partial commitments of capability. Each state involved in such a contest can accept defeat with only minimum disturbance, since it knows in advance that even the most unfavorable outcome will leave it in a viable position for further action.

We will recall that the cost/risk calculation requires that the analyst never give himself the benefit of any major doubts and that he be prepared to pay the maximum probable cost for the objective he is seeking. Since the individual decision-maker has only a limited ability to reduce cost factors in a situation over which he has only minimal control, the only way in which he can rationalize an unfavorable cost/risk computation is by scaling back his objective to one he can afford. Once again prudence dictates restraint on decision.

THE RELATIVISM OF DECISION

What we have been saying in the past few pages points to one clear moral. Absolute calculations and absolute decisions have no place in rational policy-making. A high degree of relativity in all phases of decision and action is a characteristic of the skillful and successful statesman.

There is only one absolute criterion of value in foreign policy to which all states render homage: success. A foreign policy is "good" or "bad" only in the extent to which the state moves toward its objectives and in behalf of its national interest. Since the objectives themselves and even the basic postulate of interest are creatures of value and change in response to shifts in mass preferences and situational dynamics, policy-making is a constant exercise in relating many variables to each other. There is no room for any fixed and absolute generalizations about the nature of the political world, the nature of the problems facing the state, or the substance or the methods of the responses the state must make.

Were all policy-makers equally prudent, international politics would remain confined within parameters of safety and would never approach or surpass the boiling point. But history suggests many examples of over-optimistic leaders who misread the probabilities of a situation, and some who were persuaded that they had the key to the final significance of history and could reshape the destiny of man. The international political system could tolerate such leaders in a simpler day when failure was confined to the offending state and explosion was local.

Today mankind is the loser each time imprudence takes command of the policy-machine of a state. Wags have suggested a psychiatric examination as a prerequisite to high public office, but most leaders are less than enthusiastic about aspersions on their sanity. The best most of us can hope for is that prudence will continue to shackle the hand of recklessness and adventure; the stakes are too high to permit any but the cautious to play the game of survival in an age of thermonuclear bombs.

Bibliography

Brierly, J. L., *Law of Nations: An Introduction to the International Law of Peace.* London: Oxford University Press, 1955.

Butterfield, Herbert, *Christianity, Diplomacy and War: An Introduction to International Politics.* New York: Abington-Cokesbury Press, 1951.

Carr, Edward Hallet, *Twenty Years' Crisis, 1919–1939: An Introduction to the Study of International Relations,* Second edition. London: St. Martins, 1946.

Corbett, Percy E., *Law and Society in the Relations of States.* New York: Harcourt, Brace and Company, 1951.

————, *Morals, Law, and Power in International Relations.* Los Angeles: The John Randolph Hayes and Dora Hayes Foundations, 1956.

De Visscher, Charles, *Theory and Reality in Public International Law.* Princeton: Princeton University Press, 1957.

Gould, Wesley L., *Introduction to International Law.* New York: Harper & Row, Publishers, 1957.

Jessup, Philip, *Modern Law of Nations.* New York: Macmillan and Company, 1948.

Kelsen, Hans, *Principles of International Law.* New York: Rinehart and Company, 1952.

* Niebuhr, Reinhold, *Moral Man and Immoral Society.* New York: Charles Scribner and Sons, 1960.

Nussbaum, A., *Concise History of the Law of Nations,* Revised edition. New York: Macmillan and Company, 1947.

Stone, Julius, *International Conflict in the Twentieth Century: A Christian View*. New York: Harper & Brothers, 1960.

Thompson, Kenneth W., *Christian Ethics and the Dilemmas of Foreign Policy*. Durham, North Carolina: Duke University Press, 1959.

————, *Political Realism and the Crisis of World Politics*. Princeton: Princeton University Press, 1960.

* Wright, Quincy, *Contemporary International Law*, Revised edition. New York: Random House, 1961.

* Indicates paperback edition.

Nine

War in the Modern World

In Parts I and II, we have analyzed the rationale of foreign policy as conceived and executed by individual states, and we have examined the general characteristics of the international political system within which states move. In both discussions, one primary consideration has affected everything we have said: under the standardized conditions of interstate life, it is impossible for a state to operate and for the system to function except on the fundamental basis of physical coercion or violence most clearly expressed in war. At every turn we have come upon the analytical and practical centrality of military judgments; the system as we know it today is postulated on the right and on the capacity of states to work their will by force if they so desire.

And yet, today, the process of international politics is in the grip of a strange paralysis—to which we have occasionally alluded. Foreign policies, particularly those of major powers, do not receive the vigorous and powerful implementation one would expect them to; interstate disputes only seldom reach the clean-cut resolution in power terms that the system would seem to demand. Small states display an unwonted independence of choice and action, while great powers continue to cast about (with only indifferent success) for ways to make their putative dominance again a reality. To a great extent the political world has been, if not completely turned upside down, at least knocked off balance.

The major reason for this unprecedented state of affairs is, of course, the blighting effect of new theories of warfare on interstate political relations and the weapons that have given birth to these theories. Statesmen wrestle almost in a frenzy with the problem of fitting modern military doctrines and techniques within the framework of foreign policy and international politics. Up to this point, they have not succeeded; the old ways of war are outmoded, and the new warfare has not yet found its political niche. It is no wonder that international relations carry a larger and larger cargo of futility and that statesmanship frequently finds itself in a vacuum.

In this chapter we shall examine the nature of the military dilemma, both in terms of its own components and of its impact on the political process. One of the more interesting developments in the study and teaching of international politics in recent years has been the great increase in emphasis given to military matters. While this chapter can do no more than skim the surface of the vast subject of military science, it is designed to acquaint the student with at least the basic vocabulary of contemporary military discussion and to relate these concepts to the larger context of international political affairs.

Total War and the State System

What have been the specific effects of total war upon the state system? How has the new warfare affected the general pattern of international politics? In general terms we have already answered both questions, but certain basic considerations merit a second look.

THE POSSIBILITY OF CATASTROPHE

It is often overlooked that war became a normal and regular aspect of international politics because it provided a final answer to problems *within the system itself*. That is to say, war balanced the political process but never endangered it. Even World War II, with all its destructive and disruptive results, nevertheless ended with a recognizable political system still in existence. Modern total war with nuclear missiles and other technological niceties, now raises the grim possibility of destruction of the political system and perhaps of civilized existence itself.

Advocating a technique for the resolution of an international dispute that might effect complete disaster for mankind is too much like recommending decapitation as a cure for headache. No purely political goal is so important as to justify risking survival. Put thus starkly, it would seem obvious that considerations of risk—assuming an optimistic cost calculation—would be absolutely prohibitive of a decision for total war. At least, it has seemed obvious to all statesmen who have faced the choice since the dawn of the nuclear era.

There are, of course, many learned and persuasive arguments that total war would not in fact obliterate mankind or the monuments of his civilization, but rather that the recuperative capacity of industrial society would permit the world to recover relatively rapidly from a thermonuclear holocaust. These contentions receive a moderately sympathetic hearing as long as they remain no more than intellectualized speculation. No government, however, has been willing to gamble its existence (and that of the entire world) on the validity of these hypotheses. The possibility of utter catastrophe looms large in all military calculations today.

THE INVALIDATION OF "VICTORY"

With the possibility ever in mind of utter debacle, and with the certainty of monumental devastation no matter what the course of the war, the classic military objective of "victory" has been substantially stripped of any meaning. Victory in battle has always meant the submission of the enemy; victory in war has always meant the achievement of the positive or negative political goal for which the war was fought. These classifications verge on the meaningless with respect to total war.

The destructiveness of thermonuclear war is simply beyond belief. If one state loses 75 per cent of its people and 90 per cent of its productive capacity, will the survivors be consoled by realizing that the enemy lost 85 per cent of its people and all its productive capacity? Will victory in such a case be sweet or—in the words of a leading theorist of nuclear war—"will the living envy the dead?"

One possibility of achieving victory continues to tantalize military theorists. If a state can gain enough initial striking power in one blow to eliminate an enemy's capacity to retaliate, perfect dominance will have been achieved with no damage in return. But—as we shall see in our discussion of the arms race—this margin of superiority is exceptionaly difficult to acquire, and its employment so contingent upon the attainment of absolute surprise, that it remains an illusory goal.

In any other terms, "victory" in total war today is a notion without content. This also exercises an inhibiting effect, since no war comes unless some statesman makes a decision to initiate it. With no likelihood of bringing about a real triumph, the urge to begin combat never will grow very strong. Total war is unattractive enough at best; without victory to give it point, it finds no political justification today.

THE RETHINKING OF POLITICAL VALUES

International politics has long depended for its motive force on the primacy of political values over all competing notions of good. Men were expected to support the state's efforts at whatever cost to themselves, even to sacrificing their lives. Now that war may have lost its point, the justification for patriotic death is no longer self-evident. Men might die for God or for posterity with good consciences, but to die knowing that only nothingness will follow has thrown the entire process of mental and emotional commitment out of plumb. An empty death in a fiery cauldron seems like a poor reward for all the panoply and collective enthusiasms of nationalism.

In much of the world a serious rethinking of political values has been launched. With the greatest sacrifice a man can make for his state, his very life, reduced to a mockery, many once self-evident truths about the purpose of foreign policy are undergoing reanalysis and drastically different answers are being advanced to old questions. If traditional national interest and diplomacy can promise only a fireball followed by cinders as the seal of negotiation, some men are suggesting that perhaps the content of political life needs overhauling in the direction of making it more directly responsible to individual needs and aspirations. Although no more than a ripple at the present time, this trend could conceivably develop into a wave that would sweep away many of the underpinnings of traditional international politics.

THE DISAPPEARANCE OF DECISION

With war no longer a good policy investment, the state system is deprived of its only efficacious method of reaching a clear decision in a direct confrontation between states. States today repeatedly get themselves in positions from which only a successful war could extricate them, but the inhibitions on warfare prevent them from taking the critical step. Unable to go forward and unwilling to retreat, the contestants remain locked in an uneasy and unwilling embrace and the issue remains stalemated and unresolved.

International politics since the end of World War II has seen one issue after another go to the point of maximum bearable reciprocal pressure and then remain hanging there in an agonizing and unrewarding suspension. Cultural lag prevents most states from recognizing and acting on the implications of the loss of decision capability in the system. They persist in embarking on policies whose full fruition might require war, and remain condemned to baffled annoyance when they feel themselves trapped. Some smaller states, recognizing both the opportunities and the limitations inherent in such an era, however, have had great success in pursuing active policies that are clearly cast in a frame of implementation that excludes the possibility of war.

DECISION BY CONSENSUS

With war stripped of its role as *ultima ratio*—"ultima" it may be today, but "ratio" never—some effective substitute is obviously necessary if the international political system is not to collapse from sheer inanition. The most broadly applicable alternative to war has been found in the institutionalization of consensus. Speaking primarily through the General Assembly of the United Nations but on occasion through special conferences or other *ad hoc* instrumentalities, from time to time a cohesive and articulate body of supranational consensus has exercised a controlling effect on crisis situations. Although the method of its formation and the general direction of its influence are often unpredictable and capricious, there is little doubt that consensus has to a considerable extent taken over the final-decision capability once monopolized by military power. Obviously if this process goes to completion the international political system will become a vastly different phenomenon than it was for three centuries.

Political Effects of the New Warfare

We have considered some of the effects of total war on the operation of the state system. Of equal importance in an understanding of the impact of military technology are the influences to which it subjects the statesman engaged in a policy decision on behalf of his own state.

THE "BALANCE OF TERROR"

Probably the most important consideration affecting foreign-policy decisions by large and small states alike is the existence of the so-called "balance of terror." This situation flows from the present distribution of military capability in the world in which two great states have built up such awesome arsenals of new weapons that they far outclass all other states, and yet each remains incapable of mounting an adequate superiority over the other. This allocation of military power inhibits everyone to the same extent if not exactly in the same way.

The great powers, as we have already seen, cannot develop a situation to the point in which either may contemplate unleashing war on the other. Both the United States and the U.S.S.R., in other words, have a vested interest in avoiding war. There is little philanthropy or charity in this self-restraint, only the most elementary calculations of the prospects for survival on the cost/risk scale.

Neither may, furthermore, make safely indiscriminate use of its great military power against lesser states. In the first place, a large proportion of the smaller powers are already under the protection of one or the other of the giants, and any overt pressure on one of these would bring its great leader into the dispute. Nor do the so-called "neutral" or "unaligned" states offer any more tempting target; neutrality in the cold war is a carefully worked out status that exists only because the major bloc leaders are willing to tolerate it. Any attempt by either cold-war camp to exert military coercion on almost any neutral would also bring in the opposite bloc and once again polarize the military situation.

If the cold-war giants are inhibited by the balance of terror, so—
if less obviously—are the smaller states themselves. Neither nuclear
leader can view calmly an outbreak of war anywhere. Both find
common ground in denying smaller powers the capability to reach
decisions by violence that they are themselves denied. Their reasons
for this preference of peace are the same as those governing their
direct confrontation: a war which cannot be won, or, more precisely, a war in which the prospects of real victory are remote and
difficult to visualize, is of no value to them. A small war may well
spread and involve either or both in a massive risk for small possible
profit. Both prefer to keep the lid on the cauldron of combat and
take their chances in other areas. Thus it may be said—and we shall
be examining some of the implications of this statement in a moment—that modern weaponry, at least as long as it is distributed as
narrowly as it is today, is a poor way to fight a war but a remarkably effective device for preventing one.

THE DECLINING CREDIBILITY OF MILITARY FORCE

The balance of terror not only makes war irrelevant to policy,
but it also deprives military power of much of its credibility as a
coercive or persuasive technique in the course of ordinary policy
confrontation. The credibility of the threat of violence as a tool of
policy is today realized to be no more than partially a function of
the magnitude of the threat; of even greater importance today is
the likelihood of its being made a reality. The sheer enormity of
threats today, at least those mounted by nuclear states, is far and
away greater than at any earlier period of history. Their impact on
affairs, however, is almost negligible, since we already have seen
how unlikely the threatening state is to make good its menace.

We see the consequences of this development at every turn.
Threats of dire consequences, whether veiled or open, made by
nuclear states against lesser opponents are dismissed as empty bluster
and casually disregarded. Even among non-nuclear powers, where
one might suppose the more traditional calculations might yet hold
sway, the variety of restraints that operate today vitiate once-
dominant military superiorities. The operative range of military
action today would appear to be truly bipolar and to consist either
of total war at one extreme or military paralysis at the other. Of
the once-luxuriant in-between area of gradations of force there

is little or nothing left. Nor does the threat of nuclear obliteration, even if made seriously by a reckless government, have much policy utility. The size of the threat itself, so out of proportion to any rational policy purpose, deprives it of all effect.

THE END OF STATUS

The disappearing credibility of military power has also eroded (but not, be it noted, entirely eliminated) the status system that so long regulated the relations of states. The old easy classification of states into categories of rank and privilege based upon their respective military capabilities has been substantially invalidated. A great power cannot receive the deference once its due if it cannot act in the way great powers were formerly supposed to. The result has been a new and potentially devastating sense of what we might call international egalitarianism that has spread widely since the balance of terror began to exert its influence.

States of all military levels approach each other today on an *a priori* basis of substantial status equality. Whatever deference and privilege each may enjoy in a particular relationship is a function of the specific situation and their respective range of capabilities and cannot be inferred in advance from any generalized characteristics or self-image. The essence of a status or class system is a fixed stratification of groups, and military capacity long played the role of the determinant of what level a state occupied. No universally accepted criterion of rank has yet risen to replace military power, and the international social system as a result is more fluid and less structured today than it has been since its inception. There are no accepted "leaders," no "inner circle" of dominant powers that give shape to the patterns of world politics—except insofar as the nuclear states can keep attention riveted on themselves by virtue of the awful destructive capacity they control.

THE UTILITY OF MILITARY FORCE TODAY

Are we then arguing that military force and the institution of organized armed conflict has lost all relevance to contemporary world politics? In strict conceptual terms, the temptation is strong to argue exactly that position, but a glance at the world of reality suggests that in a limited number of special cases military power retains much of its capacity to render a decision. To make a brief catalogue of these instances not only measures the relevance of war today but also vignettes some of the salient characteristics of the contemporary political world.

The first situation in which military force is useful today is one in which a leader of a major bloc in the world uses armed force to subdue a rebellious or recalcitrant satellite. The classic instance of this was Soviet intervention in Hungary in 1956. In such a case the rigidity of the bloc's international position effectively inhibits the likelihood of any attempt at penetration from any outside source, specifically from the other bloc.

A second situation, illustrated by the Indian invasion and capture of the Portuguese enclave, Goa in 1961, is action by an anticolonial state against a (usually small and isolated) remnant of a colonial empire. Here the military state has the protection of anticolonialist ideology and thus a considerable pre-formed consensus supporting its action. If its military venture is rapid and clean, opposition and resistance develop so slowly that the entire operation is over before anything can be done about it. Unless the move is made quickly and crowned by success, however, international complications may set in that would serve to vitiate its effect.

Third, we must mention intervention in support of one side or the other in a civil war, thus giving rise to what today is called "war by proxy." This is no more than an indirect application of military power, since most examples of this technique have been confined to the supply of materiel and economic and political support rather than the overt commitment of military manpower. Probably the most conspicuous example of this device was the extensive Communist support given North Korea during the Korean War of 1950–53; the pattern here was fulfilled by the appearance of Red Chinese "volunteers" who fought a large part of the battle. Less extreme involvements in recent years have included Soviet-Chinese support of the Viet Minh and Viet Cong in the civil war in Vietnam, of the Pathet Lao in Laos, of the Antoine Gizenga group in the Congo, and of the FLN rebels in Algeria. The United States has retaliated in kind in Vietnam, in Laos, and in the Congo and has long sought other opportunities to apply its military power in this way.

Most significantly, however, modern experience has clearly indicated that military power may be safely and overtly used to obtain political decisions only by groups of small states acting under authority given by the United Nations. The two most successful applications of military power to the problem of obtaining a political decision have been the United Nations interventions in the Suez Canal Zone in 1956 and in the Congo crisis in 1960. In both cases, the collective nature of the action, the relative small and weak (and therefore non-disturbing) nature of the involved states, and the general air of disinterestedness evoked by the combination of small powers and the United Nations, contributed directly to the accomplishment of the military mission and its political goal. In Suez, the UNEF did no fighting; in the Congo, the force was committed to direct and successful (but sharply limited) operations against the seccessionist regime of Katanga province. Whether by its sheer presence or by a battlefield victory, however, the United Nations military force has shown itself to be capable of making decisions by military means.

Beyond these few cases, however, the range of effective military action is remarkably narrow today; and even these instances are all so special and so much the products of accidental and epicentral circumstances that no great conclusions can safely be drawn from them. The problem of relating contemporary military capability to foreign-policy objectives still defies solution and promises to do so until military specialists and political leaders alike learn more about the implications of modern technology as applied to war.

New Doctrines and the Military Dilemma

We must not suppose, however, that military experts have remained suspended in bemusement at the massive effect the new technology of warfare has had on their profession. On the contrary, in all countries military and civilian analysts have been devoting great effort to coming to terms with the drastically changed conditions of war. Out of this enterprise has come a spate of new doctrines and concepts, covering a broad gamut of situations but all alike in their attempt to develop an intellectual base for warfare in the modern world.

THE IMPORTANCE OF MILITARY DOCTRINE

The scope of modern warfare is so vast and its instruments so complex that it would be impossible to conduct a campaign without a doctrine governing the military process. In the first place, a military doctrine spells out a series of assumptions about the nature and conditions of combat and the calculations controlling its initiation, prosecution, and termination. Secondly, military doctrine resolves in advance the difficult dilemmas inherent in battlefield operations: the relative importance of conserving materiel as compared with conserving life, the respective roles of position and maneuver, the concept of "firepower" as opposed to that of occupation of territory, and so on. Military doctrine, by developing a mental framework within which operational decisions can be made, reduces the task of modern commanders to manageable size.

Military doctrine obviously has a central place in the capability judgments of a state. Since it governs the makeup of the military machine, the principles that will affect its employment, and the point of view and professional orientation of its officer corps, doctrine is one of the filters through which raw military potential must pass before a sophisticated evaluation can be made of a nation's real military capacity. American military doctrine, for example, has always emphasized fire and maneuver as the ingredients of victory and has always argued that the offensive was both less costly and more productive of results than a defensive posture. The preservation of manpower has always ranked higher than the husbanding of materiel. The maintenance of a force-in-being at all times, capable of fighting and ready to fight, is another standard American tenet. These principles contrast, for example, with the relatively low rank Chinese military thought gives to the conservation of life and the emphasis on small-group irregular tactics developed by Mao Tsetung. Russian doctrine emphasizes massed firepower and places less emphasis on maneuver and mobility. All of these considerations—to which analogues could be found in the military doctrine of all states—have a significant effect on the way the nation's armed forces are constructed and used. They are important both to the foreign policy planner who is contemplating military action and to the statesman evaluating the potential of another state.

THE DOCTRINAL CRISIS: IS THIS A NEW ERA?

The great crisis facing the scholars of military doctrine today is one that involves an estimate of the impact of the new technology on the classic principles of warfare. Do these rules of strategy and tactics, built up over the centuries and successfully absorbing earlier technological advance from the bow and arrow to the tank, the "blockbuster" aerial bomb, and the technique of "vertical envelopment" by airborne forces, still apply in the era of thermonuclear warheads on intercontinental ballistic missiles? One school of thought argues that the changes in warfare are entirely quantitative and not qualitative and that the historic doctrines of warfare need only adaptation to the new conditions. Another group contends that modern weaponry has breached the parameters of warfare and that entirely new concepts are needed before men can effectively exploit this as yet untried range of capability.

The traditionalists argue that the new weapons are no more than advanced versions of classic types. A thermonuclear bomb has the explosive potential of fifty million tons of TNT; although a frightening figure in itself, this comparison also suggests that by traditional means it would be possible to duplicate the blast of a hydrogen bomb. Missiles are no more than improved delivery systems; the entire history of warfare is one of gradual advance in delivery techniques from the individual foot soldier carrying his spear, through rifleman, cavalryman, tanker, airplane pilot, and now to the missileman. Each advance, although not eliminating the human element, has involved increases in both the speed and the reliability of the delivery of a weapon to its target. Thus, the argument goes, there is no conceptual difference between the doctrines of Caesar's legions and those of contemporary ICBM squadrons; the principles are identical and only the technical details of mobilizing and employing the manpower and materiel are new. War is thus different only in detail today from what it has always been.

The opposite position stems from the belief that destructive capabilities such as those of hydrogen bombs and delivery systems of 9000-mile range and multi-mach speeds have made a travesty of the once-established doctrines of warfare. Not only have modern weapons endangered the survival of the political system that in theory they are to regulate, but they have also made war a cruel deception and a recipe for holocaust.

The advocates of new doctrines go in two different directions from this basic premise. One school contends that a new theory of total war must be developed, founded on different principles than historic practice and emphasizing the major characteristics of the new weapons: destructiveness and rapidity of delivery. The other group contends that war has been rendered obsolete and that the principal military mission of the future is to prevent any recurrence of combat rather than winning war if it should start.

The doctrinal dispute wages unabated, and statesmen remain suspended between the poles of passivity and recklessness while the experts wrangle. There seems little likelihood that any normally prudent policy-maker will take the risk intrinsic to modern war until he has to his own satisfaction resolved the doctrinal dilemma. So long as the military specialists themselves continue to deepen the gaps between the several schools rather than to narrow them, the use of armed force on an organized basis by any major state remains only a remote possibility.

DOCTRINES OF TOTAL WAR: DETERRENCE

One of the most pervasive doctrines of the new military era is that of deterrence. By deterrence is meant the capacity of modern weapons to deter another state from initiating warfare. Of course this notion has always been part of military lore, but the peculiar qualities of the new techniques make deterrence more significant than ever before.

Much thought has gone into the ramifications of the deterrent mission of modern military establishments. At least in the United States, two rival theories of deterrence have been voiced. One, called the "finite deterrent," argues that a nation's retaliatory capacity should be increased to such a point that—regardless of the damage inflicted by an initial strike—the enemy would immediately receive an unacceptable amount of damage in return on his cities, his industrial capacity, and his clusters of population. This so-called "city-busting" theory has been opposed by the "counterforce" concept that bases deterrence on the development of sufficiently well-aimed and sharply-targeted capability to destroy the enemy's military capacity while leaving his cities and his population relatively intact. In practice, all states with the necessary productive capability have attempted a policy that partakes of both points of view.

Deterrence is the mission for which—as we have already noted—modern weapons are extremely appropriate. Their indiscriminate and uncertain effect and the fact that the "new generation" of weaponry has never been used in combat, make policy-makers extremely cautious and susceptible to being deterred. It is paradoxical that such refined and sophisticated military technology has proved to be best suited for making war an unwise gamble rather than for winning it.

DOCTRINES OF TOTAL WAR: THE NATURE OF RESPONSE

Conceptually part of the deterrent concept, but a considerable doctrinal issue in its own right, is the question of the nature of the response a state should take to a military-political provocation. As in deterrence also, several different approaches have been developed to this question. We shall look directly at the way the controversy has been prosecuted in the United States, although all major states are seized by the issue.

One school of thought is that of "instantaneous response," more popularly known as "massive retaliation." Americans advancing this argument have contended that any direct Soviet-American armed conflict is inevitably a total war and they have urged that whatever strategic advantage lies in the first strike should be retained by the United States. Its theory of response, therefore, is that the moment a Soviet provocation crosses the threshold of tolerability, the full weight of American nuclear capability is to be unleashed on the entire spectrum of targets in the U.S.S.R. This doctrine, its advocates insist, not only ensures the optimum basis for accepting total war but also contributes largely to the efficacy of deterrent dispositions. No aggressor, certain that total war would result from an unbearable provocation, will risk breaching an admittedly unclear line of tolerance.

The contradictory position was originally identified with the doctrines of limited war that we shall examine in a later section. More recently, however, they have developed a more sophisticated position known generally as "flexible response." Its basic rationale is

that the United States should not commit itself to an all-out immediate response to a challenge but should in the first place allow
itself a "pause for decision" before taking action and then respond
only at a level adequate to neutralize the immediate threat. In this
way the responsibility for escalating the conflict will rest upon the
enemy and the United States will be free from the danger of
initiating an unnecessary total war.

American policy, long officially committed to the instantaneous
response, has recently been shifted to a version of flexible response.
This has been widely hailed as a basic doctrinal overhaul, but it is
noteworthy that the United States yet overtly retains the right to
initiate nuclear warfare in the event of an unbearable but non-
nuclear provocation from the Soviet Union. With this proviso built
into the doctrine, the differences between past and present policy
are not very great.

DOCTRINES OF TOTAL WAR: "FIRST STRIKE" OR "SECOND STRIKE"

Another doctrinal issue of great importance is that of the relative
merits of the "first strike" as opposed to the retaliatory or "second
strike" posture. It is generally conceded that there is not yet any
reliable defense against nuclear attack and that only retaliation can
deter. The doctrinal issue is whether a nation, in view of this dangerous situation, can safely adopt a second-strike strategy.

The United States, of course, has done so, and there has long
been an intense controversy over whether or not this decision was
a wise one. Opponents of the American willingness to "give the
enemy the first blow" contend that the possibility exists that the
enemy might in one assault cripple either the nation's will to fight
or its capacity to strike back; this, they say, is too great a risk to
take and they urge a revised American doctrine that permits the
United States to strike first in a "pre-emptive" or "preventive" way.
Defenders of the established American position point to the increasing invulnerability of the retaliatory weapons systems the United
States is developing—such as the *Polaris*-carrying nuclear submarine
fleet—and argue that any change in the American doctrine would
itself be viewed as a dangerously provocative move by the Communist bloc.

For a status quo state like the United States, the first-strike argument is a cruel one. Strategically the United States is more interested in deterrence than in initiating any war; it must, therefore, maintain great retaliatory capability and yet avoid increasing tension and the probability of war. Yet, if deterrence fails, it must be capable of winning the war that has been forced upon it and dare not lightly forego the advantage of the first strike. American second-strike strategy is more of an optimistic verdict on the probability of successful deterrence than it is a rationalized theory for fighting total war.

DOCTRINES OF TOTAL WAR: DEFENSE AND SURVIVAL

Estimates of the casualties that would be produced by a nuclear attack on an urbanized state are all guesswork, since nobody knows what would actually happen; but all are gruesomely high. The prohibitive cost in human life has produced considerable doctrinal effort in the areas of passive defense to nuclear attack and the prospects for national survival after suffering a major blow.

The discussions cluster around two major points. One concerns the defensive measures civilian populations might take, including evacuation, shelters, permanent underground installations, fallout and radiation protection, and so on. The entire subject suffers from a number of conceptual and practical difficulties. There is no reliable experience on which to build, the extent to which the theorists and responsible officials are themselves persuaded of the utility of the measures they urge is debatable, and public fatalism and widespread apathy reflect a profound belief that the initiation of nuclear war is simply the end of everything. No major nation has more than scratched the surface in the field of passive defense.

In like fashion, the theorists of recuperation have little evidence to support their dogmas. Their usual criterion is how rapidly the attacked state might be expected to restore its productive plant to pre-attack levels, and estimates vary not only according to the optimism of the analyst but also in response to the political exigencies of the moment. Only a few students have addressed themselves to the question of the human response to a destructive attack and have inquired into the extent to which a battered remnant of survivors would continue to be eager to perform their allotted public tasks of reconstruction after their private lives had been shattered. It is generally agreed, for example, that the first casualty of a nuclear onslaught would be the destruction of political democracy and individual freedom. How would a population accustomed to an open society respond to the imposition of an authoritarian regime in the midst of smoking ruins and wholesale death?

The problems of defense, survival, and reconstruction have not yet received their definitive doctrinal formulation. Students will continue to wrestle with them, for they are in the simplest sense inescapable as long as total war remains a possibility. Until they are solved the initiation of total war will remain a ghastly risk of unpredictable dimensions.

DOCTRINES OF LIMITED WAR: "CONVENTIONAL" WAR

For the past few pages we have scrutinized the doctrines advanced and developed by the theorists of total war. There are, however, other doctrinal positions developed by analysts who challenge the ubiquitous destruction of all-out nuclear conflict and who contend that under the umbrella of the balance of terror and reciprocal deterrence there remains a place for politically relevant warfare that is less than total. This is the province of the theorists of limited war.

Limited war doctrines accept and embrace the deterrent implications of the nuclear absolutes, but challenge their universal effect. Adherents of this position argue generally that all nuclear weapons can deter is a nuclear attack, but that—strong words to the contrary—no nation will ever unleash an all-out response to a relatively minor provocation. The limited war thesis contends that sub-nuclear challenges can and should best be met by sub-nuclear responses and that the ensuing conflicts can be fought to a political decision without escalating into an apocalyptic conflagration.

The most common formulation of the limited war position is cast in terms of so-called "conventional war"—war fought with high-explosive rather than nuclear weapons or at least with so-called "tactical" (up to a half-kiloton yield) nuclear warheads. The argument is developed along lines that suggest that the balance of deterrence is absolute and that conventional and traditional military calculations can proceed to fulfillment almost as if nuclear weapons had never been invented. This argument has its obvious and natural appeal to all traditionally-minded military thinkers and particularly to those branches of service—such as the ground forces of the army —who fear eventual displacement by modern "gadgetry."

Conventional warriors in the western world have pressed their case with great skill and determination, but the Soviet line has not been encouraging to their position. Recent Soviet pronouncements have suggested that Moscow feels that any direct Soviet-western conflict would rapidly escalate into all-out nuclear exchange and that conventional military doctrines cannot provide any rationale for such a struggle. The possibility remains, of course, that this Soviet position is part of Moscow's own deterrent strategy, and perhaps the limited war theorists are correct. In the face of such a grim warning, however, few western leaders are willing to gamble their survival on their ability to keep an open clash with Moscow from becoming a total war.

The conventional war theory suffers from two practical inhibitions. In the first place, the task of developing a situation appropriate to testing its validity has proved extremely difficult. However convincing its rhetoric, no doctrine has any functional utility unless it is applicable in the real world on a bearable cost/risk basis. Second, the record of the cold-war period indicates that the West can meet Communists on the battlefield without the war becoming total; this was the experience in Korea, in Vietnam, and in certain other crisis points. But keeping a war between nuclear powers at a sub-nuclear level can be done only at the price of virtually abandoning the possibility of a political victory. This lesson was learned in Korea and in other cases. Since limited war seems feasible only if allowed to deteriorate into a stalemate, it is difficult to see why it should win the sympathy of success-minded statesmen.

DOCTRINES OF LIMITED WAR: GUERILLA WARFARE

A second line of attack of the limited war theorists is today represented by doctrines of guerrilla warfare and other irregular and "paramilitary" (in the United States sometimes called "counter-insurgent") techniques. If limited conventional war carries too many risks, then paramilitary techniques may well provide a safe and useful way to apply force to the accomplishment of political ends.

Modern theories of guerrilla warfare are products of communist thought. The most widely-read treatise on the subject today was written by Mao Tse-tung.* The obivous success of Communist action groups in using guerrilla tactics in southeast Asia and other trouble spots has awakened much interest in the West as nuclear deterrence and the risks of conventional warfare have closed the more familiar avenues for the exercise of military power. The principles of small-group action, irregular formations, hit-and-run tactics, and a long-term war of attrition have become familiar to western military analysts.

Yet the current enthusiasm for paramilitary techniques should not blind military thinkers to the central fact that guerrilla warfare is not a technique of war at all but rather a technique of revolution. It is a political, and not at all a military, procedure. This means that it is not a form of strategy applicable under a great variety of conditions, but rather only in those special situations where the basic ingredients are present: a population alienated from its government and gripped by widespread disaffection, and a government that lacks both energy and efficiency in dealing both with the guerrilla threat and the socio-economic-political conditions that spawned the revolution itself. As such it is of limited relevance to those states, including most of the leaders of the western bloc, whose interest lies less in overturning governments and promoting revolution than in stabilizing and harmonizing relationships. Counter-guerrilla activity—strategically a doctrine of defense rather than attack—has an unquestionable military dimension, but just as the guerrilla problem has its roots in social unrest, so campaigns against guerrillas must be based initially on social reform and use military operations only as a fringe effort rather than as their ideological and operational center.

The Arms Race and Disarmament

With the logic of military action so subject to question under contemporary conditions, it is not surprising that all states have been raising the basic issues of how to secure some release from the grim pressure of potential destruction. Two interacting political trends

* Samuel B. Griffith, *Mao Tse-tung on Guerrilla Warfare* (New York: Frederick A. Praeger, 1961).

have accompanied the doctrinal and conceptual discussion of military matters since the dawn of the nuclear era: on the one hand, the major military powers have embarked on a massive arms race conducted primarily in the categories of new weapons and delivery systems. At the same time, significant efforts have been made to discover workable formulas for arms reduction, arms control, and —at least in principle—eventual total and complete disarmament.

Each of these disparate enterprises is really an almost instinctive attempt on the part of governments to develop a larger margin of relative security in a world grown more dangerous. In these terms both are understandable and merit sympathetic analysis. Yet in a peculiar way, each tends to cancel out the other and leave the system on balance much as it would have been in any case. Neither the arms race nor disarmament has made the world any more secure.

THE ARMS RACE

The arms race between the communist world and the western bloc has been in full swing for more than a decade. It is essentially a technical rather than a military contest. The advances each side seeks are in quality rather than in quantity of weapons. The major categories of effort have been the increase in explosive "yield" of large nuclear bombs, the miniaturization of nuclear warheads for tactical purposes, the improvement in delivery systems—primarily in longer-range but more accurate missiles, and the development of detection and anti-missile systems.

The most obvious dimension of the arms race has been the series of subterranean, surface, and atmospheric tests that all nuclear powers have undertaken in order to prove the effectiveness of their new weapons. As weapons have grown larger and yields have increased, the psychological and physiological harvest of resentment from all non-nuclear powers and well-organized groups of private citizens has grown. Between 1958 and 1961 the United States and the Soviet Union maintained an informal moratorium on nuclear testing that remained unbroken even when France began to test in the Sahara Desert. Late in 1961 the U.S.S.R. abruptly resumed testing and the United States shortly followed suit. The arms race was again out in the open.

THE LOGIC OF THE ARMS RACE

The rationale of the arms race was and is devastatingly simple. Although military theorists generally question whether either side can ever gain a meaningful advantage over the other as long as both are actively developing their respective armories, neither side dares to relax its own effort lest the other succeed in achieving a technological and military breakthrough. Therefore, each steps up its own pace in the (admittedly vain) hope of outstripping the other. Each new move brings its inevitable riposte that in turn triggers a new move, and so on.

Ample military and scientific arguments exist to justify an indefinite prolongation of the race. There remains much that the experts can accomplish in the improvement of old weapons and the development of newer and more sophisticated devices. In this sense the arms race is actually a productive enterprise. It must not be overlooked either that every new move that makes weapons more effective and war more horrible also augments the deterrent effect of military power. A persuasive case can be made that the arms race is actually a force for peace in that it progressively narrows the range of military action states actually enjoy.

Yet there would seem to be a point of vanishing—more than diminishing—returns. When each side has developed a truly finite deterrent (when each side possesses the capacity to utterly destroy the other regardless of what else may happen) then any further refinement becomes merely supererogation and "conspicuous consumption." At this point the stakes become no more than a specious and meretricious factor of prestige with faint possibility of achieving any meaningful psychological advantage over the other contestant. One need not be a philosopher or a convinced humanitarian to wonder if the rewards that seem to justify the effort of continuing the arms race are negligible.

THE FAILURE OF DISARMAMENT

A dismal page in the history of international politics since 1945 has been the utter failure of any attempts at an agreement on arms reduction or arms control. No point would be served by following the tortuous course of all the abortive projects; different only in detail, they have all shared the same fate. Plans have been advanced for the elimination of nuclear weapons, the reduction of conventional armaments, the cessation of nuclear testing, and for various inspection schemes to reduce the probability of cheating or surprise attack. All have quickly come to inglorious ends and the arms race has been accepted by the major powers as an acceptable substitute for arms control.

Yet both East and West have explicitly embraced the principle that general and complete disarmament except for internal security forces is the goal for which all must strive. The difficulties that have made progress impossible have not been on matters of principle but on the nature and the sequence of the steps to be taken to achieve the eventual end. Each side has had an initial *sine qua non* on which it has insisted adamantly in full knowledge that the other would reject it: the U.S.S.R. had demanded the achievement of nuclear parity and the abolition of nuclear weapons by treaty before it would consider any implementing steps, while the United States has demanded full acceptance of a "control and inspection" system as a prerequisite to any consideration of the substance of disarmament. No negotiation has been able to pass over this initial hurdle and all have broken off in mutual recriminations. The Soviets claim American concern with inspection is a cloak for espionage, while the United States finds the Soviet attempt to negotiate a commitment not to use nuclear weapons in war a sinister plot to undermine American security.

THE ROLE OF POLITICAL DECISION

The root of the difficulty lies of course in the political preconceptions each side has brought to the analysis of issues of arms control. So long as both camps feel their security is better served by a continuing arms race, disarmament is a will-of-the-wisp. So long as both prefer the great but familiar risks of open conflict to the unknown dangers of living under military wraps in an untried and possibly entrapping control system, there is not enough appeal in the new to justify an abandonment of the old. So long as the Cold War retains its active growing edge, arms reduction (that would inevitably tend to stabilize relations) is of limited political relevance.

Disarmament, like the arms race, is a question much more political than military and technical. The arms race is not a cause of the tension between East and West, nor would arms control itself ease conditions. The Cold War is a political exercise, and its mitigation would demand new political judgments as well. If and when Moscow and Washington conclude that the probability has decreased of their being obliged to use military establishments in their own defense, then and only then will a climate conducive to realistic disarmament discussions be present. Only future history can state with certainty whether the tensions of the age will permit such a reassessment of the political situation. No one now alive knows if mankind has enough time to devise an escape from the military dilemma in which he has placed himself.

Bibliography

* Aron, Raymond, *On War*. New York: Doubleday and Company, Anchor Books, 1959.

Brodie, Bernard, *Strategy in the Missile Age*. Princeton: Princeton University Press, 1959.

* Garthoff, Raymond L., *Soviet Strategy in the Nuclear Age*. New York: Frederick A. Praeger, 1962.

Kahn, Herman, *On Thermonuclear War*. Princeton: Princeton University Press, 1960.

* Kissinger, Henry A., *Necessity for Choice*. New York: Doubleday and Company, Anchor Books, 1961.

* ———, *Nuclear Weapons and Foreign Policy*. New York: Doubleday and Company, Anchor Books, 1958.

* Lefever, Ernest (ed.), *Arms and Arms Control*. New York: Frederick A. Praeger, 1961.

* McClelland, Charles A., *Nuclear Weapons, Missiles and Future War: Problem for the Sixties*. San Francisco: Howard Chandler Publishing Company, 1960.

* Morgenstern, Oskar, *Question of National Defense*. New York: Random House, Vintage, 1959.

* Neff, John C. and W. F. Hahn (eds.), *American Strategy for the Nuclear Age*. New York: Doubleday and Company, Anchor Books, 1960.

Preston, Richard A. *et al.*, *Men in Arms: A History of Warfare and Its Inter-relationships with Western Society*. New York: Frederick A. Praeger, 1962.

* Schelling, Thomas and Morton H. Halperin, *Strategy and Arms Control*. New York: Twentieth Century Fund, 1961.

* Turner, G. B. and R. D. Challener (eds.), *National Security in the Nuclear Age*. New York: Frederick A. Praeger, 1960.

Waltz, Kenneth N., *Man, the State and War*. New York: Columbia University Press, 1959.

Wright, Quincy, *Study of War* (2 volumes). Chicago: Chicago University Press, 1942.

* Indicates paperback edition.

Ten

Ideology
and Prestige

One of the distinguishing features of contemporary world
politics that makes it different from the "classic" pattern of an
earlier era is the central role of mass beliefs and popular ideas to
the affairs of states. The once-exclusive control of foreign policy
exercised by highly skilled elites has been sharply diluted and on
occasion superseded by mass movements of vast size and irresistible
force. Careful strategic calculations are subordinated to simplistic
black-and-white formulations of international reality, the irrele-
vancy of which in no way mitigates the militancy with which they
are defended. Mass man is in the middle of the political process and
his ways of thinking have become an integral part of the international system.

We need do no more than glance at the history of the twentieth
century to find dramatic confirmation of the significance of popular
ideas and movements. Fascism in Germany and Italy led swiftly to
a devastating and ferocious global war, communism has spread from
its base in Russia to become one of the major forces of the age,
democracy has opened new and exciting vistas of individual worth
and free societies to much of the human race, and anticolonialism
has transformed the political map of the world and drastically modified the conditions of international politics. The process of international politics has been constrained to adapt to the "revolt of the
masses" and to the new circumstances this great phenomenon has
created.

Ideology and World Politics

The twentieth century is an ideological era. In a manner unknown to history since the great shocks of the Renaissance, the Reformation, and the Industrial Revolution washed away the underpinnings of the unified society of the Middle Ages, men have turned to all-encompassing belief systems to furnish a guide to confusing reality. In contrast to the rational man who was the ideal of the eighteenth century, and the optimistic man that characterized the nineteenth, the present century has at its center the "true believer." Individuals, adrift in a universe that grows daily more frightening and yet more difficult to comprehend and cope with, increasingly find in systematic, and comprehensive systems of belief the relief and comfort they seek.

This tendency, running through the entire fabric of social life, is sharply reinforced when questions of international relations are involved. On one hand, the world has grown uncomfortably smaller and national groups everywhere have been wrenched unceremoniously from a cultural isolation that in some cases had endured for centuries. On the other hand, however, the great increase in the number of international problems demanding solution has been accompanied by a marked decrease in the probability of their solution. Thus faced with an agonizing dilemma of impossible choices, entire societies have fled from the reality of coexistence (in its noncommunist and literal sense) to the fantasy of ideological formulations of world mission. Consciously leaving the world of rationality behind by taking refuge in an ideological Utopia, states have given the conduct of international political relations a measure of tension, of danger, and of potential explosiveness that has no parallel in history.

THE NATURE OF IDEOLOGY

An ideology may be simply defined as a self-contained and self-justifying belief system that incorporates an over-all world-view and provides a basis for explaining all of reality. It begins with certain postulates about the nature of man and his place in the world, and develops from this a theory of human history, a moral code, a sense of mission, and a program for action. Ideologies all purport to embody absolute truth, reinforced with certain supernatural (or superhuman) justification. Thus, adherence to the system is both a rational and a moral act, and disagreement is not only error but sin.

Ideologies are of course not new in international politics. Every system of government and every national group has found it expedient from time to time to ground its international conduct on what it conceived to be eternal verities. But the mass movement, defined here as an ideology with implications of social action that gathers sufficient adherents to become a real force, is a political phenomenon of the contemporary era. Ideological formulations of international issues color the bulk of the confrontations of states today.

An ideological approach to world political problems displays certain marked characteristics. (1) Ideology leads inescapably to the formulation of problems in moral terms. An international dispute thus becomes a clash between good and evil with the stakes never less than absolute vindication or total defeat. (2) Ideological controversy (which is inevitable in any contact between states embodying total belief systems) is not susceptible to compromise or accommodation, but goes on to climax in victory or defeat. No ideology permits bargaining with evil. (3) Ideologically-oriented policy can never "succeed" in the sense that strategic calculations can be crowned with success. States cannot kill ideas, only people; wiping out a population in no way destroys their unpopular beliefs.

TOTALITARIANISM AND LIBERALISM

Modern international politics has been largely dominated by the interplay of two opposing systems of belief, liberalism and totalitarianism. Liberalism in the twentieth century has been expounded primarily in the doctrines of democratic capitalism and of either Utopian or evolutionary socialism. The recent forms of totalitarianism include Marxism-Leninism in all its subtle deviant forms, fascism as exemplified in the interwar period by the regimes of Nazi Germany and Fascist Italy, and the non-systematic indigenous authoritarianisms found today in certain states of Latin America, Asia, Africa, and the Middle East.

The ideological conflict between liberalism and totalitarianism is the international-affairs dimension of the old political quandary concerning the respective claims of liberty and authority in the body politic. As it finds expression in contemporary international political discourse, this confrontation generates conflicting views on the nature of man, the form of society, and the functions of socio-political institutions.

In liberalism, the individual is of supreme value. The ultimate objectives of democratic capitalism and utopian or evolutionary socialism are the development of the talents and capacities of the individual to the utmost, the maximum satisfaction of the individual's needs and aspirations, and the realization of personal fulfillment. There is no order of preference among individuals; the equality of men is assumed as the beginning point for action. The individual, through the institution of government, is guided and aided in pursuing and determining his own destiny within the framework of "the greatest good of the greatest number." The actions of the individual are directed as little as possible by the state. Free competition is encouraged among individuals to insure them development to the limits of their capacity. Utopian or evolutionary socialism, believing in at least a minimum living standard for individuals and somewhat more equality in the realm of economics, calls for the exercise of greater control over individuals than does democratic capitalism. It is felt that this is for the protection of the individual rather than solely for the state.

In totalitarianism, all life is regulated by the state. Fascism assumes that the nation-state, the racial society, or the people (in German, "volk") is supreme. Unlike liberalism, which appraises the nation-state in terms of its utility in promoting the welfare of the individual, fascism appraises the individual in terms of his utility to the group. The state or the society comes first; the individual is secondary and subordinate, deriving his "rights" from service to the nation or racial society. The collective entity is endowed with a life of its own distinct from the rights of individuals who compose it, becoming a corporate body or a living organism by itself. Such a formula obviously demands irrational and mystical justification rather than dispassionate argument.

Fascism has not developed a consistent or uniform philosophy, but rather fragments of ideas inconsistent, vague, and contradictory.

It is essentially irrational and has a low opinion of the common man; it assumes that human nature is sullen, ignorant, and swayed by emotion. It is an ideology which sustains an economic, social, and political elite at the expense of the masses. It is authoritarian in politics and economics, although forms of private ownership are permitted to exist under rigid control.

Fascism began to develop in Italy and Germany after 1919. In Germany, its origin could be traced to the worker's party founded in 1919; Adolf Hitler became its principal organizer and changed its name to the Nationalist Socialist German Workers' Party, quickly abbreviated to "Nazi." In 1923 it became an important political group, and in 1933 Hitler assumed the Chancellorship of Germany, initiating the formal beginning of German fascism. In Italy, fascism originated in 1919 during a conference of the *Fascia di Combattiments*, a group of socialists and ex-soldiers. By 1921, the fascists became stronger in Italy and Mussolini assumed leadership of the newly established National Fascist Party. In 1922, Mussolini became Prime Minister, and Italy entered upon its fascist period.

Communism is a system of social organization based upon common property and the equal distribution of income and wealth. It is not derived from any religious or ethical assumptions, but rather from Marxist (purportedly "scientific") interpretation of human experience. It regards the changing economic structure as the foundation of social life and the working class as the bearer of the new order which would emerge on a world-wide scale as the result of historical change.

The ideology of communism is a "scientific" form of revolutionary socialism. It rests on a definite determinist philosophy of history and asserts that socialism cannot be achieved by peaceful means but only by revolution. It asserts that the behavior of a community is determined by the way it obtains its living and by the kind of living it obtains. All history is dominated by economic class conflicts between freemen and slaves, lords and serfs, wage earners and capitalists. It further contends that there are five main stages in the development of class relations and productive systems in human history: primitive communism, slavery, feudalism, capitalism, and the higher level of communism.

Communism regards the state as an organ of class domination; government is the creation of an order that legalizes and perpetuates the domination of one or more classes by another. The state prescribes political conformism and social unanimity, and depersonalizes the individual by converting him into an anonymous member of an all-embracing personality. The word "communism" acquired its modern meaning when it was used as a synonym for "socialism" by Karl Marx and Frederich Engels in the famous *Communist Manifesto* published in 1848. After 1917, communism acquired the interpretation of Marxism made by Lenin; since then a number of conflicting interpretations have developed, including Stalinism, Titoism, Maoism, and others.

THE CONTRASTS BETWEEN DEMOCRACY AND COMMUNISM

In general perspective, communism and democracy differ from each other in underlying philosophies, their definitions of man, their conceptions of the state, their methods and tactics, and their perspectives of the future of society.

While to democracy, man is an end in himself, communism regards man as the product of social experience, a datum to be manipulated for his own good. Since society is the foundation of morality, individuals as members of society are moral beings. In communist terminology, therefore, individuality exists as a part of a collective whole rather than in isolation or in an abstract concept of oneness.

In communism, the state is always viewed as an instrument of the domination of one class over another. From the viewpoint of democracy the state is either conceived as a distinct mechanism voicing the needs of all classes and acting for the good of all concerned or is considered to be in some way the mouthpiece for "the voice of the people." Consequently, contemporary communism embodies the "dictatorship of the proletariat" in the form of a pyramid of councils (communes or soviets) of worker and peasant representatives. Democracy demands a government including all-inclusive representation modeled on the parliamentary or presidential systems.

Communism anticipates a final stage where the state will "wither away" and the principle "from each according to ability, to each according to his needs" will be realized. Democratic capitalism and Utopian socialism, however, restrain the function of the state to that of an organ for the management of common interests. In Marxism, two phases of socialism are predicted: a lower phase, in which production is socialized under proletarian dictatorship, and a higher phase that is no more than a stateless communistic society. Utopian socialism, on the other hand, conceives only of socialized production under a system of political democracy.

Leninism and its later modifications clearly involve a scheme for the destruction of the bourgeois state machinery and the establishment of the proletarian dictatorship. This goal cannot be realized except by violent revolution. Non-Marxist socialism, on the other hand, epitomized by the British Labour Party and the Social Democratic parties of Scandinavia, simply embodies piecemeal reforms, and rejects revolution. Forcible overthrow of a government is out of the question and legal and political methods are relied upon. Thus the distinction is often made that communism is revolutionary in concept while democratic socialism is evolutionary.

To a Communist, in international relations the only dynamic process is the struggle between the exploiting classes and the proletariat. In industrially advanced countries, the struggle may occasionally be obscured by the exploitation of colonies and semi-colonial countries, but the respite is only temporary. Imperialism, Communists allege, transfers the class struggle to the international scene. The very effort to escape the contradictions of the capitalist economy at home sharpens international tensions and leads inevitably to an unending cycle of conflicts and wars among the imperialist powers. All international political life is thus only a reflection of a struggle induced by economic and social changes. Statesmen are powerless to alter this fact; they can only guide it or utilize it for the ends of the dominant class. Communism thus views the network of the relations between the communist and non-communist world as an equilibrium of forces in flux in which the task of the communist leadership is to tilt the scale by constant if imperceptible pressure in the direction predetermined by the forces of history.

Since the logic of nuclear technology has imposed its domination over the political orientation of states and the rejection of the war as a political means, a new vista has been opened in the relationship of the two ideologies. According to the present conception of the Soviet leaders, "the policy of peaceful coexistence is the highest form of class struggle" because it is a "struggle for the peoples themselves to see which system ensures the more rapid development of productive forces and displays the most care for man." In essence, contemporary democratic thought finds little to contradict in this idea.

Generally speaking, western thinkers argue that communism has overestimated the role of the means of production in the determination of the political destiny of man. Communism, in fact, has made man subject to the logic of modified material phenomena (the means of production). This argument is open to several rebuttals. First, there is a continual interaction between the human being and his material environment. In fact, what we call "the means of production" is not merely a set of modified material phenomena, but is also a set of intellectual operations translated into material form. Although Marx correctly indicated the underlying role of the means of production in human life, he missed a number of other important points in his further analysis.

First, Marxism claimed that it could predict the general course of history with certainty, at least in the long run. This claim is scientifically untenable because of the many variables involved. It is possible to some extent to predict what will happen if a number of conditions are fulfilled and to state in advance that predicted development. It is unrealistic, however, to ignore the possibility that conditions may develop differently and that human responses may take a different course.

Second, Marxism projected experiences of the past into the future on the scientifically untenable assumption that what happened in the past will always and necessarily happen essentially the same way in the future. This typically determinist technique fails to take account of such variables as the unpredictable potentialities of human ingenuity, determination, and organization.

Third, in denouncing the value judgments of their contemporaries and earlier generations, Marx and Engels freely expressed value judgments of their own, both negative and positive. Most obvious is their polemic emphasis that the prevailing ideals of justice and morals in each era depend on economic factors, on methods of production, and on class interests.

Fourth, in the process of interaction between man and his industrial environment, Marx made man subject to the logic of industry and incapable of avoiding its catastrophes. But, as mentioned before, industrial technology is of human origin and under human control. In a sense, what determines man's orientation to life is his own intellect as exemplified by a set of machinery, legal orders, or moral principles.

IDEOLOGY AND FOREIGN POLICY

Ideologies have historically served to fill the needs of men, usually attempting to bridge the gap between the prevailing limits of reason and the psychological needs of man within a society. Although often originally modest, they tend to grow more all-encompassing and soon claim for themselves universal Truth. Ideologies also show a propensity to become outmoded, going through the stages of being Messianic, corrupt, misused, and eventually—as circumstances change —meaningless. They often lead to the generation of their antithesis. Ideological conflict, if disaster is to be avoided, requires that militancy be replaced by toleration and animus by mutual respect.

The role of ideology in international politics or, more specifically, the degree to which ideology affects the formulation of a state's foreign policy and the resulting implications for international politics have become increasingly important questions. This issue has become especially magnified by the challenge of the communist bloc to the western world. One important question here is whether the Soviet bloc adheres strictly to a foreign policy which is formulated according to dogmatic ideologic tenets or whether it follows the traditional method of realistic appraisal of concrete situations within the context of their individual national interests and the relevant information available concerning that situation.

Another question involves the overlap of theory and reality; that is, are not both ideology and realistic appraisal present, although in varying degrees, in the formulation of foreign policy? These two elements are present in the foreign policy of almost all states; the significant difference is only one of degree. Thus every state is equipped with a priority system for the determination of foreign policy goals and tactics. That is, there are certain levels of action for every state in which either ideology or realism plays the predominant role, and certainly one between these two extremes in which the two ways of analysis achieve some sort of balance. There is, however, no fixed relationship that can be postulated; rather, there is a spectrum of foreign policies in which ideology and realistic appraisal meet in each distinct situation with different degrees of emphasis. In this parameter, ideology plays the least role in the most restricted choice situations, and on the other hand becomes increasingly effective where there is greater freedom of choice of alternative action possibilities. In attempting to discover which tendency—ideology or realistic appraisal—operates more strongly, it must be remembered that a state can remain consistent with its ideological tenets although its actions may appear strikingly at variance with its stated purposes.

What evidence, then, is there for continuity of purpose; how may we determine to what extent ideology conditions foreign policy decisions? One must presume a state's intent by the content of a whole series of actions. We must allow for a possible total discrepancy between what is said and what is done. We cannot draw accurate conclusions even from a whole series of statements. Verbal consistency does not necessarily imply consistency in action. There must be a connection, however, between ideology and action. The nature of the state dictates that its actions should be designed to implement its real purposes, but not necessarily a verbalized ideology. One cannot completely discount the possible relevance of verbalizations, but their importance is only a function of their congruence with action.

The conflict, therefore, is really between the systematic world view imposed by an ideological approach to action and the uneven, incomplete, and paradoxical fashion in which the real world impinges upon a state. Ideology and national interest are alike in that both have their roots in a system of values. They differ, however, in their compulsions to action. Ideological formulations make generous use of concepts of inevitability or impossibility and lead to one-dimensional foreign-policy thinking. A pragmatic national interest, on the contrary, is fixed only in its (possibly Utopian) view of the future, and is infinitely flexible in the intermediate goals and objectives it generates and in the tactics its advocates adopt for their achievement.

Ideology may, of course, become the source for postulations of national interest and long-range goals. If these aspirations are deeply rooted in the social dynamic of a people and if the government espousing them is adept at tactics, a successful foreign policy is possible. But if ideology intrudes into situational analysis and if the range of state action is cast in terms of imperatives of belief, statecraft in the classic sense is left helpless.

Communism and Democracy: The War for the Minds of Men

Europe has lost its place as the key arena of world politics. The entire world is now involved in a massive struggle between democracy and communism with the capture of men's minds as the prize. This conflict has become crucial because these great ideologies have become allied with the two most powerful states in the world, the United States and the Soviet Union respectively. The interaction of communism and democracy has been the key phenomenon of world politics since 1945.

Both ideologies are attempting to recruit supporters everywhere, using any method short of total war. They both offer the states of Africa, Latin America, and Asia a road to Utopia; each presents itself as the true "wave of the future." As the "revolution of rising expectations" continues to evolve, every state is influenced in one way or another, leaning in the direction of whichever they think will help them most to attain the life they desire. Thus the major antagonists seek ideological vindication by extensive use of propaganda and economic measures—both especially appropriate weapons for this type of conflict. The war for the minds of men has thus made international politics more ruthless and more conducive to stalemate.

THE CONSEQUENCES OF IDEOLOGICAL CONFRONTATION

In the era of their great struggle, both communism and democracy have undergone significant modifications. Both have largely abandoned their original intentions of destroying the other. Communism's failure to bring about the proletarian revolution in the advanced industrial states has seriously undermined the rigidities of Marxism and opened the door to major revision. The capitalist West was unsuccessful in its attempts to destroy the Bolshevik edifice immediately after 1917, and ever since has tacitly accepted the existence and the dynamic of communism. Democracy and communism have both lost almost all their original sense of expectation.

The world has seen the institutionalized versions of the two beliefs begin curiously to learn from each other. Internally, capitalist states have adopted various measures of social reforms through control, regulation, and supervision of private activity. Externally, they have actively cooperated in the dismantling of their colonial empires, at least partially to prevent communist intrusion. This trend of reformism in democracy has brought about a reciprocal moderation in communism, particularly since Stalin's death in 1953. Communism and democracy are no longer in the bondage of their earlier orthodoxy.

The West has long since ceased to live and act in accordance with the pure tenets of liberalism (if indeed it ever did). The East no longer struggles with the orthodoxies of the pure principles of Marxism (if, in its turn, it ever did). The invalidation of the goal of ideological victory by destruction, brought about by the engineering revolution, has led to a form of competitive coexistence between the two antagonistic systems. Each system is advocating its values to the underdeveloped states as the sole panacea for their development. On the other hand, each is hoping to surpass the other in technological advancement.

THE PROCESSES OF COMPETITIVE COEXISTENCE

In the course of competitive coexistence, communism holds a number of advantages over democracy in its appeal to the emerging states. The communist advocacy of liberation and economic development by revolutionary means is often in complete harmony with the anticolonial feeling which characterizes the outlook of the new states. Communist doctrine promotes anticolonialism and anticonservatism as great strides toward the achievement of true liberation. In the very intricate situation of nuclear stalemate when total war has become inconceivable, revolution has become the safest and most rapid instrument of change. Short of total annihilation and a technological breakthrough in warfare, the present ideological struggle may well be "won" by whichever camp better understands the stakes involved in revolution.

The logic of revolutions throughout history makes clear that the first cause of any revolution has always been a mystical concept of freedom. It is difficult for the West to recognize this because it owes its present organizational concepts to the nineteenth century social and economic conditions that are very unlike those of the new states. The West's revolutionary past is far behind it. Democracy proffers the emerging states evolution rather than revolution as the appropriate vehicle of change and development. The West believes that attempts to abolish poverty and solve social questions by sudden revolution are doomed to failure; the outcome is not Utopia but terror, which always spells the end of reform. Western thought asserts that no revolution ever succeeded in the establishment of a "good" government, except the American experience which was unique in that it took place under conditions of relative prosperity rather than those of mass poverty.

While it is true that the pure ideological appeal of communism in some non-western countries seems to have abated, its political approach remains attractive. It provides deracinated intellectuals with a belief into which they can release their ambitions, distresses, ideals, envy, and need for a world view. It furnishes a technique of struggle to nationalist movements, which in their own right have little more to offer than a grievance and a mystique. It capitalizes on the deep hostility toward the white man. Communism, finally, adopts the posture of victory and seems to offer a quick way to development, political maturity, and fulfillment.

The United States and its pluralistic philosophy and social system fails to bring to the backward nations of the world a simple message of salvation supported first by a dedicated and disciplined revolutionary minority and then by totalitarian control. Communism, besides its facility for exploiting a revolutionary situation, is useful in directing a revolution into desired channels through its hold on a disciplined minority of the population. The United States, even should it agree that revolution in a society is inevitable and thereupon cease its opposition, still tends to view the revolution with misgivings since a revolution out of control is at least potentially dangerous.

The communist states have still another advantage over the western powers in that their problems and achievements are more meaningful to non-western peoples than those of the West. The

Soviet Union has achieved, and Communist China is claiming, what the underdeveloped states all seek: a drastic increase in the standard of living through rapid industrialization. The communist states use totalitarian control as their instrument and communist doctrine as their rationalization and justification. Seeking the same results, the underdeveloped states are attracted by the methods which brought these accomplishments about in the communist world. In contrast, the West epitomizes a slow process, stretching over several centuries, by which it achieved a high standard of living and political democracy. The western process also requires a degree of moral restraint and economic and political sophistication which are largely absent in the methods of totalitarianism and are generally lacking as well in the emerging states.

A further disadvantage suffered by the United States is the conservative posture it assumes both internationally and domestically. Abroad, the nation is identified with the preservation of the territorial status quo; its national values are generally clustered about the protection of an already-mature system. In consequence, the United States tends instinctively to support abroad the most conservative elements in any situation because they appear to be the "safest" in terms of the preservation of the status quo. This has often proven to be a costly miscalculation, for in many of the underdeveloped nations the choice is not between the status quo and change, but rather between change under communist auspices and change which at the very least is not directly by communists.

Change in an underdeveloped society can come about either through peaceful reform or through violent revolution. Peaceful change requires the cooperation of the ruling groups, which has only rarely been forthcoming. Social and economic change cannot help but threaten the foundations of their own power. If these groups do not cooperate or—as they often do—actively oppose change, the only alternative to extremist revolution is the cultivation of alternative groups by the United States. When they do not exist, it must develop them. This is perhaps the crucial test for the ideology of western man. If the traditions of individualism and freedom can adapt themselves to the fact of revolutionary change in much of the world, the continued vitality and survival of democracy is assured. If, however, the West becomes merely anti-revolutionary, then the political future will pass out of democratic hands and into the grasp of those who do comprehend the meaning of change. This is, for the West, the real challenge of competitive co-existence.

Anticolonialism As an Ideology

Implicit in the definition of a nation-state is the presence of a set of common beliefs and values that holds the group together. Anticolonialism has become the basis for such a response in the emerging states.

Underdeveloped both economically and politically, and with social organizations inadequate to their needs, they are seeking to safeguard their independence. Unfortunately, they have achieved independence at a time when circumstances have rendered sovereignty and true independence of action an anachronism and no more than a stepping stone to interdependence.

Their lack of self-sufficiency has made it almost impossible for them really to enjoy their new status of self-responsibility. This compromises and embitters their genuine sense of achievement and frustrates their ambitions. Their legacy of many years of colonialism is provocative of resentment and mistrust of their former colonial masters. Each one of these states is seeking to develop a philosophy of change and a concept of national purpose. In concrete terms, the consequences of the cold war, the impact of Soviet exploitation, and the long-range effect of western ineptness are magnified out of proportion to their intrinsic importance in states passing through a decisive period of internal political transition. Anticolonialism is really an attempt of non-westerners to relax the pressures heightened by the East-West conflict, the response of the non-West to the American and Soviet crusades. It reflects both a deep sense of vindication and a strong urge to seize upon new opportunities.

THE NATURE OF ANTICOLONIALISM

Anticolonialism has roughly become synonomous with anti-westernism, non-western nationalism, and neutralism. It is presently employed by the new African and Asian states as a weapon against the western powers that are finding themselves morally and intellectually powerless in coping with it.

Anticolonialism is rooted in the demographic, religious, economic, and political developments of the modern non-western world. It is an ideological symptom of a reality which it disguises and symbolizes: the collision between the venerated values of non-western peoples, reinforced by centuries old traditional prescripts, and the realities and characteristics of the contemporary environment in which these parties are now required to operate. This clash is centered upon the choice of methods by which this coexistence of the traditional and the modern can be achieved. Anticolonialism is thus the outcome of the dilemma confronting non-westerners in seeking to coexist with themselves while adjusting to their new political milieu.

While it is true that encounters between civilizations have occurred in the past, such confrontations prior to the advent of the technical revolution involved states that were very much alike, differentiated mainly by relative degrees of military superiority and inferiority. The contemporary relationship between East and West is one between civilizations very dissimilar in their degree of development. Many changes have occurred in the West that do not have parallels in the East.

Philosophically, the development of Christianity led the western states away from one of the abiding elements in oriental religions, the quality of other-worldliness. The trend in Christian thought, emphasized by the Reformation and the Industrial Revolution, led to the acceptance of the belief that the world is a testing ground for those who wish to enter the kingdom of heaven, in place of the traditional notion that the world is an illusion bound to an unbreakable wheel of destiny. New ideas were advanced that the world is a creative arena in which men could prove themselves worthy of heaven by improving their lot on earth. Heaven no longer was man's only destination. The concept of progress on earth became the gospel of the West. These ideas have led to the distinctive liberal concepts of political organization that have since characterized the western approach to the individual human being, giving maximum practical application to such concepts as human dignity, individual responsibility, and personal freedom.

The meeting of East and West today is a clash of dissimilar cultures, the West largely content with its accomplishments and its institutions and the non-West anxious, resentful, and ambitious. The world into which the new states are emerging is one largely of western creation and one in which non-western peoples cannot feel fully at home. For more than two hundred years the states of European-centered culture have been impinging on the rest of the world, powerful and self-confident in the face of non-western weakness and self-doubt. The over-all impact of the West upon the world has been many-sided, but one basic consequence was the cultural disintegration of the indigenous non-western societies. What was uniquely Asian, Arabian, or African lost its vitality, to be replaced by a mixture of ersatz westernism and deep apathy.

Today a rebirth of self-awareness has occurred everywhere in the non-western world. Unable to escape their past, these peoples remain insecure and sensitive as they confront their erstwhile masters. Non-western political development is grounded on opposition to the West with a consequent shortage of positive values. The new states are yet so preoccupied with escaping from the past that they scarcely have time seriously to contemplate the future.

The difficulties the non-western states face in their task of self-analysis, self-discovery, and policy determination cannot be over-estimated. Modern non-western self assessment is searching urgently for clarity of insight, and the road is hard and long. The majority of the non-western states are underdeveloped. Their economic performance is poor, characterized by low standards of living, over-population, and a great disparity between aspirations and capabilities.

The non-western states have in common a generous portion of misery and a sense of destiny to achieve greater purposes. The controlling mood of these states is both defensive and creative. The majority of their leaders are alienated intellectuals whose western education isolated them from the main currents of their societies. By their very existence these leaders are symptoms of cultural ferment and disintegration. The resultant psychological restiveness of the intelligentsia who can no longer tolerate non-western dependence on the West is an important factor in anticolonialism. Articulate leaders have become increasingly sensitive on this score, in the face of the uncomfortable fact that such dependence is almost inevitable. The best they can do is to adopt anticolonialism, really a gesture signifying how independent of the West they would like to be. In almost all the non-western states, political advancement has outrun cultural enlightenment and self-conscious responsibility has not caught up with emancipation.

THE FUNCTIONS OF ANTICOLONIALISM

Anticolonialism begins as an ideology of the elite in the newly emerging nations. Basically, it serves the economic, political, and social ends of both leaders and masses within the non-western states. It is a rallying point for individual recognition, and at the same time it functions practically by giving direction to people whose society, traditional as it was, is being disrupted by urbanization and the large scale intrusion of western culture. As in all acculturations, this is a time of individual confusion. An ideological response to such a situation is normal, serving as a base upon which the elite can formulate a position of national and international strength and power.

Thus anticolonialism has become a matter of expediency, both domestic and international. It is the symbol by which the masses in the emerging nations identify their lives. For demagogic purposes its emotional content equals that of "the Queen" or "democracy" in western states. Even though it is negative, its lack of substance will not be recognized until the people achieve some material gains. Here lies the paradox. The leaders desire to retain their power but clearly recognize the real interdependence of nations, especially their own. They fear exploitation by the industrialized states, and anticolonialism warns the West against being too insensitive to non-western interests.

Thus anticolonialism has a national as well as an international cash value to the new Asian and African states. Operationally, vigorous anti-western statements by non-western leaders increase the possibility of generous treatment by the Soviet bloc while not appreciably diminishing aid from the West. Anticolonialism will flourish as long as it can serve as a factor of national unity within the underdeveloped states and act as a shield against western economic penetration. As the non-western world develops a workable posture *vis-à-vis* the West, and as political and economic maturity replace revolution, charisma, and self-assertion, the militancy of this newest modern ideology may well recede.

The Prestige Race

In an era such as the present, marked by great modifications in the conditions of international political life and a drastic recalculation of the ponderables of state capability, considerations of prestige acquire special significance. States normally wish to be thought well of by others and to acquire high prestige. When the coercive component of state capability diminishes in its effect to achieve state purposes, however, the relative role of non-coercive influence cannot help but increase in importance and scope. This is the especial province of prestige.

In this chapter we have considered the ideological "war for the minds of men," and the point was clearly made in our discussion that ideological conflict is no longer a struggle for the achievement of absolute Truth, but rather a competition for results with the prize going to the system that best approximates in reality the utopia promised in its preachments. Thus the two cold-war antagonists are actively engaged in merchandising their respective wares, hoping that the impression of competence and effectiveness they convey will produce meaningful political results.

WHAT IS PRESTIGE?

The initial problem involved here is the augmentation of prestige. The notion of "prestige" is itself of no specific content, and must be given meaning in more precise terms. To be "well thought of," a state must decide initially the characteristics with which it wishes to be favorably identified. It has a wide choice. It may elect to acquire prestige by military strength, by a reputation for astute diplomacy, by a high standard of living, by an advanced cultural and/or technological level, or by a conspicuous dedication to certain abstract principles, such as freedom or justice. It may indeed select several of these to make up what we might call a "prestige package." It then devotes itself to clarifying this image.

However, another difficulty arises. It is not enough for a state to decide the terms in which it wishes to be judged. It must also in some fashion persuade other states to apply the same standards. This is a far more complex task, involving the necessity of identifying the state's actions with the values of the judging state or states. A related problem arises from the differing ways in which high prestige may be demonstrated. If a state wishes to be thought prestigeful, does it wish to be respected, to be feared, to be admired, to be loved, to be emulated, or to be disliked? All are, given appropriate circumstances, equally valid ways of demonstrating high prestige; but which one a state chooses depends in large part upon the policy results it wishes.

THE RACE FOR PRESTIGE

The international scene today is one of a vast competition for prestige. The major powers are, as we have seen, involved on a global scale in a massive effort to put their best foot forward. The states of the non-West, seeking a clearer identity, are in the same fashion actively promoting whatever aspects of their own societies they feel might produce an accrual of greater respect. The older states of Europe, although increasingly preoccupied with their own problems and consequently less sensitive to the worldwide implications of political prestige, nevertheless are constantly alert to the social, psychological, economic, and cultural aspects of European prestige.

At least two troublesome aspects of the prestige race complicate the course of world politics. For many states, the prestige competition is a two-sided game in which one state may gain in prestige only to the extent that its adversaries are humbled. This approach, founded on the idea that the total amount of prestige is finite and that a larger slice for one state means a diminished portion for another, is particularly important in at least some formulations of the stakes of the Cold War. Many Americans, for example, are convinced not only that each American victory is also a defeat for the U.S.S.R., but also that a Soviet failure in some way augments America's world image completely apart from anything the United States might do.

The second complication of the prestige race is its very inconclusiveness. The relationship between high prestige and the capability of a state to accomplish its stipulated objectives has not yet been clarified; the real "influence" component of prestige is unclear. A suspicion remains that at bottom the search for international prestige by a state flows from internalized motivations and that a people obsessed with the need for greater world renown are seeking to assuage a sensed internal insecurity. If this condition does, in fact, exist, it makes the prestige race a self-defeating international enterprise. No rewards formulated in the classic framework of world politics can be derived from such a contest.

Bibliography

* Arendt, Hannah, *Origins of Totalitarianism*. Cleveland: The World Publishing Company, 1962.

* Brumberg, Abraham (ed.), *Communism After Stalin: An Anthology From Problems of Communism*. New York: Frederick A. Praeger, 1960.

Brzezinski, Z. K., *Ideology and Power in Soviet Politics*. New York: Frederick A. Praeger, 1962.

* Cohen, Carl, *Communism, Fascism, and Democracy*. New York: Random House, 1962.

* Daniels, E. V., *The Nature of Communism*. New York: Random House, 1961.

* Ebenstein, William, *Today's Isms: Communism, Fascism, Socialism, Capitalism*, Englewood Cliffs, New Jersey: Prentice-Hall, Inc., 1958.

* Friedrich, Carl J., and Zbigniew K. Brzezinski, *Totalitarian Dictatorship and Autocracy*. New York: Frederick A. Praeger, 1961.

* Fromm, Erich, *May Man Prevail?* New York: Doubleday and Company, Inc., 1961.

Hook, Sidney, *Marx and the Marxist*. Princeton: D. Van Nostrand Company, Inc., 1955.

* Jenkins, Thomas P., *Study of Political Theory*. New York: Random House, 1955.

* Meyer, Alfred, *Communism*. New York: Random House, 1962.

* Roosevelt, James (ed.), *Liberal Papers*. New York: Doubleday and Company, Inc., Anchor Books, 1962.

* Schapiro, J. Salwyn, *Liberalism*. Princeton: D. Van Nostrand Company, Inc., 1953.

Schumpeter, Joseph A., *Capitalism, Socialism and Democracy*, Third edition. New York: Harper and Brothers, 1950.

Whitaker, U., *Democracies and International Relations: Can Ours Survive?* San Francisco: Howard Chandler Publishing Company, 1961.

---

* Indicates paperback edition.

Eleven

Man and the
Forces of Nature

Men today live in a technological age. The assault of human intelligence upon the secrets of the natural world has, in the past half-dozen decades, yielded such spectacular discoveries that greater changes in the conditions of human existence have taken place during the twentieth century than in all previous recorded human history. Man is transforming the planet on which he lives and is beginning to make real progress toward his age-old goal of breaking free of earth and exploring the reaches of outer space.

Since we have already proved in dozens of instances that what we term international politics springs from deep-seated human motivations and takes its form at any specific moment from the circumstances of life in the real world that affect the participants, it should come as no surprise to us that the technological revolution of this century has had the same direct effect on the politics of states as it has had on every other feature of social interaction. We have, for example, already glanced at the tremendous impact that advanced technology has had on the theory and practice of warfare, and we have noted the extent to which long-standing postulates have been forced to undergo systematic reevaluation. This not unexpected development has been paralleled in almost every other dimension of international politics as well; the very organizing assumptions of state life have been called into question as a result of the new relation between man and the forces of nature.

In this chapter, we shall examine briefly five of the hundreds of technological developments and resulting conditions that are putting the state system under such strain. There is no implication that these few are either the most important or that they are unique in their effect. We shall note their general similarities in modifying and perhaps transforming international politics. The tentative conclusions we shall advance at the end of the chapter are almost certainly applicable, *mutatis mutandis*, to any other technological issues we might think of ourselves.

The five we have selected for brief analysis and evaluation are (1) nuclear energy; (2) the conquest of space; (3) the population explosion (a result of technology rather than a new factor in itself); (4) mass communications; (5) the new patterns in economic production, distribution, and consumption.

Nuclear Energy

Nuclear energy is most sharply silhouetted for most people against the ominous background of a mushroom-shaped cloud towering over the ghastly fireball of a hydrogen bomb explosion. The revolutionary aspect of this exploitation of the energy of the atomic nucleus is self-evident. Even if the military potential of nuclear energy is laid aside, there remains a fundamental disruptive force in the simple fact that this vast storehouse of power has been tapped by human ingenuity. If military factors do indeed cancel themselves out, it will be the so-called "peaceful" uses of nuclear energy that will be remembered by future generations as an architectonic factor in their lives.

THE ENERGY REVOLUTION

In the simplest terms, the "splitting of the atom" resulted in the discovery of a vast new and virtually inexhaustable source of energy. Without energy modern industrial civilization is impossible. The Industrial Revolution of historic fame was grounded upon the successful conversion of coal to the production of large amounts of energy in the form of heat. Prior to that time, energy came from natural or human sources in small amounts and with the great technical and economic waste of wind, water, and human energy. Coal as an energy source was much more efficient and made large-scale enterprise feasible. Since the dawn of the coal age, men have discovered other energy sources of wide utility, most importantly petroleum and hydroelectric power. It is on these three bases that modern industry has been built.

Developments in weaponry demonstrated that the potential energy locked in the atomic nucleus could be liberated. Consequently, the total amount of energy available for human use has increased to an astronomical extent. Fossil fuels are limited in amount, and reserves have been dwindling, but the raw material of nuclear reaction is great in supply. In the case of thermonuclear uses of the hydrogen atom, supplies are literally infinite. There is now adequate energy for everyone if it can be harnessed and put to work.

THE SECOND INDUSTRIAL REVOLUTION

This development is immediately relevant to the pattern of world relationships because it makes possible a "second industrial revolution." Those states that became industrial giants in the days of the coal-iron technology were those that had accidently been endowed with deposits of these raw materials, of which coal was the more important. On this base, great economic power and world political leadership was built. States without adequate energy sources were condemned to second or even lower rank.

Now, however, the amplitude of nuclear energy has gone far to equalize the conditions of competition as states race to capitalize on this new force. Nonindustrial states have the opportunity to skip the coal-oil stage entirely and to move directly into the most advanced technology. Already-industrialized states have an advantage, of course, due to their relatively large supply of scientists, technicians, and production specialists; but this is neither absolutely controlling nor permanent in its effect. Fissionable materials are relatively common and the total amount necessary for energy production is by no means huge. The new industrial revolution will result in a substantial reordering of the relative production ranks now held by states, and will also culminate in a much narrower spread between the top and the bottom than is now the case.

NUCLEAR ENERGY AND WORLD POLITICS

With reference to military uses, nuclear energy has been a factor of division and has intensified competition and tension in the relations of states. Each nuclear power has sought to confine its advances to itself and to monopolize all its rewards. And the attempt to develop nuclear energy for non-military purposes on an exclusively national basis has not been a success. The peaceful uses and implications of this new energy source have been exploited in a dramatically different way from its military applications. International cooperation in the peaceful uses of nuclear energy has been a natural development for a number of reasons.

First, the theoretical simplicity of the task has not been matched by an equivalent ease in its execution. The scientific and technological elaboration of what is already known and the steady forward movement of the frontier are extremely expensive operations. National competition in this area condemns each state to repeat each stage in the process, while cooperation enables all to build on the totality of everyone's findings.

Second, for most effective use, nuclear energy arrangements should be on a fairly large scale, larger than most smaller states can develop. Cooperation in the establishing of supranational research and development programs could obviously result in dividends beyond the capacity of individual states to muster.

A third factor is the attitude of the scientific community toward itself in almost all countries. Committed by professional ideology to freedom of knowledge and the exchange of ideas and findings in a common pursuit of gaining truth, scientists have formed a powerful pressure group urging governments into cooperative ventures.

Finally, public imagination has been captured throughout most of the world by the rosy possibilities of a future made lighter by ample energy supplies, and a not inconsiderable degree of public approbation greets each new step in its realization.

The two most conspicuous examples of international cooperation in the area of the exploitation of nuclear energy for peaceful purposes have been the International Atomic Energy Agency (IAEA), established in response to American initiatives as a specialized agency of the United Nations, and the European Atomic Community

(EURATOM), set up by the six states of the European Community. These two enterprises provide for the joint and cooperative exploitation of the possibilities of nuclear energy in peaceful ways. Up to the present their record of accomplishment is not extensive, but the nature of the task they face is one calling for a long period of preparatory work before a few visible results can be followed by an outburst of specific applications. Other cooperative efforts of less impressive scope are in the making as well.

Thus the impact of nuclear energy on world politics is clearly ambivalent. When put into military channels it threatens the world with devastation and destruction, whereas in its peaceful aspects, it promises enormous good. The sheer magnitude of the prospects either for good or ill suggests that whatever their ultimate impact, the forces locked in the atom's nucleus cannot be confined either within the national boundaries of a single state or even within the limitations of the traditional nation-state system. In one way or another the relevance of nuclear energy is a supranational one and whatever solutions are found to the problems and opportunities it presents must be on a supranational scale.

The Conquest of Space

The "nuclear age" dates from 1945, but the "age of space" has been a reality only since 1957 when—in the course of a massive multistate scientific effort under the auspices of the International Geophysical Year—the Soviet Union and the United States launched the first artificial space satellites. Since that time the attempt to gather more scientific information about the reaches of space and to launch vehicles and men deeper and deeper into the universe has become more and more concentrated. The Soviet Union in 1961, and the United States early in 1962, put human beings into orbit around the earth and brought them back safely. Plans for larger vehicles, longer flights, and eventual manned voyages to the moon and beyond were immediately announced. In view of the rapidity with which the penetration of space has been proceeding, very few nonspecialists are willing to minimize the probabilities that these and even more spectacular steps will be taken as scheduled. So accustomed have individuals become to rapid progress in space explora-

tion that very few pause to reflect how recently the entire enterprise began.

THE BREAKTHROUGH INTO SPACE

The birth of the age of space was made possible by close and intensive cooperation by many kinds of scientists and technologists
aided by generous appropriations of funds and materiel by governments on both sides of the Iron Curtain. Physicists, biologists, me-
teorologists, physiologists, chemists, metallurgists, and dozens of
other scientific specialists all made direct and indispensable contribu-
tions. In addition, every type of engineering and technical skill
played its direct part. Perhaps the two critical areas of technological
advance without which no breakthrough would have been possible
were the development and refinement of the science of rocketry
(especially in the development of booster thrust) and the sophistication of metal technology that led to alloys capable of withstand-
ing the strains of launching and the heat and friction of reentry
into the earth's atmosphere.

Spectacular landmarks in the breakthrough include the first satellite ("Sputnik"), launched by the U.S.S.R. in 1957; the successful
use of satellites as communication devices by the United States in
1960; the landing of a rocket on the surface of, and the successful
photography of, the "dark side" of the moon, accomplished by the
Soviet in 1960, the first manned orbital flight (also accomplished
by the Soviet) in 1961, and the "Telstar" communications satellite
and other orbital break throughs in 1962. In between these well-
advertised forward steps, a constant effort has been under way by
both sides to improve their techniques and their store of knowledge.

The extent to which men have already penetrated space, and the
sense of real accomplishment that is felt, should not obscure the
fact that compared to the enormity of the task men have set themselves, no more than the merest scratch has been made on the surface of space. "Space" is, of course, an infinite notion. Until now,
men have travelled little more than one hundred miles from the
earth's surface. Their deepest ranging probes have only gone a small
way into the solar system. Beyond lie galaxies and universes as yet
only dreamed of. Man dare not lose sight of his own puniness and
the awful immensity of the universe into which he is venturing.

Yet in the few short years in which space efforts have been going on, a remarkable technical and scientific harvest has already been gathered. The instruments for further action are either at hand or on the way to development; the extent of knowledge is adequate to support and justify a constant program of forward movement along this particular frontier. It is interesting that the two most active areas of scientific and technological progress today are those that focus upon the smaller unit of scientific inquiry—the atomic, nucleus—and the largest—the cosmos itself. In these two areas the most fundamental questions imaginable are being asked and extremely interesting and important answers are being received.

THE SPACE RACE

It has been an interesting commentary on the spirit of the times that the great breakthrough into space has been conceived of as a "race" between the Soviet Union and the United States. "Sputnik" was a great blow to American pride and self-esteem, the American public had somehow assumed that United States' primacy in the advance into space was inevitable and right. When the U.S.S.R. made the first triumph, a powerful reaction immediately set in. What had been a long-range program for gathering scientific data and leading only gradually to manned space flight, became transformed into a battleground of the Cold War. The U.S.S.R. obviously enjoyed the (perhaps unexpected) reputation for scientific and technological leadership it suddenly acquired, and accepted the American challenge. Since 1957, the exploration of space has been a competitive venture.

The Soviet Union has had—as our brief catalogue of major landmarks indicated—considerable success in maintaining its "lead" in spectacular breakthroughs. Their two greatest prestige-augmenting accomplishments were unquestionably their successful attempt to hit the moon and their trail blazing manned orbital flights. Most Americans are yet certain that the Soviet is "ahead" in the space race. Yet there is great evidence, freely discussed in scientific circles, that the American version of the "race" has not been quite the same as the Soviet's; that the United States has conducted a multidimensional program (including a spectacular unmanned probe of Venus in 1962) that has lagged behind the Soviet's in one or two areas, but has put the nation well ahead in over-all sophistication about space and its problems. Nor are indications lacking that the Soviet Union itself senses its relative deficiencies in these respects and is interested in changing some of the terms of the contest.

Soviet leadership is unquestioned in one important aspect: the "thrust" developed by the booster rockets necessary to put a vehicle into orbit or on its planned trajectory. From the first stages of the space race, Soviet vehicles have been consistently larger than the corresponding American ones, often by an embarrassingly large margin. Although American technologists have gone to amazing lengths in miniaturizing instrumentation so that a smaller payload could produce equivalent or greater results, the simple fact remained throughout the first half dozen years of the space race that the Soviet Union could boost heavier cargoes into space than could the United States. There was also a strong feeling that the Soviet was willing to skip more steps and take more risks in searching for breakthroughs than was the United States, and public pressure mounted for an American "crash program" to "catch up" after each Soviet success. The original design of the American program, however, remained intact although some areas have been accelerated.

American planners were confident that ultimately the course of the space race would reverse itself and that the United States would pull gradually far ahead. Their confidence was based upon the more substantial scientific foundation produced by the longer-term research orientation of the American effort, and also upon the new vehicles and propulsion systems under development. In 1961, for example, the United States embarked upon a massive effort to achieve a manned landing on the moon before the Soviet reached that goal, and prepared to commit several billions of dollars to the effort. Americans, it seemed, were unwilling to remain indefinitely in second place in the space race.

POLITICAL AND MILITARY CONSIDERATIONS

The stakes in the space race have been both political and military. The political aspects, clustering about the much-discussed but undefinable rewards in "prestige" that accrued to the state holding the lead, have been perhaps the more obvious. There is no doubt, for example, that Soviet successes have had a profound impact upon mass opinion in much of the underdeveloped non-western world and have gone far to destroy the myth of Russian technological backwardness. The frantic concern, impassioned and frightened self-analysis, and widespread dismay of segments of the American public in the face of Soviet advances has contributed as well to the possibility of a drastic revision of their respective world images.

Yet the political rewards that some pessimists in the West have been prepared to concede to the Soviet as a result of its leadership in the conquest of space have proved disconcertingly small. There has been some doubt whether "prestige" in space exploration is a politically negotiable commodity, and as well about the real extent to which Soviet success has damaged the United States (except perhaps in the eyes of Americans themselves). Moscow obviously has enjoyed Washington's discomfiture and has lost no opportunity to twit the United States, but apart from this almost routine behavior, the political consequences of the space race have turned out to be either minimal or as yet undiscovered.

The military significance of space achievements has been widely debated by both eastern and western observers. Soviet leadership in booster thrust was used for a time as evidence of a dangerous "missile gap" in Moscow's favor—although this argument was eventually abandoned by both Russians and Americans. Earlier, there was much talk about the possibilities of manned "space stations" for reconnaissance and possibly attack purposes, but their real military advantages were difficult to isolate. Military planners have sensed that somehow the breakthrough into space has military significance, but the level of scientific knowledge (and perhaps the imagination of military leadership as well) is not yet adequate to capitalize on these considerations. Both doctrine and technique are unable to explain the full military advantages of a command of outer space.

COOPERATION IN SPACE

A counter trend to the space race began to manifest itself during 1961 and 1962: a strong urge toward the cooperative exploration of space without political overtones, instead of the competitive orientation that had set the tempo for the first few years. Proposals for cooperation had been frequent during earlier stages, but the pressure for political and possibly military advantage had prevented their implementation. Proposals to declare space "out of bounds" to the Cold War and to share both the costs and the findings of further explorations were accepted in principle, but considerations of timing, prestige, or national security vitiated these incipient efforts.

The successful accomplishment of a manned orbital flight by the United States early in 1962, however, brought the race to its closest approximation of prestige parity since it began. In his message of congratulation, Premier Krushchev once again—this time in a relatively friendly manner—raised the possibility (originally an American proposal) of the two space leaders developing ways of extensive cooperation in the future penetration of space. American response was affirmative, and negotiations looking toward the formulation of areas and techniques of joint interaction were immediately initiated in a climate of relatively good will and free exchange.

The apparently sincere acceptance of cooperation in space by the two states that had previously been competing so grimly was both important in itself and profoundly suggestive. If actually institutionalized, it would mean that one dimension of an exciting but relatively unproductive dispute would be eliminated from the Cold War. Furthermore, cooperation in space would have its effect on the remaining areas of open conflict between the two; it would be difficult to maintain a complete "we-or-they" approach in political matters when both sides were at the same time working effectively in cooperation on so newsworthy and extensive an enterprise as space exploration.

Can we conclude that the proposals for joint space action signify a relaxation of cold-war tensions and the possible dawn of a new political era? Although the temptation is strong to do so—and although many optimistic observers have reached exactly that conclusion—it is too much to concede as long as the pressure for joint action comes more from the nature of the space enterprise itself than from any over-all reevaluation of the political scene by either state. Space simply must be explored cooperatively if the effort is to produce results at all commensurate with its costs.

Factors both positive and negative enter into this conclusion. Negatively, the political-military rewards to be gained by national efforts are—as we have suggested—difficult to formulate and to cash in. The possibility of either side gaining real dominance in space is

remote, but the dangers that would follow if this eventuality occurred are incalculable. Prudence argues strongly in favor of ruling
space out of the political struggle since the advantages are minimal
and the possible disadvantages great. Also prominent in the negative
side of the argument are factors of cost. An all-out space race would
be an enormously expensive enterprise even for the wealthy United
States. For the Soviet Union, it would raise serious questions of resource allocations and public expectations. Cooperation ineluctably
means a sharing of the many burdens of further expansion of effort
with a consequent saving to both nations.

Positively, many of the same opinions operative in the matter of
space are arguing for international effort in the development of
nuclear energy. There is only one science of space, not a Russian
science and not an American science. A Soviet discovery kept secret
for political reasons holds back American progress without aiding
the Soviet, while American findings retained in retaliation might well
spark a new advance by both. Science progresses in a leapfrog
fashion, each new discovery providing the basis for further development. The universe, it is argued, is a large enough arena to permit
genuine coexistence and productive effort by different social and
economic systems. This at least seems to be the concept presently
underlying the attempt of the United States and the Soviet Union
to develop a mutually satisfactory formula for such a program.

The Population Explosion

Science and technology, joining forces in the fields of public
health and preventive medicine, have brought to the world one of
its least manageable contemporary problems: the so-called population explosion. The number of human beings on earth today is by
far the largest in history. One significant study points out that one-
third of all the people born in the entire history of the human race
are alive today! In certain parts of the world, new lives are not the
blessing and the joy western peoples find them to be, but are in a
real sense an additional and crushing burden.

Only in the recent past have western political leaders become
alarmed by the steady acceleration of birth rates in many parts of

the world. Now that population has acquired a political dimension, it has become a matter of great and growing concern to many governments. Unfortunately, the degree of awareness of the problem has not been matched by any equivalent growth in facility for dealing with it.

CAUSES OF THE POPULATION EXPLOSION

The population of underindustrialized lands traditionally has stabilized at the maximum supportable by local food supplies and prerequisites of living. It has been kept in check by the so-called "Malthusian restraints": war, epidemic, famine, and disease. A predominantly youthful population, because of its short life span, a relatively low regard for the sanctity of human life, and very high birth and death rates were generally regarded as characteristic in most underdeveloped countries.

In the twentieth century, these lands began to benefit from public health measures, improved sanitation, and modern medicine. The results have been spectacular: death rates have dropped at a sensational rate, primarily in infant mortality and in epidemic diseases breeding in filth, while birth rates have rapidly increased. As more infants have survived to become parents in their turn, population figures have soared. As a result, population pressures have begun to force the hand of many governments.

We must understand that the problem of population has nothing absolute about it; there is no magic optimum figure for the human race or any part of it. Population pressure is a relative factor: a society suffers when any increase in its over-all population results in a reduction in the amount of goods and services available for any individual. When an increase in the number of mouths to feed means less food for each mouth, a population problem exists. In some states, the crisis is almost frightening: in Egypt and in India, for example, the annual increase in population is greater than that in productivity. This means that neither state can by its own efforts accumulate the surplus capital necessary to the industrial development that alone offers any hope of surcease from the maddening pressure of human biology. All states with serious population problems stand in dire need of external assistance if they are not to be drowned in a sea of undernourished bodies.

POLITICAL, SOCIAL, AND ECONOMIC EFFECTS

The consequences of the population explosion for the states directly affected are simple and devastating. No modern government (at least in the West) dares plan wholesale starvation as the preferred method of removing the incubus of excess population. All must therefore accept as their primary responsibility to keep their citizens alive. But this does not alleviate the situation, or even palliate it; birth rates remain high and each year the crisis becomes more intense. Beset by this ominous statistic, state plans for long-range development and social stabilization are repeatedly deferred in favor of frenzied annual attempts to ward off famine. Systematic and sensible social planning in such a climate is obviously impossible.

Within the society itself, the constant specter of starvation haunts everyone. For centuries this situation was accepted passively. Today, the "revolution of rising expectations" has set powerful ferments to work in once-quiescent societies. Unable or unwilling to face their own responsibility for their dilemma, mass populations now demand rapid improvement in the conditions of their life at the same time they contribute to the inability of their governments to bring such improvement about. The tenor of political discourse in these societies has grown more and more extreme as distress augments political self-consciousness. The governments, in their turn, have become less willing and able to withstand these pressures and measures more and more desperate gain steadily an attractiveness to their beleaguered policy-makers.

At this point, the problem enters among those of international politics. Governments under such pressure at home and with so little room for maneuver before their own peoples are neither forces for stability in world politics nor free to make long-term international commitments. A state containing an exploding population is incipiently revolutionary. The larger tragedy of this situation is that any such revolution is by its own terms destined to failure. Population pressure cannot be relieved by a change in government. Oversimplified but persuasive "explanations" of the problem, suggesting that the root of national difficulties lies in the machinations of malevolent enemies, may open the door to international adventures of a particularly dangerous type. Several of these have already occurred since World War II.

Thus the reproductive habits of individuals in the tropics are of direct and immediate relevance to stabilized and industrialized states of the western world. The factor of population pressure is a major contributing element in the militancy of the non-western revolution and must be faced by the more fortunate peoples as they devise a long-range response to this new challenge. The ultimate destiny of modern civilization may well rest on the success mankind has in seeing to it that all human beings are provided at least a minimally tolerable share of the world's resources.

AVENUES OF SOLUTION

It is probably presumptuous to discuss any "solution" to the problem of population; the most we can seriously consider are some possible lines of attack. Even so, we may be certain that no quick results can be expected and that the tensions population problems produce will form part of the context of international politics for a long time. But nevertheless, a combined internal and international approach does offer some promise of eventual relaxation of the grim and impersonal threat of over-population.

Internally, there is already some evidence that forthright and courageous leadership of an extensive program of education and preventive techniques can have an effect in reducing birth rates. In part this is a matter of the development of a simple and efficacious contraceptive, and much research and effort has already gone into this task. Religious and cultural barriers, however, will remain strong even after the requisite medical findings have been made widely available. Here the courage and determination of a government become crucial. The only way to develop a viable social structure may turn out to be a broadly-based campaign to modify traditional and strongly-held social customs. Only exceptionally strong leaders are likely to run such a risk.

Internationally, the population problem can be best attacked by development programs inspired by and financed by advanced states. If done on a sufficiently large scale and if digressive elements of competition and prestige-accrual are avoided, a hope exists that the vicious circle of an increase in population eating up each year's economic growth might be broken. Over the long term, only some such effort has any chance of real success; palliative techniques only defer the dread day of reckoning. This approach does not demand that every overpopulated state immediately undergo a hothouse-type industrialization, but that the economic structure be sufficiently rearranged so as to free the optimally productive portion of the population from the grim treadmill of subsistence agriculture. Specialization of some sort in a controlled economic system will make it possible for the necessary foodstuffs to be imported from more productive areas.

POPULATION PRESSURE AND THE SHAPE OF WORLD POLITICS

Some ecologists and biologists argue that the pressure of population is the most influential single factor in shaping the future of the human species. In political terms they contend that ideological and nationalistic drives are nothing when compared to the frantic search for subsistence by two-thirds of the world population. Unless this challenge is met head-on, they contend, a new wave of barbarianism will threaten to sweep the planet.

Regardless of how seriously these warnings may be taken, and after a mere cursory examination of population figures, the observer cannot escape the conclusion that the international political system must adjust to this stark phenomenon. Whether it leads to war and destruction or to a new cooperative climate for solving common problems, the rising tide of humanity is a political problem of the first order. We will hear much more of it in the years ahead.

Mass Communications

Mass communications devices and techniques are another in the long list of technological advances that have gone so far to revolutionize life in the twentieth century. It is now possible for one man to communicate simultaneously with all members of an audience numbered in the tens of millions. This capability to affect the emotions and increase the knowledge of vast numbers of people within a short time span has had a profound effect on all patterns of social life everywhere. Information, entertainment, intellectual stimulation, and political leadership are all part of the content of the mass media. Anything so powerful in its impact directly affects international politics as well.

MASS MEDIA IN WORLD POLITICS

The primary relevance of mass media to international politics we have already noted in our discussion of propaganda. The new techniques of conveying messages to an audience have led to great advances in propaganda effectiveness. We will recall that we identified four different audiences for national propaganda efforts: the state's own people, the people of its allies, the people of neutral or uninvolved states, and the people of its opponents. In reaching each of these audiences, the propagandist makes extensive use of the mass media.

At home, electronic media (radio and television) are used widely with applications varying according to the richness of the technical installations and the sophistication of the home audience. Printed and visual media—books, magazines, motion picture films, posters, and the like—also play a large role. When a foreign audience is being approached, the problem of access is much more complex; the audience is in no sense "captive" and must be approached more circumspectly. Radio is especially valuable, since home radio receivers are common everywhere and the technique of beaming short-wave broadcasts is so well developed. Television is useless without receiving sets, and these are few outside the western world. Printed media and the cinema obtain audiences inside foreign countries only by sufferance, and their effect depends upon the delicacy and deftness of their approach rather than upon the strength of the messages they convey.

Western manipulators of the mass media of communications tend consistently to aim at the largest possible audience, even if this demands a dilution of their message content. Communist mass communicators, however, tend to emphasize impact upon the individual listener more than pervasiveness of reception, and risk alienating many members of their audience in the interest of securing strong responses from a minority segment.

IMAGE-PROJECTION IN FOREIGN POLICY

Contemporary concern, especially in the West, with matters of prestige and status in international politics has led to a concern with the "image" a state "projects" in the course of carrying out its world role. Each self-conscious state tends to formulate the most desirable ego-image it can conceive and then seeks deliberately to project it and gain its wide acceptance abroad. These images vary widely according to the values each society prizes. One state may project strength, another culture, a third moral integrity, a fourth cunning and resourcefulness, and so on. The dissemination of the controlling image and its manipulation for the state's policy purposes is the major task to which mass media are put in foreign affairs.

Image-projection is a tricky business at best, even within an homeogenous society with a stable value code and with the resources of the communications industry to call on. In international affairs, the image that one state holds of another is only partially the result of the deliberate projection of such a picture by the government concerned. It tends also to be made up of historic impressions, random and uncontrollable events that come to symbolize the state, what we might call "unintentional propaganda," such as the behavior of tourists and government officials, motion pictures, and so on, and the image of that particular state that other governments for their own purposes choose to project. Here image-projection falls far short of its alleged goal.

National concern with image-projection has had a clear impact on the formulation and conduct of foreign policy. Once committed to an image, many states insist on adhering to its outline in performing the routine and special tasks of foreign policy. A state dedicated to an image of strength may overlook opportunities for successful compromise. A state conceiving itself as superior in culture may be caught in irrelevant posturing with no policy content. The dangers of "imagery" in foreign policy frequently overshadow whatever gain it may promise. Mass media do not make very effective instruments of foreign policy. An excessive reliance on these temptingly available devices may well produce many more difficulties than it solves old ones.

DESTRUCTIVE AND CONSTRUCTIVE APPLICATIONS

The methods of mass communication, like almost any technical skill, are themselves neutral and without policy significance. They may, in other words, be put to destructive and dangerous uses or they may serve constructive ends; the decision is a human one to be made by responsible policy-makers. Examples of both categories abound in the contemporary world.

Destructively (or, at least, potentially so), mass media are very appropriate for intensifying nationalist hatreds and the tension component of an international confrontation. By mass methods the people of one state may be worked into a condition of intensive hostility toward another people and great pressure may be generated. Adamant public positions on crisis issues can easily be developed; equally powerful drives for the adoption of new policies can be unleashed. Perhaps more significant than any of these is the role of mass media in filtering and interpreting the flow of information received by the audience. Whether acting on its own or as a self-conscious tool of the government, the mass-communications machine in any state is the means whereby masses of individual citizens acquire both factual data and authoritative interpretations of the problems their government faces. At any particular moment, the state of mass opinion in a modern society is to a major extent the work of the mass communicators in that society.

Constructively, mass communications media are potentially important to the construction of a supranational consensus. In today's rapidly-moving world, world opinion can focus on a particular issue in time to have an effect on its outcome only if the mass media perform their task of purveying the information widely and quickly enough. Technically, the task is relatively simple in view of the advanced state of the art today. The difficulty is due partly to the national identification of the communicators themselves and to the confusion of motivations and of evaluation that these same individual practitioners display. A cohesive international community, such as we shall examine in our final chapter, is conceivable only if individuals are tied into a single and responsive communications network. This is the great opportunity the technologists of message transmission have before them today.

Production, Consumption, Distribution

A final technological problem is constituted by the great changes in the production, distribution, and consumption of economic goods in the world. Each of these three areas has been affected directly by the same technological revolution that we have been analyzing throughout this chapter. So vast are the economic implications of modern technology that we can do no more than suggest a few of the leading considerations here.

NEW PRODUCTION TECHNIQUES

Almost every aspect of industrial technology has affected production in a remarkable way. Best known of the new techniques is "automation": the application of electronic controls and simplified patterns to the end that higher-quality goods are turned out by only a fraction of the manpower formerly needed. Even non-automated industry has been so revolutionized by new techniques that it can almost be said that any factory built before 1945 is obsolete today. This has been dramatically demonstrated by the industrial success of the war-devastated states of Europe since 1945. Forced to rebuild their industrial plants from the ground up, they have been able to incorporate new arrangements and technique with a consequent gain in productivity that is fantastic.

The principal result of the new production techniques has been a great increase in the capacity of the world economy to produce goods of all sorts. There are more goods available for consumption than ever before, and the trend is toward a continuation of the upward spiral of productivity. This phenomenon is independent of any considerations of profit margins, markets, or employment; it is simply a macroeconomic conclusion that the world, viewed as a unit of production, is increasing its gross product at a significant rate. The social and political consequences of this development are functions of decisions made in other contexts, however, and cannot be inferred from the mere fact of an upward trend in production. It is up to the statesmen of the future to decide how this new abundance can best be put to the improvement of the lot of mankind.

RISING CONSUMER EXPECTATIONS

Paralleling the revolution in technique of production is an analogous upward curve in the expectations of consumers everywhere. The so-called "revolution of rising expectations" is usually thought of as a characteristic of underdeveloped but newly-awakened pre-industrial societies, and indeed it is ubiquitous in all of them. But even in industrialized states, consumption levels have risen since 1945 and will probably continue to do so. Regardless of the standard of living an individual enjoys, on every hand he receives stimuli urging him to elevate his expectations still further. The United States, with its consumption economy of "affluence," has long set the trend for higher levels of living, but recently, western Europe, the Soviet Union, and the semi-industrialized societies in the Middle East, Latin America, North Africa, and Southeast Asia have followed suit.

The worldwide interest in consumption of economic goods has placed many governments in a grievous dilemma. On the one hand, most are committed to nationalist goals collectively phrased whose attainment will call for a significant portion of national production to be committed to the so-called "public sector" of the economy; both a heavy burden of armament and the capital formation prerequisite to industrial development require that individual consumption be limited. On the other hand, however, the increasingly vocal demand of the mass public for more of the better things of life inhibits the vigor with which the government can prosecute the themes of sacrifice and dedication so necessary to public programs. No government has yet found a satisfactory escape from this quandary.

THE PROBLEM OF DISTRIBUTION

The nation-state system divides the world into a congeries of putatively independent and self-sustaining economies. Some of these are productive of surpluses while others can do no more than budget deprivation. At the subsistence level, for example, it is agreed that food production potential today is adequate to feed the entire population of the world. Hunger exists, in other words, only because of failures in distribution.

How, within the present structure of the world economy, can distribution be rationalized so that increased productivity can be reflected in increased consumption and a richer and better life for everyone? To this question some of the world's most serious thought has been addressed in the past decade and a half. In the next chapter we shall look at these economic issues more directly; here we need only reflect in passing on the strange turns of fate that make some economies suffer from an excess of productivity and others from an excess of consumer demand, while a combination of social, economic, and political inhibitions impede the socially and politically useful distribution of needed goods.

POLITICAL SIGNIFICANCE

The political ramifications of these general observations are self-evident. The basic economic issues of production and consumption have been sharpened by the technological breakthrough of the contemporary era. Politically, the world emphasizes division and sep-arateness; economically, the maximum social advantage for everyone is attainable only in a system emphasizing unity and joint action. The economic problems of the contemporary world are insoluble on a national-state level, except in theory for a few fortunate states of great expanse and rich resource endowment. The perpetuation of the national attack on global economic issues can do no better than buy time, and possibly, far from ameliorating them, will eventually worsen them or intensify their deficiencies. Here as in other areas no automatic or guaranteed response to the challenge of technology exists. Statesmen will discover new and possibly more rewarding approaches only insofar as they are able to devise new structures for action that leave room for a broader basis of cal-culation.

The Lesson of Technology

At the risk of being redundant, we might close this rapid survey of the impact of technology on international politics by stipulating in general terms what has been apparent in our discussion of the several specific points. The essence of the technological revolution has been to bind the inhabitants of the planet more and more intimately, all sharing both discomfort and opportunity impartially and all destined for a substantially common fate. From the threat of nuclear holocaust at one extreme, to the possibilities of a higher worldwide standard of living at present not even dreamed of, technology has unceremoniously dumped the human species irrevocably into the same boat. Statesmen of the twentieth century would do well to recall Donne's preachment, "No man is an island, entire unto itself"; for neither is any nation.

Men are,—as we have had occasion to remark previously—prisoners of their own habits. The nation-state system—the international political order whose dynamic we have been examining throughout this book—is not as old as other human social systems, but its history is rich and its appeal powerful. Statesmen and other politically alert peoples have not fully grasped (or at least have not yet fully adjusted to) the meaning of technology for international politics. The fundamentally atomistic principle of "every state for itself" is yet the sanctioned basis of state interaction, in spite of the great body of evidence that the kinds of problems posed by the new technology do not yield solutions on such a basis. The current stasis of world politics reflects this lack of success that policy-makers and political leaders have had in their attempt to force the new wine of technology into the old bottles of national interest and power politics.

So the new generation of problems spawned by man's partial exploitation of the forces of nature conspire to force hard choices on the political leadership of the human race. It may be that these issues will eventually succumb to traditional forms and patterns of action. As of today, however, the weight of available evidence strongly suggests that the opposite will be true and that effective attack on major issues will first require new organizational patterns for action and response. Technology will almost certainly require that major modification in its assumptions and structure be made.

Bibliography

* Bloomfield, Lincoln P. (ed.), *Outer Space; Prospects for Man and Society*. New York: Prentice-Hall, Inc., Spectrum Books, 1962.
* Brown, Harrison, *Challenge of Man's Future*. New York: The Viking Press, Compass Books, 1956.

* Goldsen, J. M. (ed.), *Outer Space in World Politics*. New York: Frederick A. Praeger, 1962.

Gyorgy, Andrew, and Hubert S. Gibbs, *Problems in International Relations*, Second edition. Englewood Cliffs, New Jersey: Prentice-Hall, Inc., 1962.

Hauser, Philip (ed.), *Population and World Politics*. New York: The Free Press of Glencoe, Inc., 1958.

* Herz, John H., *International Politics in the Atomic Age*. New York: Columbia University Press, 1959.

* Huxley, Julian, *Man in the Modern World*. New York: New American Library of World Literature, 1961.

Laurence, William, *Men and Atoms*. New York: Simon and Schuster, 1959.

* Lippmann, Walter, *Public Opinion*. New York: Penguin Books, 1946.

* McClelland, Charles A., *Nuclear Weapons, Missiles and Future War: Problem for the Sixties*. San Francisco: Howard Chandler Publishing Company, 1960.

Moregenthan, Hans, *Scientific Man vs. Power Politics*. Chicago: Chicago University Press, 1946.

Organski, Katherine, and A. F. K. Organski, *Population and World Power*. New York: Alfred A. Knopf, 1961.

Russell, John E., *World Population and World Food Supplies*. New York: Macmillan and Company, 1954.

Schramm, Wilbur, (ed.), *Mass Communication*, Second edition. Urbana, Illinois: University of Illinois Press, 1960.

Toynbee, Arnold, *Industrial Revolution*. Boston: Beacon Press, Inc., 1956.

---

* Indicates paperback edition.

Twelve

Trade, Aid, and Development

The state has been for over three hundred years a viable action unit for the conduct of political relations among peoples. At least in the western world, the logic of statehood and the assumptions of the state system were laid down in the era before the Industrial Revolution. When this great transformation in the method of production occurred and launched the massive reorientation in the conditions of human life that is still existent, the incompatibility of the state form with rational economic life for individuals became apparent.

Granted the expectations of individuals everywhere, no state is economically self-sufficient. All are in some measure dependent upon sources outside themselves for some share of their economic goods. Resources are not distributed among states in any recognizable proportion to the demand for them; raw materials inadequately supplied in one state may be in surplus supply in a neighboring state. States differ in their productive skills and plants, so that many broadly desired commodities are obtainable advantageously or even exclusively only from certain favored states. Since all peoples today have economic goals, these differences in physical, political, and human economic circumstances lead to different and often conflicting economic policies by governments.

Economic Forces in International Politics

Economics has been one of the fundamental determining factors in the evolution of international politics. In perspective, the breakdown of feudalism, the emergence of the nation-state, the rise of colonialism, and the new force of regionalism were related in one way or another to the fluctuating nature of economic systems and the major evolutionary trends of world economic patterns.

ECONOMIC INTERDEPENDENCE VERSUS POLITICAL INDEPENDENCE

International prosperity is a function of production for use and exchange, the exchange of monetary units of different countries and the conditions for exchanging goods or services between states. Due to the state system under which each area is separately organized for political purposes, each state must perform many economic functions that place it in opposition with other states. The free movement of people and of goods so necessary to economic wealth is thus checked, the problem of supply and demand as well as the disparity between human needs and human resources assumes international dimensions.

Granted the unequal endowment of economic potential and productive capacity among the states of the world, it is nevertheless true that sheer subsistence is possible for virtually all states. People, that is, can survive even under extremely unfavorable economic circumstances. But in societies in which the population explosion that we examined in Chapter Eleven is taking place, serious pressures are already developing. Greater numbers of people often mean a reduction in the per capita food supply, when already dangerously low. At this point, such a society is thrown upon the mercies of the world economy. Its survival is contingent upon its adjustment to the vagaries of international economic relations. Since such unhappy states are with disconcerting frequency also the sites of generous raw material endowments, at least some of the ingredients of a mutually profitable economic relationship with industrialized states are already present.

The issue becomes even sharper when simple survival is not an issue; but instead, when the crucial factor becomes the ubiquitous notion of a rising standard of living. More than food is involved; a "standard of living" today is a societal value judgment incorporating individual and group economic expectations. In addition, it is an intricate blend of necessities, comforts, and luxuries that together reflect a large portion of the ethos of the society. When a people is determined to "raise" its standard of living, a powerful dynamism is added to its foreign policy, and the conflict between economic interdependence and political independence becomes sharper than ever.

MODERN ECONOMIC TRENDS IN WORLD POLITICS

From the point of view of the industrialized states of the world, recent economic trends have contributed a situation of major relevance to the course of world politics. Although these factors have been noted by communist and other Marxist analysts as explaining the entirety of western foreign policy in the postwar world, we need not be overly concerned about these strictures. It is undeniable, however, that at least some of the conditions that we shall point out have predisposed several western governments to follow certain lines of policy rather than others. The denial of a strict economic determinism does not imply that economic forces are completely without influence in international politics.

The modern economic problem begins with the fact that for most commodities, large-scale mass production is the most efficient procedure. Thus productive units are and have been growing steadily larger. This immediately creates a constant need for reinvestment growth capital and for a growing margin of fixed overhead costs.

At this point, with so much of its net worth tied up in plant and with overhead cutting deeply into profit, a typical firm feels a great need to maintain continuous operation. Adding to this pressure is the role of organized labor, which in western states has become a politico-economic force of great impact that is ever assiduous to keep production moving and thus ensure its employment. Full employment is both a social and an economic desideratum in western society.

But constant operation and steady growth require both a guaranteed supply of raw materials and an expanding market. Capitalism demands a cash profit, and markets must be found for production if the firm, the industry, and the economy alike are not to smother in a flood of unsold goods. Here still another fixed cost factor appears: the necessity of expanding the distribution, advertising, and sales aspect of the enterprise if the inexorable demands of the balance sheet are to be satisfied.

Some few nations, including the United States, are fortunate to possess a large and prosperous domestic market to furnish the consuming base of their economy. For most states, however, expansion and growth lead to the search for markets abroad. Here the dilemma runs full circle. Competition with other states, frequently conducted within the domestic market of a second economy, has its obvious political implications. It is natural—almost inevitable—for an industry pressed for new markets to beg help from its government in its foreign activities. It is equally natural for an economy "menaced" by foreign competition to seek its own protection by tariffs and other restrictive measures.

The problem is intensified for a state and an economy that has expanded production and sales under favorable circumstances and then faces a possibility of losing its advantage. This, for example, is sometimes thought to be the situation of the United States *vis-à-vis* a newly-prosperous and rapidly integrating Europe. Committed to growth and expansion, but in danger of losing markets, such an economy cannot escape from its overhead nor from its social responsibilities to its labor force. It is probably correct but often irrelevant to point out that classical economics has a solution: such an economy must rationalize itself so as to be better able to compete for markets. Given the highly structured and therefore relatively inflexible nature of modern industrial societies, however, major overhaul of a productive plant entails such massive social and political costs that few states dare to make the attempt. It is usually thought to be easier and safer, although less meaningful, to attempt political palliatives of protection and subsidy. This in turn, as we already know, invites retaliation and the vicious circle is renewed.

THE ECONOMIC REVOLUTION IN EUROPE

The one industrialized area of the world which has been able to bring about a full-scale revolution in its economic habits is western

Europe. The end of World War II found the once-dominant economies of Europe prostrate. Their industrial plants were destroyed by the war, their capital was dissipated by Nazi occupation and looting, their labor forces were dispersed and demoralized, and their economic situation with regard to the Soviet Union and the United States was no less than desperate.

What was worse, the atomic age and the new technological revolution were upon them. As individual states, they lacked the capacity, financial and technical, to conduct the basic research necessary to the exploitation of the new potentialities. The new possibilities of production, furthermore, made no sense when there were narrow national markets in Europe. The economies of such once-viable states as France or Italy, to say nothing of much smaller ones like Belgium or Denmark, had been made obsolete by the new technology. Even under the best of circumstances, Europe was out of date.

If the atomic revolution were to have an impact at all comparable to that of the coal-iron revolution of the eighteenth century, to be left out of this development would mean decadence for any such unfortunate state. Many European advocates of economic integration argue that, should their effort fail, Europe will bear the same economic relation to the United States or the Soviet Union as prewar Asia, Africa, or Eastern Europe did to the productive centers of Germany, the Low Countries, or France. What Europe needed, it was realized shortly after the end of the war, was a broader and more efficient economic base, one adequate to the new demands and the new opportunities of a nuclear era.

The consequence was the politico-economic trend of European integration. The goal of this ambitious project, already far advanced in the few years since its launching, is no less than the creation of a new entity in world political and economic relations to be called simply "Europe." Pure political and military efforts, such as the European Defense Community (EDC), and the European Political Community (EPC), have thus far failed: military cooperation with the United States via the North Atlantic Treaty Organization, while useful in security matters, has produced no real steps toward unity. It has been only in the economic realm that Europe has made real inroads into sovereignty.

The first moves were made on a continent-wide basis, with the Organization for European Economic Cooperation (OEEC) uniting fifteen states on the principle of "self-help and mutual aid" for the implementation of the American Marshall Plan in 1948. At almost the same time, the Council of Europe (1949) became the first overt expression of what was known as the "European movement." Both these ambitious projects, although contributing to the nascent sense of common interest and destiny, demonstrated that it was difficult to move toward European unity without an effective delegation of sovereignty.

It was not until a smaller core group of six states (France, West Germany, Italy, Belgium, the Netherlands, and Luxembourg) resolved to pool their sovereignty in certain specified economic fields that real steps began to be taken. The Schuman Plan led in 1951 to the creation of the European Coal and Steel Community, a merger of the steel-making capacity of the six states into a single unit independent of national boundaries. The success of this bold move stimulated the decisions in 1957 to establish the European Atomic Community (EURATOM) to pool atomic research and development, and the European Common Market—the most far-reaching step of all—that by 1972 was to eliminate all trade barriers among the six states and to create a single market of almost 200 million people.

The Common Market crowned the revolution in Europe. So powerful has been its attraction and so gripping its prospects that the other states of Europe—notably Great Britain—have begun the irrevocable process of seeking admission. Even pessimists today are virtually convinced that the European breakthrough is an accomplished fact and that the birth of a new economic entity is imminent. From this to workable political integration will be conceptually only a short step, however difficult its practical accomplishment may be. The economic lessons of the European experience have relevance to all states, and they are being closely studied everywhere. Even the Soviets, for example, have paid the European Community the compliment of imitation.

New Patterns of International Trade

The requirements of international economic life immediately raise the question of international trade: the exchange of commodities among sovereign states (or the people thereof) in response to mutual needs. As with all aspects of foreign economic relations, trade policy in all states represents some sort of compromise between the interests of individual citizens bent on private gain and the collective concern of the government for the over-all economic welfare of the society. Individuals are normally motivated by considerations of economic interest, whereas the state's approach is as "political" in the last analysis as it is in defense policy, propaganda, or direct diplomatic maneuvering. Thus the movement of goods and services in international trade at any moment in history follows patterns dictated by the several states' judgment of political expediency.

DOCTRINES OF INTERNATIONAL TRADE

In the most general terms there are two theories of international trade that reflect the conflicting points of view of individual traders and the collective force of the state. One, called in its earlier manifestation "mercantilism," emphasizes the right and the duty of the state to control the nature, the amount, and to direct the flow of trade in the national interest. It therefore demands extensive government regulation of trade and the submission of individuals to the general policies laid down by the state. The second theory, rooted in classical economics, calls for the absolute freedom of goods to move across national frontiers in response to economic laws, with no reference to government attitudes. "Free trade" thus maximizes the role of profit and individual enterprise and contends that each state and the world economy at large profit best when the volume of international trade is at its untrammeled maximum.

Mercantilism was founded on an assumption that wealth consisted of "treasure"—precious metals and stones—and argued that state policy should be directed at creating a "favorable balance of trade" that resulted in a net increase in the supply of wealth. International economic life was thus a matter of state competition, for a limited supply of treasure and economic conflict among nations was a postulate. Trade, in this context, was a zero-sum game in which one side gained only to the extent that another lost.

Free-trade theories reject the doctrine of conflict and argue that trade, if permitted to follow its natural bent, results ultimately in the maximum profit for all participants. Doctrines of "comparative advantage" call for international division of labor with each unit specializing in the production of those commodities which it can most competitively sell on the world market. Ingenious adjustment mechanisms deduced from such premises suggest that *laissez faire* is even more applicable to international economic relations than to domestic supply and demand.

Mercantilism flourished in the pre-industrial era of the state system, reaching its maximum application during the seventeenth and early eighteenth centuries. The rise of mass production and the necessity of the early industrial powers to seek markets led to the development of classical economics, the abandonment of mercantilism as a government policy, and an energetic advocacy of the principles of free trade by Great Britain. This doctrine, fulfilling the requirements of the early industrial leaders, became accepted during the nineteenth century as authoritative. British wealth and preeminence were pointed to as proof of the theory's validity.

The twentieth century, however, has seen the complex structure of multilateral trading arrangements crumble under the dual impact of economic depressions and the rise of integrative nationalism. Although all governments pay lip service to free trade as theoretically impeccable, in practice, what we might call neo-mercantilism has become the controlling principle of trade control. Almost all states since 1914 have found ample pretexts to depart from free-trade principles in the national interest, and trade has struggled for many years within a complex framework of politically-inspired restrictions. The economic theory of mercantilism is dead, but its policy and practice remain very much alive.

TRADE SINCE 1945

The economic catastrophe of World War II and the radical changes in the structure of the international political system since 1945 have had a great effect on both the theory and the practice of international trade. First, the critical economic conditions of many countries forced their governments to deal with international economics on the basis of "every man for himself"; all the resources of government were directed to halt an economic collapse, and trade suffered seriously. Second, the rise of the Cold War split the world into political blocs that soon knit together economically and diverted trade from many of its historic channels. Third, it soon became apparent that economic health could not be restored to the world on a state-by-state basis, but that some form of multilateral economic action was crucial. This applied both to the war-shattered older industrial economies and to the newly-emerging underdeveloped states. The upshot of all these interacting factors has led to the appearance of what may be called controlled multilateralism, a curious paradox in which governments, acting from nationalist motivations on behalf of collective national economies, act slowly and steadily to advance an acceptance of the principle of multilateral and liberated trade.

In the contemporary world, therefore, neo-mercantilism and free trade exist simultaneously. States seek to expand their trading opportunities and increase their volume, yet all exercise extensive controls in the interest of advancing political purposes. Only in western Europe, where the decision has been taken to liberate all intra-community trade from controls, have national interests been subordinated to some broader notion. Elsewhere this perplexing amalgam of freedom and control is dominant as governments large and small are caught by the contradiction between economic imperatives and traditional political values.

CONTEMPORARY TRENDS IN THE CONDUCT OF TRADE

The blurred contemporary doctrines of trade are clearly demonstrated by varying trends in the conduct of trade. At least four clear practices are in evidence today: (1) the general lowering or elimination of tariffs; (2) the preference system; (3) international control of buying, storing, and selling of specific products; and (4) the quota system.

Lowering or elimination of tariffs is a clear reflection of the trend toward a policy of free trade. In order to meet new conditions, various multilateral as well as bilateral and regional efforts have been made. A leading example of multilateral effort has been the General Agreement on Tariffs and Trade (GATT) which came into effect in 1948. By the terms of this agreement, over fifty trading states meet periodically to negotiate tariff reductions both general and specific. The United States has since 1934 been committed to tariff reduction by bilateral negotiation, and in recent years has made even stronger moves to gain the capacity to act quickly and extensively in this direction.

A clear example of this trend is the concept of the common market, as it has been developing in Europe and Latin America. These markets eliminate the tariffs between member states and form a unified tariff wall to the rest of the world. This policy will create a larger consumer market for member states and yet protect their internal market from outside competition. The success of this policy can be seen in the remarkable industrial growth of the member countries of the European Common Market.

The preference system is best illustrated in the Commonwealth of Nations and the European Community. This procedure was developed to encourage trade between the former colonial powers, principally Great Britain and France, and their former colonial areas. A similar pattern of preference can also be seen between the United States and the Philippines. It allows goods from the privileged area to escape tariffs other goods must pay. The advantage for the mother country is to maintain the former colony as a consumer market and as a source for raw materials. The advantage for the colony is to maintain close relations with an industrial power with markets remaining open to the underdeveloped countries. The preference system is clearly a reversion to a sophisticated mercantilism.

International control of buying, storing, and selling of specific products is carried on by international trusts. In the past, committees or international cartels were formed to control the export and trade of wheat and coffee. At present, many products, such as oil, tin, rubber, and copper are controlled by international trust or consortia made up of states that export these products. The groupings were formed to regulate production and marketing of these commodities in the interest of guaranteeing a regular return to member states. This policy is designed to escape the boom and bust cycle of single-commodity economics.

The quota policy has been developed to stabilize underdeveloped states that are producers of a single prime commodity. Large consumer states permitted producers a certain share of the market usually at a prescribed price. The producing states could count on a guaranteed sale and could thus plan production. The United

States has had extensive quota systems for sugar, tin, and copper—all important to particular producing states in Latin America.

THE UNDERDEVELOPED AREAS IN WORLD TRADE

The emergence of new states upon the world political scene has resulted in their becoming full participants in international trading relations. Freed from their colonial status, and with considerable control over their economic destinies, they bring something new to world economic relations.

Endowed as they are with relatively low-cost labor and generous endowments of raw materials, they lack only capital and technological know-how to become industrial and exporting units. In all areas of the underdeveloped world, thanks to strong leadership, the strange workings of the Cold War, and the preoccupation of the industrialized states with their former colonies, the process of production for export has begun. Although the total amount is not yet impressive, the trend is already set and the future will see a constant expansion.

The new states contribute less than 25 per cent of the world's total exports, and two-thirds of this amount is still in raw materials and foodstuffs. These are inevitably low-profit items of trade, and domestic conversion of raw materials into at least semi-industrial goods will obviously return a higher profit. Also interesting is the extent to which underdeveloped states are now trading with each other. Today, over one-fourth of the imports of underdeveloped states come from other underdeveloped countries. In this strange and unforseen way, the classical principle of comparative advantage is once again making itself felt.

The Revolution of Rising Expectations

In the last two decades, almost the entire non-western world has come into political responsibility. This political liberation has brought home to them the startling contrast between their traditional ways of life and the higher standards enjoyed by the industrial states. New dimensions of individual life are opening to them;

they are responding to new economic, social, and political pressures, and awakening to new aspirations and ambitions.

While the industrial states constitute about 20 percent of the world population, they enjoy about 80 percent of its annual income. The United States has 6 percent of the world population and enjoys 40 percent of its income. In many underdeveloped states, the average annual income is less than $100, compared to $1800 in the United States. Experts set the minimum requirement for existence at 2,000 calories a day; the average American consumes 3,000 calories, the average Indian 1,700. In the industrial countries, in general, there is one physician per 1,000 inhabitants; in Nigeria, one per 56,000. In an average industrial state, four persons out of five can read or write; in the average underdeveloped country, it is one out of five.

THE NATURE OF THE REVOLUTION OF RISING EXPECTATIONS

The revolution of rising expectations involves a change in attitude the poverty-stricken masses of the non-West take toward their situation in life. They are beginning to regard their situation as being anomalous and not inescapable. They are coming to believe that they can change their way of life to one of relative abundance. They have awakened to the possibilities of change through the influence of mass media and by increasingly frequent contact with people from advanced countries. Others, they learn, do not live as they do, but lead instead a richer and fuller life.

Non-western people feel today that their subservience to the white man is not a law of nature. They are realizing that they have as much capacity for development as the western man does and their lives are now filled with a spirit of hope and expectation for a better life, materially as well as spiritually.

This is a revolution against the nineteenth century division of the world into industrially advanced and backward countries. This division of states into rich, productive, industrialized areas on the one hand and exploited colonial empires on the other was a basis of the world economy and political system. To the practical considerations were added overtones of racial superiority.

The revolution of rising expectations is not a tangible movement lending itself to simple measurement of its stages. It is rather an elusive, intangible, nearly ineffable change in the consensus of the political society comprising each underdeveloped state. The leaders of underdeveloped countries must respond to the collective will of their followers or they will not long remain as leaders. Thus, while it is not easy to define the extent of the "revolution" in any one state, it is at least possible to take cognizance of the degree to which it is manifested in the actions of the state in the international system.

Viewed in the general context of international prosperity and well-being, the revolution of rising expectations has a dual effect. From the point of view of the industrially advanced states, it is a possible threat to their continued prosperity and well-being. To the underdeveloped states, the revolution of rising expectations is a movement toward their own greater prosperity and well-being. The industrially advanced states advocate a slow and gradual revolution; they are therefore quite cautious in approaching change, particularly since they have much to lose by making a wrong move and relatively little to gain in any case. The underdeveloped countries, on the other hand, have next to nothing in material possessions and stand to lose little in attempting to gain more. They are therefore eager to follow even an extreme course of action if it offers a remote hope for the attainment of any of their innumerable goals. In the process of recklessly seeking to improve themselves, the underdeveloped countries may very well worsen their lot; this can be seen today in cases where overenthusiastic leadership has gone seriously astray in ambitious projects.

PROBLEMS AND PROSPECTS OF DEVELOPMENT

In discussing the problems and difficulties of development, we shall examine three main issues: the dichotomy between economic reality and the idealistic aspirations of the underdeveloped areas, the prerequisite factors for economic growth, and the type of economic system most suitable to development.

The dichotomy between economic reality and idealistic aspirations is significant: non-western people aspire to goals which at this time seem almost unattainable. The populations of most of these states are growing far more rapidly than food supplies. There is poverty, hunger, disease, illiteracy, low productivity, and mass unemployment. These states are predominantly agricultural; current systems of land ownership are not conducive to industrialization or, for that matter, to any type of economic stability.

There is a very small middle class in these states, without enough influence to stabilize the economy. The poor peasant and the wealthy land owner contribute little effort to build an industrial economy. It is not in the immediate interest of the wealthy few to invest their money in long-range projects, and the peasant has no money to invest. These conditions make it difficult for the very poor states even to begin industrialization by their own efforts. On the other hand, those states that enjoy a slightly higher level of wealth can begin to industrialize, but their problem is rather how to keep the process of development moving forward.

The prerequisite factors for economic growth are numerous. The principal ones are natural resources, human resources including labor, management, technicians and educators, and capital.

Natural resources are important because the abundance or lack of them often determines what type of economy a state has, whether it has the ability to produce a variety of goods, or whether it must specialize in one product and try to export it in order to import other commodities. Many of the underdeveloped states are deficient in natural resources. This makes self-sufficiency impossible but does not make economic progress out of reach.

Human resources as a prerequisite for development are of prime importance. One of the major problems in developing technicians and managerial personnel is that when one has been educated sufficiently for one of these positions he no longer wishes to engage in this type of work. The social status of such occupations does not offer the prestige rewards of other professions, such as medicine or law, and therefore, talented people are reluctant to enter these fields. There is thus a shortage of leadership and often a distrust of innovation due to the non-mechanical orientation of these peoples.

The villager, the substance of the non-West, exists on a bare level of subsistence. The industrial worker is the victim of inadequate programs of social welfare and social security benefits. The labor force is not sufficiently stabilized; social patterns conducive to high productivity barely exist. Wages are low and inadequate, and purchasing power severely limits production. Meanwhile, rapid population growth poses a severe impediment for development.

Capital constitutes another prime prerequisite for development.

There are many types of capital, differing according to whatever stage of industrialization a state is experiencing. Tools and machinery, for example, are important types of capital as well as savings and investments. One of the major problems of the underdeveloped states is their inability to accumulate investment capital. The capital shortage is one of the largest problems of the underdeveloped states except those few that are rich in oil deposits.

With respect to capital formation, it is important to note that the problem sometimes is not the scarcity of capital, but often the effective use of capital for productive purposes. In many underdeveloped states, capital is often used for "conspicuous consumption," such as jewelry, places of religious worship, oversized armies, improvement of the physical appearances of homes, and for other unproductive purposes. Furthermore, owing to the absence of fluid capital at the disposal of the entrepreneur class, inadequate transportation and banking facilities, or skilled labor, it is difficult to find opportunities for investment in industries that will yield profits. The problem becomes one of accumulating enough foreign currency to pay for the import of capital goods with which to begin industrialization. Time, money, and technical knowledge are all necessary.

In some underdeveloped areas, a real difficulty is involved in planning types of new industry. Should industries be capital or labor incentive; that is, should they encourage the country to take advantage of its abundant labor resources, or concentrate on using machinery? This issue is complicated by the question of technical training and maintenance. To establish an urban industry demands the recruitment of unskilled labor from the rural areas. However, there is a real risk involved in selling land and moving to the city in search of employment. Unless the migration is planned by the government, the problem of adequate housing, hospital facilities, schools, and so on may become insoluble.

The type of economic system suitable for development is no less significant than capital. Communism has made a vast appeal to many underdeveloped states. Private enterprise does not seem suitable or appealing to a state that has been exploited by that system for centuries. Government regulation, supervision, and coordination are a necessity. This conclusion, so repellent to free-enterprise theorists, does not imply totalitarianism, but underdeveloped states lack the time for pure freedom of economic choice to work its effect.

As we learned earlier, the communist bloc appeals to the under-developed states because of its seemingly anti-imperialistic attitude toward the West. Communists accuse the West of economic pene-tration and have been relatively successful in propaganda attacks re-enforcing this position. Flattering the ego of the non-western world and appeasing their hunger for goods, communists pose as great benefactors.

The communist bloc has still another point in its favor: a doctrine of social equality. The peoples of the underdeveloped areas not only want a higher standard of living, but also seek full recognition as individuals and equals with all other people. They do not under-stand the sacrifice that individuality makes to equality, but they do see the vast inequalities in the western social and economic system. The communist thesis of equality of dignity and status cannot help but be attractive to sensitive psyches, and thus economic preferences come to be based on doctrine rather than on production and dis-tribution.

The Politics of Development

Similar to the tensions of international politics in the nuclear era which come largely from the inevitably frustrating effort to fit the contemporary environment into traditional political categories, the tensions of national politics in the underdeveloped states represent their equally frustrating attempts to fit the modern concept of a nation-state into their traditional institutions.

The newly-emerging states are rapidly learning that political inde-pendence alone does not carry a magic formula for prosperity; it merely opens up new horizons and opportunities for betterment. The successful development and utilization of these opportunities are dependent upon the establishment of effective national political systems. Thus the politics of development represents a larger prob-lem of underdeveloped states and their well-being in the interna-tional system.

THE MODERN SOCIETY

We must recognize at the outset of this discussion that our obser-vations on such a vast subject will inevitably represent gross judgments and hence our comments will consist of generalizations that do not necessarily apply to every underdeveloped area.

Before we examine the processes of modernization, we should define the term "modern society." A modern society can be characterized as a society with a wide human base of political, social, and economic processes. This base is founded on a complex network of communication, urbanization, literacy, relatively high per capita income, and social mobility. The political system of such a society is characterized by an elaborate differentiation, explicitness, and functional distinctiveness of political and governmental structures performing authoritative functions. Through processes of political socialization, this structure serves to create a distinct loyalty to the general political system. Yet the boundary between society and political system is maintained.

In such a society, political recruitment tends to be limited by general performance criteria. Interests are articulated through associational interest groups performing a system-wide regulatory role by processing claims in an orderly way. These are in turn organized by a party system acting as the institutional link between the legislature and bureaucracy. The party system is characterized by competing, pragmatic, bargaining parties. Political communication is performed by autonomous and specialized mass media which tend to penetrate all other structures within the political system. In addition, the boundaries between governmental structures are sharply delineated and effectively maintained.

The modern society is an outgrowth of 500 years of western historical development and experiences. Modernization, therefore, implies westernization nourished by great sacrifices, initiative, ingenuity, and brought into being by many revolutions and wars on the part of western man.

THE PROCESSES OF MODERNIZATION IN THE NON-WEST

The non-West is trying to cover a century in a decade; it is attempting to telescope the achievements of the Enlightenment and the Industrial Revolution into one generation. While the changes that are occurring are gradual in their genesis, they are nevertheless dramatic in their issue. The new non-western world is in marked institutional discontinuity with the old. The family, the king, the tribe, and religion, have outlived their usefulness as organizing prin-

ciples. The non-western people have discovered themselves in unfamiliar ways: their horizons are widened, their mental environment transformed. Yet the concurrent emergence of the Cold War
compromises and embitters their sense of achievement. Their internal weakness aggravates their frustrations. They are faced with
finding ways to retain their self-responsibility; they are searching
for self-sufficiency to maintain their national dignity. They face
two stark choices: either for their system to baptize change into
its spirit, or to renounce the relevance of their value systems to life.
Since they cannot do the latter, they must do the former.

The non-West is thus in a state of ferment; what is emerging is
confusion and, at times, anarchy. We have already learned that in
much of the non-West, a nation in the western sense scarcely can
be found included within the boundaries of any present state. These
states reflect not spontaneous political growth but rather the after-
effects of the division of the world by colonial powers. Government
is minimal in organization and in effect, and the visible symbols of
national identity are either few or irrelevant to modern conditions.
The state does not respond as a unit since there is no adequate agreement on common norms. Their laws and organizations are not effective since they do not correspond to and express a given ideological
or normative inner order. In most of the non-western states, there
does not exist a philosophy of society: basic concepts and assumptions agreed upon by people and their leaders for organizing their
experience and ordering their relations to nature and community.

This is a period of accelerated historical transition in the non-
West, in contrast to the previous 500 years when it played the part
of a mere passive recipient of historical forces. The pressure of
new ideas is explosive. The passing of the old order is fraught with
upheavals and disturbances which are in themselves manifestations
of unendurable stress. The conflict between conservative and revolutionary forces make smooth transition difficult. While recep-
tiveness to new ideas is strong, reluctance to let go of the older
ones is still greater. The search for adjustment creates both individual and national crises, for it demands a separation from that
which is familiar in order to espouse something untested. Thus there
is always the temptation to maintain traditionalist attitudes until
the crumbling process approaches completion and new and more
appropriate theories begin to find spontaneous acceptance.

Resistance to change and deliberate hesitation must be appreciated by outsiders as being subconscious devices for self-preservation, which should not be completely discarded before the new values and the old aspirations have been more convincingly attuned to each other. Such a process is inevitably a slow one, and in the beginning it cannot escape inconsistency and superficiality. The personal attitudes that govern group behavior are less easily revised than are the institutions which purport to do so in the official and sanctioned ideologies which are often exotic to the society.

The non-western states as they stand today are incapable of meeting their problems with their own resources. They are urgently seeking a metaphysic to justify their existence and encourage their progress. These states are still overwhelmingly rural, the majority of their populations are illiterate, and their per capita income is very low. Social and geographical mobility, outside the urban sectors, is severely restricted. The central structures of government are modern only in form but not in substance. The non-western societies display also a lack of political integration, partly because they are characterized by ethnic, religious, racial, and cultural pluralism and partly due to the limited and uneven operation of the processes of modernization. Furthermore, a general characteristic of non-western states is the wide gap in modernization between the masses and the elite.

The processes of change have produced a variety of political consequences in the non-West. Above all, the traditional gap between urban and rural areas with respect to the political center of gravity has been widened. National politics has become almost exclusively concentrated in the capital cities and the peasantry is left outside political action.

The disparity in standards of living between rural and urban population also has grown. As a result, the tribal structure of society is dissolving. Peasants are moving to the cities. This trend has a double effect. The new population, accustomed to a subsistence level of life in the village, cannot secure even these minimum requirements in the city. In addition, the new urban proletariat constitutes a heavy burden and a potential explosive force close to the seat of government. Many of the street mobs of recent vintage have been made up largely of such uprooted peasants.

The pace of non-western governments in coping with the processes of industrialization is lagging behind the problems that arise. Hence, the economies of these societies have not developed social or political integration, an appreciable middle class, or a stabilized labor organization. The disparity in the distribution of benefits remains great; not shared equally by all groups, it is differentiated along communal, racial, religious, tribal, or similar lines. This results in a lack of positive correlation between economic development and greater social and political integration. Finally, the processes of modernization have ushered in secularization, which stands in direct confrontation to religious traditions. Among the masses, religion remains a vital force, while the more secularized elite seek to capitalize on religious tensions.

THE FORMS OF NON-WESTERN POLITICAL SYSTEMS

Modernization in governmental structure has mainly occurred at the level of formal structure where there has developed in much of the non-West a progressive trend toward the establishment of western institutions. In most of these states the parliamentary and the presidential systems have become the favorite models of imitation, with American and French influence predominant.

Most of the non-western states have had long experience with executive bureaucratic governments, either through traditional or colonial structures. The most distinctive innovations displayed in the formal structure of most non-western political systems are two: central representative parliaments endowed with constitutional legislative power and a constitutionally secular and independent judiciary.

In practice, however, these new innovations are not operational and remain mere exotic importations. Instead, the working form of non-western political systems is characterized by two phenomena: a tendency toward unitary government with a heavy centralization of decision-making, and the continuing predominance of the executive-bureaucratic branch.

The tendency toward centralization is evident even in non-western states where federalism has been attempted. In many of these, nationally appointed agents operating in sub-units have replaced former colonial officers and commissioners. The concept of local government is almost non-existent in most of the non-West.

The predominance of the executive branch is paramount in the non-western states; the legislative and judicial branches of government consistently occupy subordinate places. The participation by Parliament in the authoritative functions of rulemaking is severely restricted. The independence of the judiciary in rule-adjudication is generally a myth, and in much of the non-West, courts are utterly dependent on the executive.

POLITICAL PROCESSES AND FUNCTIONS

The methods of inducting members into the political culture, the patterns of their recruitment into the political arena, and the manipulation of interests and political communication are all rapidly changing in the underdeveloped world.

In this respect, most of the non-western states are characterized by a fragmentation of their political cultures. This reflects two fundamental types of internal cleavage: the gap between the urban and rural elements, and the division of indigenous political cultures expressing itself in the form of particularism or provincialism.

The members of the urban society are inclined toward western political values and institutions; the rural inhabitants are oriented toward traditional political values and institutions. This disparity is further compounded by differences among the mixture of indigenous political cultures which, through colonialism and the independence movements, have become included within the boundaries of the larger territorial political systems. Consequently, channels of communication between the elite and the masses are restricted and the efforts of the elite to develop and strengthen a national consciousness face strong resistance.

The patterns of recruitment into the political arena in the non-western states present many variations. The range extends from the largely patriarchal system to narrow-based oligarchies with a varying breadth of political participation.

In the patriarchal systems, traditional leaders are recruited using such criteria as wealth, family lineages, and tribal affinities. In narrow oligarchies, leaders are recruited from the urban centers from such elements as the professional and business groups, civil servants, and army officers. This situation explains the high degree of substitutability of roles in the non-western political process. Accordingly, in much of the non-West there is little consensus as to the legitimate ends and means of political action. The intensity and magnitude of political discussion have little relationship to political decision-making. The rate of recruitment and change of social categories from which political participation is drawn, however, is becoming relatively more rapid.

The non-western states display many similarities in the manner in which interests are expressed and organized. On the one hand, non-associational groupings of a patriarchal or communal character are persistent and important in political life. Thus the character of political issues is largely dominated and determined by religious, tribal, linguistic, racial, or similar groupings. On the other hand, associational interest groups are limited in development; where they exist they have not become an integral part of the political process. Hence, particular economic or occupational interests are generally latent and are not expressed by functionally specific associations. These conditions have brought into political focus the role of institutional interest groups, such as military, religious, and bureaucratic.

In much of the non-West, political groups have very narrow bases and serve essentially as vehicles for competition either between different elements drawn from the modern sector of society or between different non-associational groupings. These political groups are generally organized around a particular strong leader. Hence the political process in the non-West is characterized by a prevalence of cliques. This special character of political loyalty gives to political leaders a high degree of freedom in determining matters of strategy and tactics. Opposition parties and political opponents can easily be presented as revolutionary movements. One-party systems tend to predominate ranging from comprehensive nationalist movements to dictatorial parties. A multiple party system is only seldom found and usually only conceals rather than replaces the struggle of modern elites against non-associational groupings.

In much of the non-West, the political sphere of life can hardly be differentiated from the spheres of social and personal relations. The lack of a clearly differentiated political arena prejudices the clear orientation of political parties to distinct points of view. Hence, political parties tend to take a world view and feel they represent competing ways of life. Instead of engaging in internal reform programs, they concentrate almost exclusively on issues of foreign policy. Outside the local communist parties which are generally dependent on Moscow or Peking, whatever local ideological parties exist usually combine a communist structure with a fascist orientation and a vaguely defined theoretical socialist program. They are untroubled by the joining together of incompatible ideas; since they conceive of their problems as purely theoretical, they resort to empty posturing in the belief that they have thus settled all problems. They seek a way out of the present through a disguised return to a dead past.

In much of the non-West there are gross discontinuities in political communication revealing the cleavages between communal groups and the gaps between the modern and traditional sectors of the non-western states. Within communal groups there are near-autonomous communication systems strengthened in their isolative tendencies by linguistic distinctiveness or lack of a well-developed network of transportation. The cleavage is sharp between the modern sectors where mass media are developed, where political participation is high, and where the rural areas are predominantly traditional. Thus in much of the non-West there does not exist a single, unified communication system. National leadership must therefore appeal to an undifferentiated public.

Bibliography

Almond, Gabriel, and James S. Coleman (eds.), *Politics of the Developing Areas*. Princeton: Princeton University Press, 1960.

Baran, Paul, *Political Economy of Growth*. New York: Monthly Review Press, 1957.

Black, Eugene R., *The Diplomacy of Economic Development*. Cambridge: Harvard University Press, 1960.

Bowditch, John, and Clement Ramsland (eds.), *Voices of the Industrial Revolution*. Ann Arbor: University of Michigan Press, 1961.

Brand, W., *Struggle for a Higher Standard of Living*. New York: The Free Press of Glencoe, Inc., 1958.

Cairncross, A. K., *Factors in Economic Development*. New York: Frederick A. Praeger, 1962.

Hirschman, A. O., *Strategy of Economic Development*. New Haven: Yale University Press, 1958.

Johnson, H. G., *International Trade and Economic Growth*. Cambridge: Harvard University Press, 1958.

Kautsky, John H. (ed.), *Political Change in Underdeveloped Countries; Nationalism and Communism*. New York: John Wiley and Sons, Inc., 1962.

* Pentony, De Vere, *Underdeveloped Lands: A Dilemma of the International Economy*. San Francisco: Howard Chandler, 1960.

* ————, *United States Foreign Aid: Readings in Problem Areas of Wealth*. San Francisco: Howard Chandler, 1960.

Rockefeller Brothers' Fund, *Foreign Economic Policy in the Twentieth Century*. New York: Doubleday and Company, Inc., 1958.

Shils, Edward A., *Political Developments in the New States*. New York: Frederick A. Praeger, 1962.

Staley, Eugene, *Future of Underdeveloped Countries*. New York: Frederick A. Praeger, 1961.

* Triffin, Robert, *Gold and the Dollar Crisis: The Future of Convertibility*, Revised edition. New Haven: Yale University Press, 1961.

* Indicates paperback edition.

Thirteen

The State Form
in Transition

We have already learned that the nation-state is a human device for satisfying the needs and enchancing the welfare of a society. Its organization provides the response to prevaling needs through the performance of specific functions. The state form has thus neither finality nor a perfected form; its changes are a record of man's experience with it and of his own changing needs.

In purely functional response to the chaos resulting from the collapse of the Roman administration in the fifth century A.D., western man developed the institutions of feudalism. The new conditions in Europe during the breakdown of the medieval synthesis saw feudalism gradually replaced by another organizational concept, the national state. Today, the impact of new technological conditions on the state system has launched man on a new process of organization in response to the new needs and conditions of national and international politics.

Should we then assume that the nation-state has become obsolete today? If it is obsolete, what has replaced it and why? What trends has the new organizational transition assumed? To what degree will this prove beneficial or detrimental to the future development of humanity?

Obsolescence of the Nation-State

The problem of the obsolescence of the nation-state might best be examined in respect to the present changes in its original objects and functions. The state is by no means the same organization it was in the sixteenth century. New missions have been given to it, and many historic functions have gone through a metamorphosis.

THE BROADENING OF THE ORIGINAL OBJECTS OF THE STATE

The basic objects that stimulated the emergence of the nation-state have been modified beyond their original scope. The new dimensions of economic, military, social, political, and scientific realities are forcing states to establish tighter control over national life and evolve greater purposes with regard to their development.

In the realm of economics, the national state as an independent economic unit is presently almost non-existent; the international system is rapidly reaching a point where it is more advantageous to disregard the state as the basic economic unit and concentrate upon supranational units of several types. These organizations have already proved themselves of great value to small as well as great nations. An interesting and provocative question growing from this development is, will economic federation pave the road to political federation or will it instead completely split the world in half?

In the military domain, the nation-state's ability to provide military security for its inhabitants is no longer a reality; any territorial state can be totally destroyed today. Military strength only conceals but does not cure this impotence. The alterations in the theory and practice of war during this century have done much to vitiate the previously held notion of unilateral defense and bring again to the fore the concept of collective security. The search for measures of collective defense has played an important part in the devaluation of the centrality of the national state. No longer can a nation concentrate on protecting itself; it must participate in protecting the entire world if it is to have any real security.

In the social and cultural field, significant changes can be foreseen.

While nations continue to develop their respective cultures and civilizations, and continue to take pride in their traditions, the clear trend is toward an increasing emphasis on the artistic, intellectual, and ethical aspects of mankind as a whole. While it is true that as a unit of social association, the nation-state is very much alive, individuals are increasingly beginning to regard themselves as members of some larger group: the West (or the non-West), Europe, Africa, Latin America, and so on. The intellectuals of the world in particular often transcend their respective national loyalties. They as well as the masses seem to crave association with others of the same social strata regardless of national identification. These and other social forces today, both conservative and revolutionary, are combining to push the nation-state more and more out of the spotlight.

In the purely political area, the assumptions upon which the state was originally formed have changed considerably. The logic of the technological revolution is progressively restricting the area of choice open to states.

Science is the force that has been most injurious to the cause of the nation-state. The new Industrial Revolution has altered the world economy, the concept of war, and the ability of peoples to communicate. This has been a unifying as well as a divisive force. Today it can cause the total annihilation of mankind (or at least civilization as man is familiar with it today), or it can unite the species in a new ascending spiral of progress. Space and its mysteries, for example, are one of the major hopes for the unification of the world.

THE EXPANSION OF STATE FUNCTIONS

Traditionally, the minimum functions of the nation-state in world politics—to provide security and protection to its people—were fulfilled and satisfied, because one could delineate the source of authority possessing the power of protection against the interests and aspirations of other states. In other words, security could be approximated because power could be graded, calculated, and compared. The radical developments in military technology, however, outstripped the ability of the nation-state to keep abreast of the new economic, political, and social relations engendered by this revolution. Today, no nation is self-sufficient, militarily secure, or immune from political and ideological penetration.

In the light of the revolution in communications and technology, the thesis that the nation-state has an objective national interest that is static, unchanging, and permanent—the basic content of which is the satisfaction of its needs and wants through the maximum use of its power—becomes irrelevant to reality. To equate national interests with national security and to assume that power is both the ends and means of state action is a position that is simply untenable. The impact of technology in the nuclear age has made it impossible to measure "power" in the old way and to make effective use of it for traditional ends. The familiar struggle for power to attain maximum security can only have one final consequence in the modern world—constant turmoil, mutual frustration, and perhaps chaos and annihilation.

From the above examination, we can conclude that the function of the nation-state has been altered to one of providing stability and protection by means other than the pure, sheer unadulterated calculus of power. The nature of the contemporary world is such that no dominant national actor can make a decision that fails to take into consideration the interests of other national actors. The revolution in technology and the instruments of warfare have produced a situation where the basic interests of a single nation are almost indistinguishable from the interests of the other actors in the international system. The classical goals of power and prestige are no longer the cardinal feature of national interest for sophisticated societies. Rather, the emphasis is on the discovery of means to regulate and limit them for meaningful purposes and common ends. National goals and interests have become broadened so that they must take into account various other needs at the individual, national, supranational, and international level.

The impact of technology in the nuclear age has placed a variety of restrictions and limitations on state action. Although the ends of national interest remain the same—to provide security, prosperity, and peace—the means to attain them have undergone a profound change. War, as an ultimate use of a nation's actual or potential power, can no longer be rationally or safely employed to satisfy a state's needs, grievances, or achieve the fulfillment of aspirations.

At the same time, the impact of technology has released a whole host of problems that defy the human imagination. While the possibility of a millenium remains in man's grasp as a result of the wonders of technology, complete and utter destruction of civilization is also a frighteningly real possibility. This factor, along with the paralysis of world politics as a result of the East-West and North-South schisms, has increased world tensions to unprecedented heights.

While the two dominant powers, armed with nuclear weapons and divided by conflicting ideologies, are struggling for a world in which their respective ideologies can prevail, the North-South conflict, between former colonial powers and the culture they represent on the one hand and the emerging nations on the other has enlarged and expanded the scope of the world conflict. Rampant nationalism, imbedded in the revolution of rising expectations is clamoring and demanding its share of the fruits of technology and industrialization, and has further complicated an already tense situation.

In summary, several conclusions can be reached. While the nation-state remains the basic unit in the international system, the world is on the verge of reconsidering, reevaluating, and re-defining its role in satisfying the needs of mankind. The nation-state does not provide security and protection because there is no escaping the possibility of a nuclear holocaust which will invariably affect all of mankind. There is no place to hide.

At the same time, the new and emerging nations, freed from colonial rule, are paradoxically intensifying their efforts to create the myth of the state which the West is discarding. While East and West are both striving to close their ranks and for greater military, political, economic, and social collaboration in the form of supranational organization, the emerging nations are acting independently in exploiting the East-West conflict. Yet in spite of existing conflicts and tensions the significant trend of all national actors in broadening their national interests is a process that cannot be minimized. In this age of acceleration and nuclear technology, the challenge of universal survival or universal destruction has brought mankind closer together than ever before in attempting to find solutions to the pressing problems that divide the world. Human needs have thus become universalized, and nation-states have been forced to work collectively.

Approaches to Organization

The dynamic nature of change in the present milieu of international politics is intensifying the search of men and governments for new concepts of organization. The combined consequences of the technological revolutions make organizational modernization in the present international system imperative. As individual governments have broadened their areas of effective control, corresponding areas of international activity must necessarily be subjected to regulation and standardization. The jet-propelled pace of international activity on all levels cannot be satisfied with the traditional horse and buggy devices of international politics.

In order to operate, the new organizations need secretariats to issue directives, gather and disseminate information, conduct research, and foster public relations. Diplomatic practice has been to a great extent superseded by more complex structures as diplomats have lost their freedom of action by the increasingly ritualistic role they play, the rise of "summitry," and chronic backseat driving from their home governments.

The recent proliferation of new states illustrates further the utility of the new organizations. These new states are better able to assume their international role through such formal processes as adhering to the provisions of several international conventions. There are then established practices from which novice states can learn, there are patterns upon which they can build, and there are standards of mature conduct to which they can aspire. Knowing that a world-wide organization is watching and evaluating every move is a profoundly sobering influence on any new state.

THE SEARCH FOR A NEW ORDER

A man's right and ability to defend his person, his property, and his family, has been, throughout history, the ultimate exercise and proof of man's freedom. The distinction between self-defense and aggression for defensive purposes has always been unclear. Being a social animal, man has naturally extended this first principle to the various forms of communal organization which have characterized his heritage. Following the emergence of the nation-state as the primary unit of organized society, this exercise of self-defense was collectivized in the form of modern war. In this form, however, the freedom which the individual intended to preserve was cruelly wrested from him. The state, artificially created to bring him security, clearly outgrew its usefulness. Men found that although within the state the individual could find a relative degree of security from his immediate neighbors, his remaining task was to control the dangerous dynamics of inter-group existence. For this purpose, supranational organizations, in myriad forms and for multifarious interests, have been created.

From a theoretical viewpoint, the development of new organizational forms has been embodied in the efforts toward international organization. These efforts have been conducted from two major positions: the federalists, and the functionalists. The federalists seek a world government. They base their hope for world order on the premise that it must come, before it is too late, by a voluntary leap by all nations from long-held sovereignties to allegiance to some form of universal parliament or council. The functionalists, on the other hand, postulate that the future can be assured only by the gradual expansion of cooperation on broader levels in response to specific needs.

International organization, in the sense of the voluntary submission of action competence by sovereign states to an outside and common authority, is a relative newcomer on the world political scene. In spite of its novelty, however, its logic and its force ensure the long life of the idea. Furthermore, given time, it appears likely that the trend toward wider and greater forms of international organization will continue until, minimally, the war-making capacity of the nation-state is eliminated and men can turn to the solution of other abiding problems with the new zest that will follow release from the specter of destruction.

It had been the general historical practice, prior to the League of Nations, to formulate international agreements for the purpose of concerted action against a particular power or alliance, either defensively or offensively. Implicit in the observation that the League opened a new era of international organization is the fact that no previous international agreement had sought to encompass the whole of the international system. Nor had any international compact undertaken to embrace as broad a range of interests as did the League. When, after World War II, the United Nations replaced the League, it was not thought at all remarkable that this "second try" at general international organization should take on an even broader scope of responsibility.

It is on the subordinate levels that the real novelty of modern international organizational forms can be best observed. Such present day organizations as the International Labor Organization, the World Health Organization, or the International Monetary Fund on the governmental level, and the World Federation of Trade Unions, the Inter-Parliamentary Union, or the International Organization of Journalists in the private sector are representative of the character of the new form of international organization. None of these action areas were conceived of in the early days of the state system; all are reflective of current trends and requirements. Functionalism, breadth of scope, and specialization thus are the major characteristics that differentiate contemporary organizations from such earlier international arrangements as the Concert of Europe, the Holy Alliance, and other eighteenth and nineteenth century European associations.

The evolution of organizational forms has touched off a growing controversy over the relative advantages of regional as opposed to universal systems. Regionalism has been supported by those who contend that the universalist ideal is far too ambitious and perilous because it assumes an allegiance to a community which is, in fact, not in existence. Universalists, on the other hand, contend that the regional approach is no more than an extension of the old and dangerous balance of power, by nature doomed to a repetition of its failure. Recognizing the revolutionary changes and needs of modern society, the universalists maintain that only through equally revolutionary political breakthroughs can men hope to find peace. Regional organizations, however, have continued to coexist with such universal bodies as the United Nations.

The functionalists have gained their greatest impetus from the astounding success of the European Common Market. The developments in Western Europe have also strengthened the idea of regionalism. Most contemporary supranational organization has, indeed, been a combination of the regional-functional approach.

New Organizational Forms

To enumerate the various military, economic, social, and political organizations which have proliferated in the last decade alone would be superfluous. We have selected two of the new organizational forms for detailed discussion, the European Community and the United Nations. These two have developed more elaborate institutions than the others and hence provide better models for analysis.

THE EUROPEAN COMMUNITY

Before World War II, efforts in the direction of European integration were either confined to theoretical speculation or to ultimately abortive structures of hegemonic domination by force of a single power. Following the war, the idea of European integration gained popular favor in the form of the European movement.

On April 18, 1951, France, West Germany, Italy, Belgium, the Netherlands, and Luxembourg signed the draft treaty of the European Coal and Steel Community. The treaty established the first European organization with a federal structure. Previous organizations, which were composed of representatives from member states, based their decisions on a compromise between national viewpoints and national interests. For the first time, the Coal and Steel Community created a common European authority, independent of governments, and able to make its own decisions. To this body, the governments have thus transferred some of their sovereign power.

In the decade since the launching of European integration by the Coal and Steel Community, the six participating members have formed two other bodies, the three now making up the European Community. The first is EURATOM (the European Atomic Energy Community), which was created to further the use of nuclear energy for peaceful purposes and insure that Europe does not lag behind in the coming atomic revolution. The second is the European Economic Community (the Common Market), formed on January 1, 1958. Its aim is to establish a vast single market for all products, with a broad measure of common economic policies. This would bring into being a powerful productive unit generating a steady expansion and providing greater stability and a more rapid rise in living standards.

In terms of industrial potential, trained people, and long tradition, Europe should be able to play an important role in this century of radical change in the world order. The structures inherited from past centuries have been breaking up under the impact of nationalism, war, science and technology, and communism.

The Schuman proposal of 1950 which created the ECSC must be seen in this perspective. The driving forces behind European integration have been both political and economic. Individually, the European countries cannot compete as equals in world trade against the United States and the Soviet Union. But were an economic union of 170 million people to be created, Europeans could hope to play a full role in developing their own economies and those of the developing nations who look to them for aid.

The task is not simply to permit trade in goods between separate economies, but to merge existing markets, and establish in their place the conditions and characteristics of a single market. This means the abolition of the traditional barriers to trade (customs duties, quotas, etc.) and less obvious hindrances, such as discrimination and private agreements to share out markets, the control of the conditions in which imports from the rest of the world can enter the new economic area (a common external tariff), and the maintenance of free movement of persons, capital, firms and services. Gradually separate and divergent national policies must be merged into a harmonius whole (particularly in the field of agriculture) while moving towards a common economic policy for the Community as a whole.

To establish a single market and work out common policies the European Community has established an institutional system whose basic structure is federal: a European Executive Commission, independent of the member states, a Council of Ministers, in which sit representatives of the Governments, a European Parliament entrusted with democractic control of at least some issues, and a Court of Justice.

The activity of these institutions, set up to work out and apply the common rules of the Community is in fact political in nature though economic in its field of operation: it aims not only at integrating the actions of producers, workers, and businessmen, but also at harmonizing the policies of the national governments and the major role they play in determining the conditions of economic activity.

THE COMMON MARKET: A BALANCE SHEET

In general, the European Community has enjoyed high levels of economic activity, trade, and growth since its formation. Trade within the Common Market has been expanding dramatically, and trade with the United States and the rest of Europe has also grown. The Community has enjoyed an economic growth rate higher than the United States or Britain, it has expanded its share of world trade, and has steadily built up its monetary reserves.

In part this prosperity reflects the continuation of economic stimuli which have been operating on the Continent for some years. But the Common Market also has clearly had its direct impact. Since its formation, trade between members has increased even more rapidly than before. Businessmen of the Community and outside investors as well have been acting on the premise that a full customs union would exist within the Community by 1970 or earlier. They assume that the EEC will continue to expand at high rates. Such private decisions backed by investment dramatically reinforce the trend toward integration.

The political development and consequences of the Economic Community are more difficult to appraise. The operations of the Community are doubtless less "supranational" than the European federalists might wish but the Executive Commission plays a major role. While the final power of decision rests more with the Council of Ministers than under the Coal and Steel Community and the Executive Commission works closely with the member governments in developing its proposals, its treaty right to submit proposals and its close realtions with the European Assembly enable it to exert direct pressure on the members of the Community. Moreover, the Commission's proposals aim not only merely at the reconciliation of national policies but at the development of common policies for the Community as a whole. This concept of building a strong new entity is crucial and is not seriously questioned within the Community.

At French initiative, the Six have been considering ways to co-ordinate political policies, though differing seriously on methods and objectives. Among the Six there are differing views of proper methods or institutions. France prefers a "Europe of fatherlands," with maximum sovereignty retained in each state, while Italy and the Benelux countries favor a real supranational body. The problem has become more complex with British requests for admission to the Community.

Britain's decision to affiliate is in many respects the clearest possible evidence of the growing political and economic significance of the European Community. The decision is an historic break with the long tradition of British policy toward the Continent. Economically and politically, Britain is motivated not simply by the disadvantages it sees for itself in standing aloof, but also by the positive gains to be won by combining with the Six.

Any great increase in membership will alter the character of the Community. The change will be in large measure simply a function of increasing the size and decreasing the homogeneity of the group. To some extent it will be the result of the redistribution of the balance of interest within the Community. The United Kingdom would bring with it a complex of worldwide economic and political commitments, a different legal system, and a host of other institutional and historical differences.

As the Community members continue to merge their economies and develop their capacity for acting as a unit, they approach for the first time the role of an equal partner with the United States, sharing equitably in the responsibilities and burdens which have hitherto rested mainly upon the latter. The European Community therefore offers an effective way for the developed countries of the West to join together in discharging some of their common obligations and responsibilities. The European Community can work with the United States for the creation of a more viable world order which can accommodate the needs and interests of the less-developed nations in their gigantic effort to modernize. The two groups can also concert more effectively for military defense against aggression and for a common political approach ultimately designed to bring about basic changes in Soviet purposes and objectives.

Fulfilling this promise of the European Community depends on three conditions:

First, the members of the Community must develop their readiness and ability to act as a unit. This is, of course, implicit in their ultimate goal of European federation or confederation. The Community seems likely to progress gradually to that goal. In the shorter term, this means that the central institutions of the European Community, particularly the Commission, must be given more power, and must develop the capacity to act on behalf of the members in their external relations. So far, the Six have made limited progress in this respect. More will have to be done once the United Kingdom and others have joined.

Second, the development of an effective and enduring bilateral partnership between the United States and the enlarged European Community is of fundamental importance. This partnership would cover the major economic, political, and military problems confronting the United States and the enlarged Community.

Third, the partnership must face outward toward the rest of the world. The building of their own resources and unity is valuable not merely for its own sake but to enable the Atlantic nations to discharge more effectively the crucial tasks facing them. A close partnership need not and must not prevent a broader community of nations and must be handled in ways enabling the others interested to participate.

Thus the opportunity offered by the European Community imposes heavy obligations on both Europe and the United States to see that it does come into being as rapidly as possible, that it grows in strength and influence, and that the United States and the European Community are able to work together effectively in pursuit of common purposes and in the discharge of common tasks.

THE UNITED NATIONS

The United Nations is composed of six principal organs that operate through a number of committees, commissions, and boards. The principal organs of the United Nations are: the General Assembly, the Security Council, the Economic and Social Council, the Trusteeship Council, the International Court of Justice, and the Secretariat.

The General Assembly is the largest organ of the United Nations in which all member states are represented. It meets every year in regular session; special sessions can be called by a majority of the states, the Security Council, or one member with the concurrence of a majority. Every member of the United Nations has one vote in the General Assembly. Recommendations on important issues require a two-thirds majority and on less substantial issues only a simple majority is required. It functions as a world forum to maintain international peace and security, to advance international economic and social cooperation, and to promote welfare of non-self governing and trust territories. In addition, the General Assembly regulates budgetary matters.

The Security Council is composed of five Permanent Members (China, France, United Kingdom, Union of Soviet Socialist Republics, United States of America) and six members elected by the General Assembly for two years. It functions continuously, and each member has one vote. Resolutions on procedural matters are passed by any seven affirmative votes, and resolutions of "other" (substantive) matters require seven votes including the concurrent votes of the permanent members. This is the famous "veto"; a negative vote by a permanent member on a non-procedural question. The Security Council has primary responsibility for the maintenance of peace and security. It therefore undertakes the pacific settlement of disputes and also is authorized to take preventive or enforcement action in cases of "threats to the peace, breach of the peace, or act of aggression."

The Economic and Social Council is composed of eighteen members elected by the General Assembly for three years. It normally holds at least two sessions a year; each member has one vote, and decisions are arrived at by majority voting. The Economic and Social Council works to improve standards of living everywhere and is concerned with the solution of international economic, social, and health problems. Its operations are also directed to promote cultural and educational cooperation, and the universal respect of human rights and freedoms.

The Trusteeship Council is composed of all members holding trust territories plus China and the Soviet Union (who hold none) and an additional number of members to balance the number of trust-administering states. These additional members are elected by the General Assembly for a period of three years. It meets twice a year; each member has one vote and decisions are arrived at by majority voting. The Trusteeship Council carries out the function of the United Nations regarding trust territories except those areas which are designated as strategic.

The International Court of Justice is composed of fifteen judges elected concurrently by the General Assembly and the Security Council for nine year terms. Except for judicial vacations, the Court is permanently in session at The Hague; nine judges constitute a quorum. It functions as the judicial organ of the United Nations.

The Secretariat consists of a Secretary-General and such staff as the United Nations may require. The Secretary General is the chief executive officer and administrator of the United Nations and acts in this capacity in all meetings of its principal organs except the International Court of Justice. He is appointed by the General Assembly on the recommendation of the Security Council for a period of three years. The Secretariat is the administrative agency of the United Nations.

THE CHANGING ROLE OF THE UNITED NATIONS

The United Nations, as its founders well realized, is not a world government and has a limited function in the settlement of conflicts of interests between states. The preservation of the peace by the United Nations was postulated upon the principle of unaminity of great power interest which was hoped for following World War II. The United Nations emphasized the necessity of disarmament where the League of Nations had emphasized collective security.

The United Nations was designed to be a balancing force in international politics through the maintenance of the status quo and the grand design of the victorious powers. While in reality the United Nations has failed to balance world politics or to maintain the status quo, it has demonstrated a high degree of flexibility in adapting itself to new circumstances and has become an institution for change. In becoming the midwife of change, the United Nations system has taken on the dual role of institutionalizing new factors in world politics and of communicating their impact to the system at large. As a result of these developments in the character of the United Nations, a new vista opened in the life of the General Assembly and the office of Secretary-General, both of which assumed new roles and functions. These two organs became the main regulatory centers of the process of change, clearing houses of postwar conflicts and accommodations.

The shift from the early conception of the United Nations prevalent at San Francisco—that of an aristocratic organization animated by the spirit of dominance of the chief victorious powers—to a diverse and curiously democratized institution reveals some of the difficulties and dangers which the western world in general and the United States in particular will encounter in the future. In fact, the major contemporary criticisms of the United Nations have focused on the great differences of aim and purpose between the fifty-one founder members and many of the fifty-nine newly independent countries which were later elected to membership.

The founders laid the whole emphasis on the organization of peace through collective security, to be achieved by great-power cooperation. The great powers were chosen as permanent members of the Security Council in the expectation that they would agree on how to keep international order, and work together against any breach of the peace by the smaller powers through united decision and coordinated action. In the event of disagreement among them, each was armed with a veto on action by others. The optimum results of this system would be the successful defense of the status quo; the worst possible outcome would be stalemate.

The supposition was in error. The Soviet Union's decision to subordinate the main purpose of the organization to its own national ends was the first breach in the spirit of the Charter. At the same time the United States hoped to convert the United Nations to an instrument of its foreign policy, often attempting to overburden the organization with responsibilities clearly outside its competence. The rise of anticolonialism was another important factor of change. The new countries are placing their campaign for the end of all colonial rule above the "international peace and security" implications of the Charter.

The newly independent states who were not active participants in international politics during World War II know little of the depth of feeling that brought the United Nations into being and the reasons for the presence in the Charter of each long-debated article. The Allied states that sent their delegates to San Francisco in 1945 held strong beliefs formed from their experiences in two world wars and their previous attempt and failure to create an effective world organization. They were determined that there must be a new international organization and they knew that it must demand more from its members than the League of Nations in order to be effective.

The majority of the new states of Asia and Africa were spared these experiences, and looked on what the Allied nations had tried to do at San Francisco in their own special way. Their whole history, insofar as it was politically conscious at all, had been dominated by one concern: the struggle for independence. They are less interested in what often seems to them theoretical formulas of how world peace is to be preserved than with the immediate problems of how they can give their new independence a stronger economic and social base and help other colonial peoples to attain independence. They still mistrust all ex-colonial powers, including the very ones now rapidly freeing their colonies. Since the same powers are prominent in the effort to preserve the integrity of the United Nations they have deep suspicions about their motives and actions.

In addition to these factors of change, the impact of the Cold War on the United Nations can hardly be overstated. When great power harmony was abandoned the Security Council—the main center of guarantee for the maintenance of the status quo—it began to lose the prominent role which the framers of the Charter had planned for it. In addition, the Cold War stripped the United Nations of any effective leadership. Its effect on the structure of the United Nations was to produce significant changes in the function of both the General Assembly and the Office of Secretary General.

In short, today, no one of the organization's key bodies—the Security Council, the General Assembly, or the Secretariat—is functioning as was planned at San Francisco.

The Security Council, which was intended to act as the United Nations executive organ with primary responsibility for the maintenance of international peace and security, is held in a state of chronic stalemate. Because the Security Council has been so completely frustrated, the General Assembly has moved into the gap to take leadership in political matters. Landmarks in this process include the "Uniting for Peace" resolutions of 1951 that authorized the General Assembly to take jurisdiction of a political-security question on which the Security Council was unable to reach a decision, the development of a military action capability under General Assembly control in the 1956 crisis in the Suez Canal Zone and in the Congo affair of 1960–61, and the open assault on colonialism in Africa launched in 1960 and further developed during the next two years.

The Secretary-General's office has developed in response to these trends as well. Particularly during the tenure of Dag Hammarskjold, but clearly evidenced under his successor U Thant as well, is a determination to make the Secretary-General a significant political force in his own right. The dominant majority in the General Assembly is sufficiently powerful to provide the Secretary-General with a political base from which to work. He is sometimes referred to as the "foreign minister of the world's fourth great power," as he moves about the political map applying the name, the prestige, and the influence of the United Nations to political problems.

Finally, no more clear proof of the changing character of the organization could be adduced than the dramatic erosion in the notion of "domestic jurisdiction" that has taken place. Originally written into the Charter as a protection of sovereignty against external inquiry, it remains intact in principle but has been riddled with exceptions in practice. The long-standing principle in this connection has been that each state is the judge of what in fact constitutes its domestic jurisdiction, and is capable of rejecting international intervention into such issues as it chooses to except. Ever since the ex-colonial states have assumed membership, however, the scope of interest of the General Assembly has widened to include many questions once considered clearly out of bounds. Without ever resolving the ticklish legal questions involved, the organization has simply taken account of whatever questions seemed important to it and has let the protests fall where they may.

This is by no means an unclouded benefit, for trampling on sensitive nationalism always engenders strife; the United Nations, it is said, has begun more controversies than it has solved. But it is beyond doubt that the vast bulk of its members conceded, whether happily or gloomily, that the scope of action of the United Nations has broadened widely. The organization has more to say about questions of peace or war than it was ever dreamed it would in 1945.

Organization: The Escape from Disaster?

An assumption implicit in the entire discussion in this book, made explicit as well at many points, is that the political world today is undergoing extensive, rapid, and in some cases, violent change. New forces of far-reaching import have been released on mankind, and statesmen are grappling with the consequences. The structures and patterns of international politics, like those of any social system, were developed originally on the basis of and in response to certain prevailing social conditions. Now that conditions have changed so drastically, serious questions must be asked about the relevance of familiar institutions to unfamiliar circumstances.

The international political system, as we have remarked often, is a relatively loose and underinstitutionalized order, nicely calculated to limit without nullifying the inescapable dynamics of state inter-action. The inhibitions on state freedom of choice were long ago set at the precise minimum necessary to preserve the integrity of the system while allowing for a wide range of adjustment and stability. Created in the era of absolute monarchy and the musketeer, the systems and processes of world politics proved capable of adapting to such explosive forces as the rise of nationalism, the development of world empire, and the creation of mass armies. Why then are we suggesting here that their viability has been seriously compromised today?

This question also has been repeatedly answered in the preceding pages. Contemporary challenges overtax the competence of the state form and international conflict threatens constantly to spill over the limit of tolerability and safety. The new means of action open to states are too dangerous to use, while the old techniques are inappropriate to the problems. The great questions of international life today find no answers within the traditional confines of the state system.

Nor can it suffice merely to write off such insistent problems as the escape from destruction, the demands of the non-West, the challenge of communism, and the implications of nuclear energy as insoluble and therefore not fit matters for concern. So powerful are the new dynamics of international life that either answers will be found for them or they will find their own answers. The simple issue facing political man is whether he will discover methods and mechanisms to dominate and shape events or whether he will ultimately be dominated by them.

In these terms the problem of organizing human effort for the solution of these long-term problems becomes central. The familiar state form has both legal and mystical underpinnings, but in the last analysis its only rational justification is utilitarian. It must, in other words, get the job done; if it fails, other structures and other principles must be found to replace it.

The process of experimentation has already begun. New organizational forms have been developed, new processes initiated, and new solutions attempted. Only a very few of these, however, incorporate a fundamental break with the past; most remain tentative and reluctant steps that seek to preserve the psychic component of sovereignty while restricting its actual force. It is a tribute to human ingenuity that so many ways have been found to have man's cake of sovereignty and eat it too.

But no serious observer feels today that such half measures have proved their effectiveness or demonstrated their efficacy. Such proof may yet be forthcoming; it is premature to argue flatly for the outright abandonment of the sovereign nation-state in favor of an unproved vision of world government. But it is crystal clear that no over-all rationale for international politics yet suggested or attempted meets the requirements of the contemporary era. What has taken place up to now is a massive purchase of time, time for innovation and—hopefully—time for hard thought. The era of difficult decision and new ways of action lies ahead.

Some way must be discovered to cope effectively with the new forces of world politics if man is to win release from the excruciating tension of contemporary life and to move out from under the mushroom cloud of nuclear destruction. New ways of organizing human effort across national lines must precede any direct attack on the problems. History teaches that both success and renown are the rewards of those that most quickly and most powerfully respond to the challenges civilization faces. To this end students of international politics can enthusiastically dedicate themselves. The penalty for failure may mean disaster; the reward for success may be a better life on this planet for everyone.

Bibliography

Bailey, Sydney D., *General Assembly of the United Nations*. New York: Frederick A. Praeger, 1960.

* Buchan, Alastair, *NATO in the 1960's: The Implication of Independence*. New York: Frederick A. Praeger, 1960.

* Cassirer, E., *Myth of the State*. New Haven: Yale University Press, 1961.

Claude, Inis, *Swords into Plowshares*, Second edition. New York: Random House, 1959.

Eagelton, Clyde, *International Government*, Third edition. New York: Ronald Press Company, 1957.

Frank, Isaiah, *European Common Market*. New York: Frederick A. Praeger, 1961.

Frye, William, *The United Nation's Peace Force*. New York: Oceana Publications, Inc., 1957.

Goodrich, Leland M., *United Nations*. New York: Thomas A. Crowell, 1959.

Goodspeed, Stephen S., *Nature and Function of International Organization*. New York: Oxford University Press, 1959.

* Lawson, Ruth C. (ed.), *International Regional Organizations: Constitutional Foundations*. New York: Frederick A. Praeger, 1962.

Miller, Richard, *Dag Hammarskjold: A Study in Crisis Diplomacy*. New York: Oceana Publications, Inc., 1961.

* Reuter, Paul, *International Institutions*. New York: Frederick A. Praeger, 1961.

Robertson, A. H., *European Institutions*. New York: Frederick A. Praeger, 1959.

Ward, Barbara, *Interplay of East and West*. New York: W. W. Norton and Company, Inc., 1957.

---

* Indicates paperback edition.

Index